IMPRESSIONS IN LIFE

IMPRESSIONS IN LIFE

NETAJI SUBHAS CHANDRA BOSE

GYAN

Published by

GYAN

Gyan Publishing House
5, Ansari Road
Daryaganj, New Delhi-110002
Phone: 011-47034999, 9811692060
E-mail: books@gyanbooks.com

Distribution Network
gyanbooks.com
India, USA, Canada, UK, Australia

ISBN: 978-93-7316-327-7 (PB)

First Published, 1947

2nd Impression 2026

Printed at: Gyan Press, Delhi.

IMPRESSIONS IN LIFE
Author: NETAJI SUBHAS CHANDRA BOSE

IMPRESSIONS IN LIFE

By

NETAJI SUBHAS CHANDRA BOSE

Announcement

We have produced a number of books on current national problems and biographies of some of the finest men in India. If you are not already in touch with these books please let us have your name and address on a postcard. We will intimate to you without any obligation, of all our publications as and when they are published

To

★ **STARVING**

★ **STRUGGLING**

★ **TOILING**

★ **MILLIONS**

PUBLISHERS NOTE

Netaji Subhas Chandra Bose has spent greater years in Europe and other foreign countries than any other Indian Political Leader. He was exiled from India in the middle of 1933 and during the four years of his stay in Europe he visited practically all the countries of the west including Ireland, Germany, Italy, France, Poland, Switzerland etc. Where ever he went he tried to study the political movements and organisations, met important personalities and tried to understand the economic, social and political life of those countries and as far as possible enlist their moral support for the Indian Political movement. In letters to friends in India and also in the form of press articles he had been giving the account of his travels in the western countries and also his impressions about the conflicting political ideologies in Europe. Sometime he contributed illuminating articles to reputed foreign journals about affairs in India. Occasionally he wrote for friends at home of his own reactions to the political developments taking place in India and abroad from time to time. The present volume is a record of these letters and articles and it is hoped that they will provide a true reflection of the working of the mind of India's greatest revolutionary.

Some of his writings about Forward Bloc are also appended to enable the reader to understand his plan and programme of revolution.

CONTENTS

I.	Impressions of Ireland	13
II.	Impressions of Rome	20
III.	Impressions of Poland	24
IV.	Impressions of Aden	28
V.	Problems of Japan	32
VI.	The Future of Europe	60
VII.	Impressions of Vienna	83
VIII.	A visit to Berlin	89
IX.	Impressions of Egypt	94
X.	My Impressions of Abyssinia	103
XI.	Impressions of Britain	138
XXI.	India in the World Affairs	142
XIII.	Anti-Indian Propaganda in Europe ...	163
XIV.	Need for Foreign Propaganda ...	167
XV.	India and the League of Nations ...	172
XVI.	Reuter's Propaganda tactics ...	181
XVII.	India and China	184
XVII.	Meeting with a Philospher Thinker and a Dreamer in Geneva ...	187
XIX.	An interesting personality in Rommania...	198
XX.	Sidelights from Vienna	202

XXI. Analysis of Political Situation in India ... 209

XXII. New Reforms in Europe—An Article ... 214

XXII. Bengal of My Dreams ... 234

XIII. Political Views 255

XXIV. Forward Bloc 277

XXV. Indo-British Trade Relations ... 340

IMPRESSIONS OF IRELAND

I

IMPRESSIONS OF IRELAND

I am grateful to President De-Valera for the permit of visiting the Irish Free State and thereby fulfiling long cherished desire of mine and also for the warm and cordial reception I received at his hands in Dublin. It was the desire and command of the late Mr. V. J. Patel that I should visit Dublin before returning home and attempt to receive the activities of the Indo-Irish League which he had helped to found. I hope that my visit to Ireland has served some useful purpose in that direction.

While in Ireland I endeavoured to meet as many parties and personalities as I possibly could in order to get a correct picture of the social and political life of the country. I believe I have seen and learnt much that will be useful and interesting to us in India.

In the Dail—the majority party is President De-Valera's Fianna Fail, which has also the support of the Labour party, led by Mr. Norton. The opposition party is Mr. Cosgrave's 'Five Gael' party. Mr. Cosgrave's party is looked upon as a pro-British party and practically all the old Unionists support it. Mr. Cosgrave's party has been weakened by the defection of

General O'Duffy, the organiser of the Blue shirts, who has founded the national Corporate party on Fascist lines. This has naturally strengthened the position of 'Fianna Fail' in the country.

"Fianna Fail and Republicans"

The only unfortunate feature in Irish politics to-day is the breach between Fianna Fail and the Re-publicans. The republicans allege that President De Valera is not moving towards the republic which he had promised and that his government is persecuting the republicans—25 of whom have been put in prison. The feeling of the government is that the republicans are too impatient and tactless and are blind to the realities of the situation namely the existence of Pro-British party in the country which makes it difficult if not impossible to declare a republic atonce. The members of the Fianna Fail party aver that they will stand for republic and are working for it but that the actual declaration of it must depend on several factors and conditions.

Interview with Ministers

Besides having prolonged discussions with Mr. De-Valera I met individually most of the Fianna Fail ministers. All of them were exceedingly sympathetic, accessible and human. They had not yet become responsible. Most of them had been on the run when they were fighting for their freedom and would be shot at sight if they had been spotted. There was no official atmosphere about them. With the Minister for Lands I discussed how they were abolishing landlordism by buying up the big estates and dividing the land among the peasantry. With the Minister for Agriculture I discussed how they were trying to make the country self-sufficient in the matter of food supply. It was interesting to know that wheat and sugar were now being cultivated in large areas and the development of Agriculture was making the country less dependent on cattle rearing—and therefore less dependent on the English Market. I also discussed with him the question of restriction of Jute cultivation in India and he gave me valuable suggestions as to how he would tackle the problem if he were put incharge. With the Minister for Industry I discussed the industrial policy of the Government. He explained to me that they wanted to make the country self-sufficient not only in agriculture but also in industry. This would make for the economic prosperity of the country and at the same time make them less vulnerable should they have to face economic reprisals in future. A colosal amount of work had already been done within a few years to build up new industries. While appreciating all that the government had done and were doing for industrial regeneration, I felt that possibly they could have gone in for more state enterprise in the sphere of industrial revival. On the whole I found that the work of Fianna Fail Ministers was of interest and value to us in India when we would have to tackle the problems of nation-building through the machinery of the state.

There was so much to learn in Ireland and my stay was so short. I was surprised that so few of our countrymen who spend years in England, ever care to go over to Ireland which is next door. Ireland is quite a *different world from England.*

I was agreeably suprised to find that all the Irish parties were equally sympathetic towards India and her desire for freedom regardless of their own internal differences. I was glad I was able to do some publicity on behalf of India while I was there. At several receptions and public meetings, I was able to talk about the present day conditions in India and about our fight for freedom. Outside their own shores the two countries which interested them most, were India and Egypt.

(2)

India and Ireland

press report regarding Mr. Bose's visit to Ireland :

The death of Brian-Le-Valera has naturally forced Mr. Subhas Chandra Bose to make slight alterations in his programme here. Since writing to you on Friday last he has seen several other prominent men in the country. He was to see Mr. De Valera this afternoon, as the two leaders wanted to have final talk before Subhas Babu leaves for Havre tomorrow night. His conversations with Mr. Ryan, the Minister for Agriculture, are of great importance to India. He discussed with him agricultural policy of the Finna Fail party and its attempt to make the country self contained in foodstuffs. Mr. Bose was particularly interested in obtaining the views of Mr. Ryan on the question of 'jute restriction' in India in order to give the agriculturists a higher price for the jute they grow.

There were several questions of common interest which made Mr. Bose spend considerable time of his afternoon on Friday with Mr. Sean T. O. Kely, Minister for Local Government, and Vice President of the Cabinet. However, the most important talk that the Indian leader had, was with the Dublin Trades Council. It is a powerful body working as the Central trade union committee for Dublin. The council acquainted Mr. Bose with the useful work that it had been doing for several years for the upliftment and social amelioration of the working class of this country.

Apart from these conversations, Mr. Bose finds himself surrounded by Irish pressmen, representatives of political, social, women's organs and magazines. They all want his views on different Indian subjects. With great difficulty, because of want of time—he could give an interview referring to the women of India. In the course of this interview he has told the Irish nation that the women of India have been aspiring to take their proper place in the social and political movements. Woman Movement in India, according to him, has three main lines of activity. Firstly, there is the movement for giving Indian women literary, artistic, and practical training through institutions like the Seva Sadan of Bombay, Indian Women's University of Poona, the

Saroj Nalini Association of Calcutta. Then there is the movement for women's rights run on feminist lines; and the political movement which is closely associated with the Indian National Congress.

Mr. Bose delivered another public lecture under the auspices of the Indian-Irish Independence League. He was enthusiastically received by the large crowd of Irishmen and women. "As in Ireland" he said, "British Imperialists have tried to force their language and culture on the people of India, but so far as the cultural domination of India is concerned, the worst is over. In India today we have a revival of our own culture adapted to modern conditions. We are told now that all is quiet on the Indian front, that is not true. That is British propaganda. In fact, the movement for independence in India is going on different lines, from those of the past."

"The British Government in India," Mr. Bose continued "has profited by its experience in Ireland. As it is unpopular for it to have martial law, it has had all the regulations normally found under martial law made the permanent law of the land. Before the new constitution for India is planned these emergency ordinances have been made the permanent law."

Madame Gonne MacBride who presided, said that telegrams had been received from Mrs. Despared and from two Indian groups in the welcome to Mr. Bose.

Missing Page

II

IMPRESSIONS OF ROME

From Naples I came to Rome, and spent about a week there. For me Rome was a fascination, because it is a blend of the old, and the new. Last year, when I visited Rome, I had devoted considerable time to sight-seeing as well as to study of the Municipal administration of the city. This time I tried to study something of the work of the Fascist party, and how it was working in co-operation with the Government, for the uplift of the nation. I was given all facilities for going round the party offices, examining the party administration, and organisation, and putting innumerable questions to party officials for eliciting the sort of information I wanted.

I could see and feel that the Fascist party was out to create a new nation according to its ideas, and ideals. The party takes charge of every individual in the state, regardless of age or sex. No individual is isolated from the state, and it is the function of the party to train citizens for the state. Thus, the state, the party, and the individual are organically related, and the party is but the organ of the state. Every institution, whether intellectual, cultural, or physical is controlled or influenced by the party. Further every profession, every association is under the control or influence of the party —the party functions as the watch dog or moral trustee of the state. The thoroughness of the party organisation is amazing indeed. To me coming from a different land, and belonging to a different organisation—what was of greater interest was not the ideal of Fascism,— but the thoroughness of this party organisation. We have our own national ideals, which we do not need borrow from elsewhere. But what we do lack is organisation and discipline, and the methods of organisation we shall have to learn elsewhere. The sooner we realise this, the better for us, and our country.

Disciplined Organisations

Even before I came out to Europe in 1933, it was my conviction that the ramshackle organisation of the Indian National Congress should develop into a disciplined organisation based on modern methods. What I have seen in Europe, since has only confirmed that former belief. In India, we want a party, that will not only strive for India's freedom but also produce a national constitution and after winning freedom, will put into operation the whole programme of national reconstruction. There can be no question of a Constituent Assembly for drafting a constitution. The first that Lenin did when he came to power, was to dissolve the Constituent Assembly. Likewise there can be no question of giving up power as a stroke of generosity, where freedom is won by the party. I think it was Pt. Jawaharlal Nehru, who once suggested that when the Congress won freedom for India, it should dissolve itself. If Turkey had not done this is 1922, Mustapha Kamal would no longer be the head of the Turkish Government today, and Turkey would have been in the depths of chaos. The experiences of the Spanish people today should be an eye-opener to us in this connection. Much of Spain's trouble is due today to the fact that there is no strong and stable party there to put into effect the programme of national reconstruction, for which the revolution had taken place. Can we in India, evolve a stong and disclplined party, pledged to strive for and win freedom and thereafter to build up a strong and powerful state, and create a new nation—all according to our national ideals? If we can do that, we have no need to be pessimistic about our future.

There was another interesting experience I had in Rome, namely, my interview with ex-king Amanullah of Afghanistan. His Majesty received me with the utmost cordiality and we had a long talk. He wanted to know the latest news about Mahatma Gandhi, the Indian National Congress, and the political situation in India. He condemned communalism strongly and supported the cause of Nationalism. I found that His Majesty's whole heart was with his people. He did not seem to care what happened to him so long as his people were prosperous and happy. He was optimistic about the ultimate future of Afghanistan. He conveyed his warmest wishes for the welfare of the Indian people. He imdressed me profoundly as being truly a patriot king.

In all the newly awakened countries, that I have visited in Europe, one factor is common, namely, the self-confidence, the courage, and the dare-devilery of the youths. Will our youths also develop these traits ?

III

IMPRESSIONS OF POLAND

During my journey in Poland 1933, I was fortunate enough to meet several interesting personalities, some of whom were greatly interested in India. The general attitude was one of sympathy for India's struggle for national emancipation. The Poles, having struggled long for their freedom and having won it quite recently —are in a position to sympathise with another nation struggling for its national freedom. I remember that I was once taken in a car by some Polish friends in Warsaw to see peasent life in the interior. We were taken to a village agricultural school—one of the new schools established by the Government, for giving the children of the peasantry an education in modern scientific agriculture. We were shown round by the care-taker, an old woman, and at the end of our visit, she asked very kindly about the health of Mahatma Gandhi and what he was doing at the time. It was touching.

One of the efforts of the Polish people at present is to industrialize their country as rapidly as possible. For this purpose, they built a port of their own—Gdynia, which has made them independent of the former German port of Danzig, which has now been internationalized. They are also attempting to develop their connection; they have been opening Consulates in different countries. The Polish Consulate in India was opened in 1934. The Textile industry in Poland is highly developed, one of the important textile centres being Lodz. Recently the Iron and Steel Industry has been making rapid progress.

There is an Oriental Society in Warsaw, the capital of Poland, which is specially interested in Oriental culture. I was invited to a social gathering under the auspices of the Oriental Society and I spoke about our desire for a Polish-Indian Society which would endeavour to foster cultural and commercial relations between our two countries.

The students, both men and women, were wide-awake. The women were particularly enthusiastic in the matter of developing contact with foreign countries including India. They wanted information about students and youth organisations in India. Their organisation was called the LIGA. Within the Liga, they had a separate circle for each country, with which they wanted to develop contact.

In this brief article I shall refer particularly to one interesting personality whom I met in Warsaw—Professor Stanislaw F. Michalski, who has devoted his whole life to the study of Sanskrit and Indian literature and is a lover of India. Prof. Michalski-Iwienski was born in 1881 in Poland. He studied Sanskrit language and Indian literature under Professor Leopold V. Schroder in Vienna from 1905-1911 and in Gottingen, in Germany under Prof. Oldenburg in 1914. For several years he delivered lectures on the Sanskrit Language and Literature at the Polish Free University of Warsaw-Wolna Wazcchinca. In 1920 he took part as a volunteer in the war against the Bolsheviks. Since then, Prof. Michalski has been giving his whole time to literary and scientific work. In 1923, together with some. Polish Orientalists he founded the Oriental Section of the Warsaw Scientific Society.

Prof. Michalski is the author of a number of books in Polish on India and Indian culture. The following are some of them :—

(1) Bhagwad Gita, 1912; second edition—1920; third edition 1926.

(2) Upanishads (Selected), 1913, second edition —1922.

(3) Rama's Longing (One chapter from the Ramayana). 1920.

(4) Dhammadadam (Translated), 1924.

(5) Forty songs of the Rig Veda, 1914.

(6) Atmabodha, 1923.

(7) Bhagwad Gita (Text in Sanskrit with Introduction and Remarks), 1921.

In the introduction of a Polish Edition of Odyssea (Warsaw), 1935—Prof. Michalski has referred to the relations between the Ramayana and the Odyssea and has pointed out the necessity of studying the Ramayana in connection with research work about Homer...

During the last few years Prof. Michalski has been engaged in bringing out a big Polish Encyclopedia in which he has written several articles about India, Indian Language and Literature, Indian Geography, Indian History, etc. Many pictures and multi-coloured maps have been appended to the big article on India

In 1924, the Professor gave a discourse in Warsaw about the Epic poetry of India. In 1935 he gave a discourse about a general survey of India before the Warsaw branch of the Rotary Club.

The Professor has been collecting a library about India during the last few years. The library contains at present over 2,000 books on the Sanskrit Language and Indian Literature—ancient and modern.

As a host, Prof. Michalski was exceedingly hospitable He treated me to a sumptuous dinner and as a parting *dakshina* gave me a big bundle of his own publications.

It is interesting to know that another Polish Professor, Prof. Stasiak of Lwow, is now on a visit to India. Prof. Stasiak is a well-known Orientalist, and has spoken at several important centres in Europe on Ancient Indian Literature and Philosophy.

The ground has already been prepared for a Polish-Indian Society in Poland—with a corresponding branch in India. All that is wanted now is that somebody should take the lead.

IV

IMPRESSIONS OF ADEN

On the 13th January, 1935, when M. N. Victoria of Lloyd Trienstina called at Aden on her way to Europe from Bombay, some Indian residents of Aden arrived and invited me to accept their hospitality for a few hours. I did so with great pleasure. When I went ashore in their company, there was an agreeable surprise for me. I had seen Aden last in 1919 on my way to England, but what a pleasant contrast. Now there were beautiful roads (probably asphalted), street-lighting with electricity and many imposing buildings to greet the eye. On enquiry I learnt that the population of Aden was over 50,000 and the Indian population well over 2,000. The Indian settlers were businessmen and the majority of them hailed from Kathiawar. Aden is a flourishing port and trade-centre and the volume of trade is steadily on the increase. Raw materials like hides as well as articles like coffee, are brought from the interior and shipped to Europe. Manufactured foods, including textiles, which are symbols of so-called civilization, are imported from Europe and sent into the interior of the Arabian Peninsula. The administration is British in personnel in the higher grades. In the lower grades the employees are partly Arab and partly Indian. At present

Aden is under the administration of the Government of India.

The problem that has been worrying the Indian settlers in Aden is the proposed separation from India. They are genuinely afraid that their interests will suffer greatly if they are cut off from India and therefore lose the support of public opinion in India. I tried to find out what was at the back of the mind of the authorities in launching this proposal. So far as the Indians were concerned, they were of opinion that the motive was political. The Government wanted to convert Aden into a Colonial possession so that even if India got Swaraj at some time in the future, Aden would be safe in their hands. Aden and Singapore were the two naval gateways of India and these two gateways were to be kept under full Imperial control. There were some Indian regiments in Aden formerly, but they had been sent back and there were only British troops, numbering about 2,000 left there. There was also a strong contingent of the Royal Air Force stationed at Aden. The territory within a radius of 25 miles from Aden was under British protectorate and beyond that was independent territory.

Besides the strategic importance of Aden as commanding the entrance to the Red Sea, the place is also interesting because of its picturesqueness. Aden is sheltered in the bosom of some rocky hills. The major portion of the town is situated at the foot of hills, but some of the nicest buildings are built high up and there are winding roads, quite modern in construction, leading up to them. Tunnels have been built through some of the hills with a view to improving communications.

Rainfall is very scanty in Aden and hence the acuteness of the problem of drinking water. This problem was solved by the Arabs long long ago in a clever way. The rain falling on the hills used to be collected in a huge stony reservoir constructed out of natural rocks lying at the foot of the hills and throughout the year water used to be drawn from the reservoir for drinking purposes. Besides this supply of water, there were very deep wells, of the same sort that one would find in Indian villages. The day we reached Aden, there had been a heavy shower and the reservoir was pretty full.

I was glad to find that the Indians in Aden were keenly following events at home. They asked me for the latest information. At the group meeting—after giving me all the information I wanted about Aden—they requested me to speak on the Congress programme. I delivered a short address on the constructive programme adopted at the Bombay Congress and on the Khadi movement in India. The meeting over, light refreshments were served and I was then driven round the town. A pleasant farewell ceremony took place at the jetty and I then returned to my boat M. N. Victoria. By midnight we were once again on the high seas.

It would encourage the Indians in Aden greatly if prominent Indians take the trouble of landing at Aden, and meeting their fellow countrymen there. They remembered gratefully the visits paid to them by Mahatma Gandhi and Pandit Madan Mohan Malaviya. There is also considerable room for cultural propaganda among Indians there and any Indians visiting Aden for that purpose are sure to be warmly welcomed. At present Pandit Kanhaya Lal Misra of Benares is engaged in that work there, but he is to leave soon.

It is the desire of Indians in Aden that there should be a strong agitation in India against the proposed separation. Whatever may ultimately happen, there is no doubt that public opinion in India on this question should make itself heard without delay.

PROBLEMS OF JAPAN

Every now and then we open our daily papers to read about some clash between China and Japan. Many pass over the columns as something happening too far away to interest us in India. Others go through the columns as a matter of routine. But I wonder how few of us understand the significance of the happenings reported.

The islands which form the homeland of the Japanese race are overpopulated. They have to support a population of about 70 millions with the result that there is over-crowding and too much pressure on the land. But that is not the end of the trouble. The Japanese are exceedingly prolific and their population has been growing by leaps and bounds. The number of people per square mile in China is 100. In Japan it is 313. Moreover, Japan's birth-rate is twice that of Great Britain. Hence Japan wants more territory for her children to settle in—more raw materials for her growing industries and more markets for her finished goods. No one will make her a present of these three things—hence the resort to force. The only other solution for Japan is to restrict her population through birth-control and live within her own resources—but that solution does not ostensibly appeal to her. This is, in short, the *raison d'etre* of Japanese impearialist expansion.

Japanese expansion can take place only in the face of Chinese, Russian, British or American opposition. If she expands on the Asiatic mainland she is bound to incur the wrath of China or Russia. If she expands southwards—towards the Philippine Islands or Australia —she is bound to come into conflict with the United States of America or Great Britain. As far as one can judge, Japan seems to have decided in favour of the first course, notwithstanding the appeal made by Lt.-Commander Ishimaru in his book *Japan must Fight England* to the effect that she should make up with China, Russia and the U. S. A. and concentrate on fighting. On the Asiatic mainland the territory on which Japan can cast her eyes belongs either to Russia or to China. To attack Russia would be folly for Japan because under Soviet rule, Russia is fully reawakened. She has, moreover, a first class military machine, both in Europe as well as in the Far East. Therefore, the only alternative left to Japan for satisfying her imperialist ambitions is to expand at the expense of China. But though she may expand at the expense of China, that expansion can take place only in the teeth of Russian opposition, for reasons that will be explained below. So far as Britain is concerned however much she may dislike the growth of Japanese power on the Asiatic continent, she will put up with the nuisance, knowing full well that the only alternative to it would be expansion to the south, bringing Japan into direct and unavoidable conflict with her, and in her present mood, the U. S. A. will certainly not go to war with Japan over her "interests" in the Far East.

Being an Asiatic country and living in close proximity to a huge continent, it is but natural that Japan should look primarily to the mainland of Asia to fulfil her impercalist requirements. There she finds a huge state —formerly the Celestial Empire and now the Republic of China—ill-managed and disunited and with more natural resources than she can herself develop. The vastness, the potential richness and the internal weakness of China constitute the greatest temptation for Japan.

The conflict between the two Asiatic countries is more than forty years old. It began towards the end of the last century. By that time, Japan had modernised her state-machinery with the help of modern methods and had modern weapons of warfare. She found that all the big European Powers had begun to exploit China and to enrich themselves at her expense. Why, then, should not Japan, an Asiatic Power living next-door, do the same and keep out the Western Powers from draining the wealth of East? This was the imperialist logic which started Japan on her race for expansion.

During the last forty years, Japan has not lost a single opportunity for wrestling concessions from the Chinese Government and during this period she has been undermining the influence of the Western exploiting powers slowly and steadily. Her greatest rivals were Russia, Britain, the U. S. A. and Germany, During the Russo-Japanese War of 1904-1905, she was able to checkmate the Czarist Empire. During the Great War she was able to wipe out Germany from the map of China. But she has not been able to tackle Britain and the U. S. A. And in the meantime Russia, which was once beaten, has come back into the picture as a Soviet State, newly armed and considerably strengthened.

The disintegration of China began during the latter half of the nineteenth century. European powers like Britain, Russia, Germany, etc., and the U. S. A. put pressure on China and obtained "treaty-ports" like Hong Kong, Shanghai, etc., which virtually amounted to annexation of Chinese territory. Just before the end of the last century, Japan appeared on the scene and also adopted western tactics in her dealings with China. The island of Formosa lying to the south-east of China was acquired by Japan in the war of 1894-95 with China. Port Arthur in Southern Manchuria and the Southern half of Sakhalin Island, then belonging to Russia, passed into Japanese hands after the Russo-Japanese War of 1904-1905. About the same time Japan took over the Kwantung Railway and the southern part of the Chinese Eastern Railway running through Manchuria, thereby making South Manchuria a Japanese sphere of influence. Korea, formerly Chinese territory, was annexed by Japan openly in 1910 and it is interesting to note that Japan had professed to secure its independence when she went to war with China in 1894. During the Great War, Japan declared war on Germany and immediately proceeded to seize Tsingtao and other German possessions in the Shantung peninsula. In 1915, when she found all the Western Powers up to their neck in the war, Japan presented 21 demands to China and extorted several concessions from her. After the war, Japan received as her share of the spoils, the mandate for the ex-German Pacific Islands, the strategic importance of which lies in their position athwart the direct sea-route from the United States to the Philippine Islands. Then there was a lull in Japanese expansion for a period, since Japan wanted time to assimilate what she had annexed. The next period of feverish activity began in 1931 with the conquest of Manchukuo (Manchuria), when Manchukuo, formerly as a Chinese territory, was set up as a nominally independent state, just as Korea was in 1895. The present expansionist drive which has been continuing since 1931 can be traced to the now famous (or rather notorious) Tanaka memorandum of 1928 in which plans for Japan's future expansion on the Asiatic mainland were clearly laid down. From this brief historical survey it should be clear that Japan's detemination to find more elbow-room for herself in this planet of ours is unshakeable. Outward circumstances can hardly thwart this imperious drive and can at best determine the direction and speed of her expansion.

A scientific examination of the internal economy of

Japan will clearly explain Japan's military aggression since 1931. It is easy to understand her need for fresh territory when her population is growing and her existing territory is already too scanty for her present population. Looking to her industrial system, one finds that Japan has to import all her important raw materials, *viz.*, cotton, wool, pulp, iron, oil, etc., from a great distance. The expansion of her industrial system, like her need for territory, is necessitated by the growth of population. Therefore, to maintain her large population, Japan requires a safe and regular supply of raw materials. The expansion of industries, again, requires new markets. Now, how are all these needs to be fulfilled ? Will China of her own accord give up territory for colonisation to Japan ? Will she allow Japan to exploit her vast resources in raw materials and her extensive market ? Certainly not. Both national honour and self-interest will stand in the way. Further, the European Powers and the U. S. A. will not voluntarily permit Japan to monopolise China—her resources and her market. They will insist to the last on the "Open Door" policy in China which permits all powers to share the Chinese spoils. Hence Japan has to seize Chinese territory by force. She has been doing this by stages, biting off one slice at a time and taking time to digest it. Each attack is preceded by certain border incidents, which are carefully stage managed in order to serve as a pretext for Japanese aggression. The tactics are the same, whether one observes the north-western frontier of India or

Walwal in Abyssinia or the Manchurian frontier in the Far East.

Japan's imperialist needs and demands in the Far East can be fulfilled only if she can establish her political hegemony over China to the exclusion of the white races and by virtually scrapping the "Open Door" policy. Time and again, her politicians have said as much in so many words. For instance, Japan's spokesmen have often said that she has special interests in the Far East which cannot be compared to those of the any other Western Power—that it is Japan's mission to umpire the Far East and maintain peace in that quarter, etc. etc. No doubt, besides the purely economic motive, the Japanese are inspired by the desire to found an Empire and the consciousness of being an unconquered race whets their imperialist appetite. Incidentally, the foundation of an Empire abroad enables the fascist elements in Japanese society to get the upper hand.

If China could somehow persuade herself to accept the political and economic suzerainty or patronage of Japan, the Sino-Japanese conflict would end in no time. This is what Hirota, Japan's foremost diplomat has been trying to achieve for the last three years. His speeches have been extremely conciliatory on the surface with a constant appeal for Sino-Japanese co-operation. Now, what is the objective of this co-operation? Obviously, the enrichment of Japan and the virtual enslavement of China. But this naked truth cannot be blurted out—hence the slogan is "Co-operation in a joint defence against Communism." This slogan not only serves to cloak Japanese motives, but at the same time conciliates all anti-socialist elements whether in Japan, China or elsewhere. Thus, the Indian papers of the 7th August, 1937. gave the following account of Hirota's foreign policy :—

> "Declaring that a major point in Japan's requests in China was co-operation in a joint defence against communism, M. Hirota in the House of Representives said, he believed that Sino-Japanese co-operation was possible if the radical elements in China, particularly the Communists, were effectively controlled. He added, the Japanese Government wished to settle the North China incident on the spot and the same time to effect a fundamental readjustment of Sino-Japanese relations."

And similar statements in similar language have been made ever since Hirota first became Japan's Foreign Minister a few years ago.

Can China submit to this demand even if it brings her peace ? My own view is that left to himself, Marshal Chiang Kai-shek, the Dictator of the Nanking Central Government, would have done so. At heart he is violently anti-Communist and since the split in the Kuomintang (Chinese National Party) in 1927, when he managed to establish his supremacy, he has spared no pains to exterminate the Chinese Communists and their allies. But Marshal Chiang has encountered consistent opposition from two quarters. The Western provincss of China, known as the Chinese Soviet, being practically independent of Nanking, have kept up the fight against Japan and, on this point, have faithfully echoed the feelings of the Chinese masses. Secondly, the Western Powers with their vast interests in China, and with their prestige to maintain before the Eastern races, cannot easily persuade themselves to scuttle. The foreign investments of U. S. A. in China are, in point of magnitude and importance, second only to its investments in Latin America (Central and South America). Regarding investments in China, the following extract from the London *Times* of the 19th August 1937 is illuminating :—

> "British direct interests in China are worth about 250 million pounds, made up of 200 million pounds in business investments and 50 million pounds in government obligations. Of the total sum, about 180 million pounds is tied up in Shanghai and of this 180 million a high proportion is in the Settlement district north of the Soochow Creek. This is the district now being most heavily shelled and bombed. It is where most of the Public Utility offices and works and where most of the large mercantile businesses are established."

The *Times* writer goes on to point out with dismay that whilst previously this district has been policed under British superintendents, the police stations have been evacuated and occupied by the Japanese. The white races are consequently alive to the fact that Japanese hegemony over China will mean not only the subjection of the latter but their own exclusion from the Far East.

Since the geography of a country often determines

military strategy, it is necessary to note the sa features in the geography of China.

China's most important lines of communica are her three great rivers: the Hwang-ho (or Ye River) in the North, the Yang-tse in the Centre the Si-Kiang in the South. The entrance to the Si-K is controlled by the British port of Hongkong; to Yang-tse by Shanghai, which is jointly held by foreign powers with Britain and America predominat The entrance to the Hwang-ho is dominated by Ja entrenched first in Korea and now in Manch (Manchukuo) as well. The one practicable land r into China is that from the north. Along this route Mongols and the Manchus entered China proper, and the years preceding the Great War, both Russia Japan had their eyes on it. Since 1931, Japan has b aiming at the possession of this route and the coun adjoining it and since July 1937, fighting has been go on in this area. It should be remembered in this c nection that high mountains separate China proper fr the western part of the Republic (*viz.*, Sinkian or Chin Turkestan). The consequence of this is that the l route to China proper is from the north and we find t historically the power which has controlled Manchu has always been in a strong position to dominate Chi

In order to understand in their proper perspect the events in the Far East since 1931, it is necessary understand the broad lines of Japanese hegemony China though peaceful penetration was not possib

Japan laid down her plans for a military conquest of China, or at least for military pressure on her. To achieve this objective, Japanese strategy had to work along two lines—firstly to break up Chinese unity and secondly, to make it impossible for any other power to come to the aid of China. This purpose could be served only if Japan could seize the entire northern part of the Republic, including Manchuko, Mongolia and northern China proper. These territories taken together from a compact mass, cutting of Russian Siberia from China proper (the valleys of Hwang-ho. Yangtse and Si-Kiang rivers). A reference to the map will show that if Japan holds this area, she can in the event of war with Russia, penetrate through Outer Mongolia and cut the trans-Siberian railway at Lake Baikal. And if Russia can be effectively isolated, no other country can come to China's rescue in an emergency. We shall see how Japan has progressed in the task of absorbing this area since 1931.

It is necessary to note at the outset that Japan never lays all her cards on the table and she proceeds with her aggression cautiously, taking care that she is not attacked by any other power when her own hands are full. Moreover, she always manages to stage some "incident" in order to give her a pretext for seizing Chinese territory. The first "incident" was staged on September 18th, 1931, by Lieutenant Kawamoto of the Japanese Imperial Army who was reconnoitring along the South Manchuria Railway track. This led to the seizure of the Mukden, pus the next day of the whole of Manchuria within a short period. At that time, the whole world was in grip of an acute economic depression and Russia was feverishly pushing on her first Five-Year plan. Japan was, therefore, sure that there would be no effective challenge to her predatory moves. The Lytton Commission sent out by the League of Nations reported against Japan and following that, the League Assembly condemned the Japanese seizure of Manchuria. But Japan snapped her fingers at the League and walked out. This was followed by the sale of the Chinese Eastern Railway to Manchukuo by the Soviet Union in 1933, and in 1934 the Russo-Manchukuo Waterways Agreement was adopted. Though Manchukuo was not given *de jure* recognition by the other powers, she obtained *de facto* recognition from most of them.

Manchukuo is a huge territory with plenty of room for colonisation, though the climate is severe, it is rich in several raw materials including coal. Moreover, it is exceedingly useful as a jumping-off ground for Japan in the event of war with Soviet Russia. Many people thought it would take Japan years to develop Manchukuo and in the meantime, there would be peace in the Far East. But they were mistaken. Both on economic and on strategic grounds, Manchukuo cannot stand by itself. Only a part of the raw materials desired by Japan can be found there and the Manchukuan market is not big enough for Japan. Moreover, strategically Manchukuo is exceedingly weak, there being hostile territory on all sides. Consequently, to satisfy her economic needs and to ensure the safety of the new state, Japan had to continue her aggression further.

In 1932, another " incident " was staged in Shanghai and the Shanghai war between China and Japan started. The upshot of it was that China was forced to demilitarise a certain area near Shanghai and submit to a few other Jananese conditions. The strategic importance of Shanghai was not so clear in 1932, but the present war (1937) has brought it to light.

By 1933, the consolidation of Manchukuo under the puppet Emperor, Pu Yi, was complete and Japan was ready for a further extension of her frontiers. Fighting took place in North China outside the frontiers of Manchukuo. The Japanese troops seized Jehol and a slice of Chahar and marched up to the gates of Peking (now called Peiping). Vanquished in battle, the Chinese had to bow to the inevitable and see another slice of their territory annexed by Japan. The war ended with the Tangku truce in 1933.

The year 1934 was comparatively uneventful but hostilities broke out again in 1935. As always happens with Jappan, a fresh act of aggression was preceded by conciliatory speeches and a show of moderation in foreign policy. On January 23rd, 1935, Hirota delivered an address, advocating a policy of non-aggression and the addoption of a " good neighbour " policy with a view to effecting a rapprochement with China. This time, the slogan adopted by the Japanese was an autonomous North China (like an autonomous Manchukuo) and the Central Government of Nanking (new capital of China) was told not to interfere with Japanese activities and negotiations in North China. But Nanking could not wholly oblige Japan and the people of North China did not want to walk into the Japanese trap as blindly as the Manchurians had done in 1931. The result was that the Japanese plans did not succeed. Nevertheless, when the conflict was finally liquidated, it was found that China had virtually lost another portion of her territory. In 1933 Jehol and a part of Chahar had been absorbed by Manchukuo. Now, a demilitarised zone was created in Hopei province with its capital at Tungchow, 12 miles east of Peiping, called the East Hopei autonomous area. In charge of this area was a Chinese renegade, Yin Ju-Keng, and the territory was under Japanese domination. (Later on, large-scale smuggling went on within this area presumably with Japanese connivance, with a view to evading the Chinese customs.) Further, the remaining parts of Hopei which (contains Peiping and Tientsin) and a portion of Chahar were combined into a separate administrative unit under the Hopei-Chahar Political Council, headed by General Sung Cheh Yuan, the strongest leader outside Nanking. The Council, while afraid to oppose Japan openly, did not sever its connections with Nanking.

In February, 1936, there was a military revolt in Tokyo and, for a time, the Japanese Government had its hands full at home. Nevertheless, it was not altogether inactive. With a view to strengthening her position internationally, Japan entered into a Pact with Germany—the German-Japanese-Anti-Comintern Pact. Towards the end of the year, in November, 1936, an attempt was made to push into Inner Mongolia down the Peiping-Paotow Railway, but the Mongol-Manchukuo mercenaries of Japan were held at bay in the province of Suiyan by General Fu Tso I, with the aid of Nankings troops.

It should be clear to any student of history that since 1931, Japan has been growing increasingly assertive not only in the Far East, but in world affairs in general. If she had not felt strong in the international sphere, she would never have ventured an aggression against China. We have already referred to her withdrawal from the League of Nations after the seizure of Manchuria. Prior to this she had allowed the Anglo-Japanese Alliance to lapse, probably because she felt that she was powerful enough to do without it. In the Washington Naval Treaty, Japan had agreed to the ratio 5 : 5 : 3 in the matter of warships etc. as between Britain, U. S. A, and hereself. When this treaty lapsed in 1935, Japan insisted on parity and since this was not agreed to by the other Powers at the London Conference, she contemptuously walked out of it. When Britain wanted to bring about an economic understanding with Japan in the matter of world-markets, Japan refused to discuss any markets except those which were directly controlled by the former, and the London Conference of 1935 between the two Powers broke up. From all these facts it will be clear that when 1937 dawned, Japan was morally and internationally prepared for a major conflict in the Far East.

But sometimes even the most well-informed are led astray. Between March and July 1937 Japan lulled the whole world into the belief that she was passing through an economic crisis and was therefore unable to launch on any military aggression against China. Articles appeared in several American journals to show that while the rest of the world was enjoying an economic recovery, in Japan it was the reverse. Owing to this recovery, the price of all raw materials had gone up considerably. Japan had to buy them at a high price and so her cost of production had gone up—making it virtually impossible for her to compete in the world-markets successfully. (This statement is disproved by the remarkably low prices of Japanese textiles in India at the present time.) American journalists took pains to argue that because of this economic crisis Japan had decided to go slow with China and was therefore offering her the hand of friendship. It was further argued that owing to the same reason, extreme militarists were out of favour for the time being and moderate politicians were getting the upper hand in Japan. It now appears that Japan's moderation was simply a cloak to hide her real intentions in order to lull her enemies to a sense of security. Japan chose this particular moment for attacking China for obvious reasons. Neither the U. S. A. nor Britain nor Russia is yet ready to challenge Japan in war. All of them are preparing feverishly and are piling up armaments and two or three years later, the outlook for Japan may be gloomy. It was therefore a case of "now or never" for Japan, and she struck. She carefully prepared for this attack by a period of sober talk and moderate action. And when everybody felt convinced that Japan was thinking in terms of peace, she launched her attack. Thus, writing on April 24th 1937, the well-known journal of New York, *The Nation*, said: "The prospects of peace in the Far East are greater than at any time since 1931." Writing on June 26th, the same journal remarked that there was a lull in Japan's offensive against China. But little did the writer know then that it was merely a lull before the storm.

Apart from Japan's general preparedness for another drive, certain factors precipitated the persent crisis in the Far East. The Scian coup and the kidnapping of Marshal Chiang Kai-shek in December 1936, prepared the ground for a "United Front" policy in China. There seems to be little doubt now that before Chiang was released by his captor, an understanding had been arrived at between the Chinese Soviets and the Nanking Government on the basis of a common resistance against Japan. This understanding meant the completion of the unification of China for the first time in recent history. The Chinese Soviets were to give up their Communism and Separatism and submit to the direction of Nanking. Chiang was to lead united China against Japanese aggression and the Communist leaders, Chow En-lai and Chiang's own son, were to fall in line with him. Japan came to know of this and attacked, before united China could proceed further with the work of consolidation.

This time is opportune for Japan in many ways. Though British. Russian and American rearmament is proceeding apace, as already stated, neither of them is yet ready for a conflict. It will still take time for Britain to complete her Singapore base. The Neutrality Act adopted by the U. S. A. is a clear indication that she wants to keep out of every international conflict. The Russian Army, according to Fascist reports, is seething with discontent and in any case is not as formidable as it appeared twelve months ago. The clash on the Soviet-Manchukuo border followed by the withdrawal on July 4th, 1937, of the Soviet troops from the disputed islands which belonged to Russia under the 1860 Agreement with China—was a further proof that the Soviet Government was not prepared for a war.

Three days after the withdrawal of the Soviets troops from the Amur River, a fresh "incident" was staged near Peiping and the attack on North China was resumed on July 8th, 1937.

Man is proverbially wiser after a calamity has befallen him. It is now reported by well-informed journalists that Japan had been preparing for this war for some time past. She is not satisfied with the occupation of Manchukuo. This country is too cold for Japanese immigrants. It has contributed only a small proportion of the raw materials needed by Japanese industry. It has, no doubt, brought some increase of trade to Japan, but this has been offset by the cost of administration and the losses incurred as a result of the competition of Manchurian products in the Japanese market. On the other hand, economically North China (*viz.*, the provinces of Shantung, Hopei, Chahar, Shansi and Suiyan) offers far more than Manchukuo. There are iron deposits in Chahar, Shansi and Southern Hopei. Shansi has also high-grade coal. Moreover, tin, copper, gold and oil are scattered throughout the five provinces. The Yellow River (Hwang-ho) valley is suitable for the cultivation of cotton which is now imported into Japan from India and America to the value of 400 million yens annually. And the climate is more favourable to Japanese immigrants than that of Manchukuo, as well as cattle-breeding.

The Japanese drew up plans for the exploitation of this territory some time ago, but Japanese capital was loath to come in as long as the area remained under Chinese sovereignty. Hence, milictarism had to come to the aid of capitalism.

Apart from the economic urge behind the present

aggression, there lurks the psychological factor. American journalists were partly right when they wrote during the earlier part of this year about the economic crisis in Japan, but their conclusions were wrong. Contrary to what they wrote, economic difficulties may instigate a "totalitarian" government to launch on a war abroad in order to stave off discontent at home. (The same crisis may overtake Germany in the not distant future.) In the case of Japan, it may be averred that the economic difficulties which she encountered in the recent past as a result of her declining trade balance, made a revival of war paychology necessary.

Further, since the defeat of the Japanese-directed expedition against Suiyan (a province in North China) in November, 1936, it became apparent that the strategic areas of Inner Mongolia could only be obtained if the whole of North China were brought into subjugation. Without controlling Chahar and Suiyan, in particular, it is impossible to push into Inner Mongolia from the direction of Manchukuo.

. . . .

Why is Japan so keen about Inner Mongolia, a barren country of little economic value? The reason is strategic rather than economic. It has been remarked above that Japan has been aiming at a compact mass of territory comprising Manchukuo, North China and Mongolia. Now, in the meantime, Soviet diplomacy has not been idle and two big provinces of the Chinese Republic have passed under Russian influence—Sinkaing (or Chinese Turkestan) and Outer Mongolia (the upper portion of Mongolia adjoining Soviet Russia). Sinkiang is not of much strategic importance to Japan (though it is to Soviet Russia owing to its proximity to India)—but Outer Mongolia is. With Outer Mongolia under her control, Soviet Russia can easily descend into North China. The only way to prevent this and cut off Russia permanently from China proper is to seize Inner Mongolia (the Southern part of Mongolia) and North China and thereby form a compact corridor from West to East, separating Russian Siberia and Outer Mongolia from China proper. To annex this territory is at present Japan's objective. Once she succeeds in this effort, her next endeavour would be to build a strategic railway through this newly acquired territory from East to West. If she is able to consolidate her position there, she may then think of moving into Outer Mongolia. What would then happen, it is difficult to predict. At present, Outer Mongolia is a Russian sphere of influence and the Soviet Government have declared very plainly that any move on the part of Japan within this territory would be tantamount to a *casus belli*.

But Japan has not given up all hope of uniting the Mongols under her suzerainty sometime in future. Hence, Japanese agents often talk of "Mengkukuo" as a worthy political ideal for all the Mongols. This plan, if it ever materialises, will be a counterpart of Manchukuo. It will give the Mongols their own state, with the Gilbertian facade of autonomy of course, but in reality under Japanese tutelage. There are approximately five million Mongols in the Far East. Two million live in the Hsingan province of Manchukuo. A million live in Outer Mongolia—a territory half as large as the United States, but mostly desert. Another million live in Inner Mongolia, while about a million are scattered in Sinkiang (Chinese Turkestan), Tibet and Soviet Russia (Buriat Republic). The nucleus of the future Mongol State of "Mengkukuo" has already come into existence with a Mongolian Political Council. Among the Mongol leaders who are under Japanese influence are Li Shouhsein and Prince Teh.

But while an "autonomous" Mengkukuo may be a future project for Japan, an autonomous North China is her immediate objective.

Since the annexation of Manchukuo, Japanese influence in North China was steadily growing and this must have led them to hope that without a major conflict, another puppet state would be set up in the near future comprising the five provinces of North China. But the absorption of Canton province within Nanking's zone in the recent past, followed by the reported understanding of Marshal Chiang with the Chinese Communists in December last must have dashed Japanese hopes to the ground. A strong and united China was, at long last rising before the world's eyes and that China would not give up her northern provinces without a fight. Since January 1937, Nanking began to assert its influence over North China officials.

She interfered with the Japanese-protected smuggling through East Hopei. She dared to order the suspension of the new Tientsin-Tokyo air-line. established by Japan with Chinese consent. In Northern Chahar there was a small-scale rebellion of Manchukuan and Mongolian troops against Japanese domination. Anti-Japanese incidents were thus occuring with increasing frequency and not settled by abject submission to Japan's demands. To crown all, there was the report of an understanding between Nanking and the Chinese Communists which would bring into the field against Japan, the 90,000 seasoned soldiers belonging to the latter.

On July 3rd, 1937, the Japanese Ambassador, Shigeru Kwagoe, started negotiations with Nanking. Japan trimmed her sails and proposed the relinquishment of Japanese political control in North China, provided Nanking would recognize Manchukuo *de jure* and undertake "economic co-operation" with Japan. Nanking is reported to have rejected this proposal and her counter-proposals fell short of Japanese requirements. No further proof was needed that a new China had come into existence which would soon exercise its full authority over the northern provinces. Therefore, Japan struck without delay and an "incident" was staged at Lukouchaio, about 18 miles west of Peiping (Peking) when Japanese troops engaged in night-manœuvres clashed with units of the Chinese Twenty-Ninth Army stationed in that area.

Looking at this incident legally, there can be no doubt that the Japanese were in the wrong. Though the Boxer Protocol of 1901 entitled them to station troops in the Piping Legation quarter and at certain points in the Peiping-Tientsin railroad, they sent their troops outside the specified areas and obstructed rather than maintained communications with the sea—the purpose for which the protocol was designed. However, soon after the clash, the Japanese Government made the following demands :--

(1) Withdrawal of the Twenty-Nine Army from its present lines west of Peiping.

(2) Punishment of the Chinese responsible for the conflict.

(3) Adequate control of all anti-Japanese activities in North China : and

(4) Enforcement of measures against Communism.

It is reported that the Hopei-Chahar Political Council submitted to these demands on July 19th and the terms of the settlement were published in Tokyo. on July 23rd. The expectation on the Chinese side was that both the Chinese and Japanese fighting forces would withdraw from the zone and it is extremely probable that Nanking would have reluctantly endorsed the above settlement. But when the Japanese troops did not leave the area, the subordinate officers and the rank and file of the Chinese troops refused to withdraw. On July 26th, the Japanese military issued an ultimatum that the Chinese troops must withdraw by noon, July

28th. The latter refused to budge and the Japanese thereupon proceeded to evict them by force. Thus the war was started.

Though Marshal Chiang, the Nanking Dictator, is not ready for a war, he has stood up to Japan and it is not likely that he will give in without a fight.

Japan is preparing for a long fight and the Japanese Diet has already voted large sums for the campaign. It is reported that she will spend up to £117,650,000 in order to carry on the war till the end of January, 1938.

The latest development in the Far Eastern War is the extension of the fight to the Shanghai area. On the 9th August a fresh "incident" took place at the Hungjao aerodrome near Shanghai. Two Japanese naval officers were shot dead while attempting to enter the aerodrome. Thereupon, Japanese naval forces took drastic action to avenge the shooting and the Japanese Admiral demanded, among other things, that all Chinese troops should be withdrawn to a distance not less than 30 miles from Shanghai and that all defences prepared within the area should be immediately dismantled. The Chinese response to the demand was the movement into the Shangbai area of the 88th Division from Nanking in order to reinforce the local troops. The Japanese regarded this as a flagrant breach of the 1932 Agreement—but the Chinese retorted by saying that the Japanese themselves by posting troops in Chinese territory and provocatively bringing a large fleet to the scene, had absolved China from any obligation to observe the terms of that agreement.

Thus the war is going on along two fronts—Peiping and Shanghai. A moot point in this connection is as to which party desired the extension of the war to the Shanghai front. In all probability the Japanese.

The Japanese, being blocked on land, as they were when Nanking troops moved into Hopei province, turned to the sea. The semi-circle of armies which Marshal Chiang threw round Peiping (under Japanese occupation) based on a well-prepared line of forts, was a bold and important strategic move. The left flank of the Government Army is at Nankow, the famous pass, where the Peiping-Paotow railway cuts through the hills. The centre of the semi-circle depends on Paotingfu, 100 miles of Tientsin, also under Japanese occupation. The task of forcing this semi-circle—this "Hidenburg" line—is a formidable one. Hence, the decision from a strategic point of view to undermine Chinese resistance by attacking Shanghai.

If China has a heart, it is the financial and commercial centre at the mouth of the Yang-tse. Japan is attacking this heart in order to disorganize the foreign controlled industrial, commercial and financial centre of China with a view to imperilling the economic basis of the Central Government, demoralizing national feeling and terrifying the Chinese bourgeoise. Shanghai is virtually at the mercy of the Japanese navy and an attack on this prosperous and ever-growing city is the obvious way to bring the war to a rapid conclusion. But the effectiveness of this thrust will depend on the extent of the dislocation of trade and of the material damage accruing from the war.

The war will go on for some time. Japan will try "to paralyse the heart of China in order to amputate the limbs. China must stand or fall, therefore, by the war in Shanghai"—as an eminent strategist has declared. Will China be able to survive this blood bath? If Canton remains open for supplies of armaments and the loss in revenue due to the fighting in Shanghai is not too serious—China may, perhaps, keep going sufficiently long to be able to endanger the social and economic stability of Japan. As against this consideration is the fact that the Japanese Navy is attempting a blockade of the Chinese ports and further, that there is a war fever among the Japanese people and there does not seem to be any difference between the aims of the military and the civilians in Island Empire.

China has appealed once again to the League of Nations, as she did in 1931. But what is the value of this moribund League in such an emergency? World opinion is, of course, on the side of China—but world-opinion is not of much value when pitted against machine-guns. The outlook for China is gloomy indeed. The mellow view that time is on China's side is not correct any longer. To-day China is fighting against time. God grant that she may succeed.

Japan has done great things for herself and for Asia. Her reawakening at the dawn of the present century sent a thrill throughout our Continent. Japan has shattered the white man's prestige in the Far East and has put all the Western imperialist powers on the defensive—not only in the military but also in the economic spheres. She is extremely sensitive—and rightly so—about her self-respect as an Asiatic race. She is determined to drive out the Western Powers from the Far East. But could not all this have been achieved without Imperialism. without dismembering the Chinese Republic, without humiliating another proud, cultured and ancient race ? No, with all our admiration for Japan, where such admiration is due, our whole heart goes to China in her hour of trial. China must still live—for her own sake and for humanity. Out of the ashes of the conflict she will once again rise phoenix-like as she has so often done in the past.

Let us learn the lessons of this Far-Eastern Conflict. Standing at the threshold of a new era, let India resolve to aspire after national self-fulfilment in every direction—but not at the expense of other nations and not through the bloody path of self-aggrandisement and imperialism.

September 19, 1937.

VI

THE FUTURE OF EUROPE

It is customary in modern Politics to classify the different nations as the 'Haves' and 'Have-nots.' The 'Haves' are those, like Great Britain and France, that have profited as a result of the Treaties of Versailles, Trianon and Neuilly, following the Great War. The 'Have-nots' are those that have lost territory under some of these treaties or have specific grievances against their provisions. In Europe, Great Britain, France as well as the succession states that have been carved out of the former Austro-Hungarian Empire are among the 'Haves.' On the other hand, Germany, Italy, Hungary Austria and Bulgaria are among the 'Have-nots.' Though Russia lost much of her territory as a result of the last War, she is now interested in maintaining the *status quo* and is therefore classified among the 'Haves.' And though Italy acquired territory from the Austro-Hungarian Empire at the end of the War, she is nevertheless regarded as a 'Have-not' because she was expecting a greater share of the spoils of war. Italy was cajoled into joining the Allies in 1915 by the terms of the Secret Pact of London, wherein Britain and France promised her several things including the Dalmatian Coast which later on was assigned by the Peace Conference to Jugoslavia (called in the Peace Treaty the kingdom of the Serbs, Croats and Slovenes).

Though Austria should be one of the principal 'Have-nots,' she seems to have resigned hereself to her fate and does not cherish any irredentist dreams. Austria is therefore no longer an explosive force. The Government Party, led by Chancellor Schuschnigg, which has the backing of the Catholic Church and a section of the peasantry, is interested in maintaining the integrity of Austria's present frontiers. The younger generation who do think and dream of a change, look forward to an 'Anschluss' or Union with Germany. Occasionally one hears that the Government Party is thinking of reverting to the monarchical from of Government with Archduke Otto as Emperor. Though Austira is not herself an explosive force, she is unwitting unwrittingly a disturbing factor, inasmuch as Germany wants to annex her, while France and Italy want to preserve her independence. And behind both these parties, moves the youthful and sinister figure of Archduke Otto, who from his Belgian retreat, plots and schemes for the throne of his ancestors.

Of the the other 'Have-nots,' Bulgaria is the quietest. She lost territory to all her neighbours (Roumania, Greece and Servia—now Jugoslavia) as a result of the Balkan War of 1912 and the Great War as well. But she nurses her grievances in secret and sighs for better days, though she feels helpless within a ring of hostile powers. Hungary is more active, so far as propaganda goes. Her protagonists roam all over Europe and endeavour to canvass support among the Big Powers for revision of her frontiers. From the military point of view, Hungary is not an important factor today, having lost more than half of her former territory and population to Czechoslovakia, Jugoslavia (formerly Servia) and Roumania.

Till recently, Soviet Russia would have been regarded an as explosive force of gigantic proportions, busy in stirring up revolution all over the world. But such is not the case today. After the death of Lenin and the elimination of Trotsky, Soviet Russia under the guidance of Stalin is interested only in building up Socialism within the Soviet frontiers. The sudden insurgence of Germany has helped to accentuate this tendency. Russia has therefore joined the League of Nations, which by the way is dominated by the capitalist powers, under slogan of 'Collective Security and Peace,' is doing everything possible to prevent a disturbance of the *status quo* in Europe.

The really explosive forces in Europe today are Fascist Italy and Nazi Germany. Ranged against them are Britain, France and Soviet Russia. On the complicated chess-board of Europe interminable moves are going on and the scene is changing from day to day.

Before the Great War, the *status quo* was preserved by maintaining the 'Balance of Power.' The powers interested in preserving the *status quo* would have a secret alliance among themselves and would endeavour to play against one another the potentially hostile ones who refused to join them. The League of Nations which was constituted in 1919 was meant to put an end to secret diplomacy and to the division of the world into rival groups of powers, which served to keep up the bogey of war. In its place, was introduced a new technique, whereby all nations were to be brought into the League and made jointly responsible for the maintenance of 'Collective Security and Peace.' Both the League of Nations and its new technique seem to have failed in their objective, because there are powers that do not feel interested in preserving the *status quo* and among them, Japan and Germany are no longer members of the League—while the most powerful factor in international politics, the U. S. A., has never been a member.

To understand the meaning and purpose behind the recent disturbances in Europe, one has to comprehend the aims of Fascist Italy and Nazi Germany. Since Mussolini came to power in 1922, Italy has been thinking aggressively of expansion—of a place in the sun—of a revival of the Roman Empire. But till January, 1935, Italy did not herself know which direction her policy of expansion should follow. She had grievances against Jugoslavia who had robbed her of the Dalamatian Coast. She was snarling at France who had taken the Italian Districts of Savoy and Nice and was in possession of Tunisia, in North Africa, with a large Italian population and of the Island of Corsica which belongs geographically to Italy. She was hostile to imperialist Britain who was in control of Italian 'Malta' and had French acquiescence, converted the Mediterranean Sea into a British lake. The tension between Italy and France was particularly acute, with the result that both sides of the Franco-Italian frontier were heavily fortified and guarded. Then in 1933, the Nazi Colossus suddenly appeared on the scene and changed the whole aspect of England for support and alliance against the new danger. But Britain was non-committal. Perhaps in her heart of hearts she relished the idea of a check to French hegemony on the Continent. Perhaps she was simply following her traditional policy in international affairs. However, France was nettled and in annoyance, she turned to Italy and Soviet Russia. France wanted to withdraw her troops from the Italian frontier, and concentrate them against Germany and she wanted, further, an ally on Germany's Eastern flank. Thus there came into existence the Laval-Mussolini Pact and the Franco-Soviet Pact.

The Laval-Mussolini Pact in January, 1935, decided for Italy the direction of her future expansion. Italy squared up her differences with France and gave up territorial ambitions in Europe. In return France agreed to give her a free hand in Africa. The result was the rape of Abyssinia.

After the conquest of Abyssinia, Mussolini made a speech in which he declared to the world that Italy had now become a 'satisfied' power. The annexation of Abyssinia had been regarded by Britain as an encroachment on her preserves in Africa and the speech appeared as a pointer in the direction of the renewal of an Anglo-Italian friendship. That expectation was not fulfilled however. Though Britain had at first challenged Italy over the Abyssinian question and then beaten a quick retreat before the bluff and swagger of Mussolini—she had not forgotten the humiliation. In order to repair the damage done to her prestige among the Mediterranean and Near Eastern nations—she set about strengthening her naval and aerial bases in the Mediterranean. The first Lord of the Admiralty, Sir Samuel Hoare, went on a tour of inspection in the Mediterranean and concluded it with a public declaration that Britain would not withdraw from that zone. Other Cabinet ministers, like Anthony Eden, also made pronouncements to the effect that the Mediterranean was Britain's life line—that it was not merely a short cut, but a main arterial road. It is this determination on the part of Britain to maintain her position in the Mediterranean and to strengthen it further which has irritated and antagonised Italy—for Italy is equally determined to increase her influence in the Mediterranean through the expansion of her Navy and Air Force and this could take place only at the expense of Britain. It should therefore be clear that the present Anglo-Italian tension is not a product of Il Duce's ill humour nor is it a passing phase. It will continue until the question of the future hegemony over the Mediterranean is finally solved through the voluntary withdrawal or defeat of one of the two rival powers. Fraternising letters may pass between Neville Chamberlain and Signor Mussolini, Ambassadors and Foreign Ministers may shake hands—but a political conflict born of objective factors and forces will continue, so long as the causes remain.

Italy's reply to Britain's renewed interest in the Mediterranean is her intervention in the Spanish Civil War. It would be puerile to think or suggest that Italy has plumped for Franco because of her sympathy for the latter's Fascist aims or her hatred of Communism. Political sympathy she would have for Franco in any case but she is pouring out her blood and money for Franco primarily for strategic reasons. The same is true of Germany and whoever does not realise this, understands nothing of the Spanish Civil War.

In spite of her progress in rearmament, Italy is no match for Britain. British rearmament throughout the world has made Italy's position weaker since the end of the Abyssinian War. In any case, Britain through her control of Gibraltar and Suez can, in the event of a war with Italy, bottle up the Italian fleet and carry out an economic blockade which may prove disastrous to the latter. Italy has to import most of her raw materials like coal, iron, oil, wool, or cotton etc. and two-thirds of her sea-borne trade comes from the Atlantic, while eighty per cent of her imports come over the Mediterranean. Her coastline is long and vulnerable and she can maintain contact with her African possessions, Libya, Eritrea and Abyssinia only if she dominates the

Mediterranean. For all these reasons, an economic blockade combined with an attack from British naval stations, like Malta and Cyprus, can create havoc for Italy and even strangle her. She may retaliate by attacking British possessions in the Mediterranean or British trade passing through that sea, but she can neither attack Britain nor touch Britain's sources of raw materials and food which lie outside the Mediterranean zone. Thus, matched against Britain in war, Italy is virtually helpless and can play a primarily defensive role. And as long as Spain remains friendly to Britain, or even neutral, Italy's helplessness will remain unrelieved. Only with the help of Spain can Italy escape from her fatal strategic position. With Spain under her control, Italy could take the offensive against Britain. She could destroy Gibraltar and menace both the trade routes of Britain—the Mediterranean route and the Cape route. What is more, she could get over the blockade by using the land routes over Spain in order to bring imports from the Atlantic side. As the advent of Air Force more than compensated Italy for the weakness of her navy, *viz-a-vis* Great Britain, during the Abyssinian campaign, so the control of Spain, or even a foothold in Spanish territory, would enable her to convert her present, fatally weak and defensive position into a strong offensive one, in the event of a future war.

Thus Italy is fighting Great Britain. She is helping Franco in order to get a foothold in Spainish territory.

After considering these strategic factors, one need not be surprised that Italy is so greatly interested in Franco's success. Rather, it is surprising that there should be people in England who sympathise with Franco and the rebels. As Captain Liddell Hart, the well-known British strategist says in *Europe in Arms:*

> "Strategically, the danger (to British interests) is so obvious that it is difficult to understand the eagerness with which some of the most avowedly patriotic section of the British public have desired the rebels' success."

This is probably a case of political prejudice (*viz.*, hatred of the Socialists and Communists) overriding the dictates of self-interest.

Notwithstanding all that I have just said, it has to be pointed out that Italy today is on the whole a satisfied power. She resents British superemacy in the Mediterranean and she thinks that, as in days of yore, the Mediterranean should be a Roman lake. But she will not go to any extreme in her conflict with Great Britain. Intervention in the Spanish Civil War is all right for her, because she knows full well that none of the big Powers is yet ready for an International War. Mussolini is far too shrewd a politician to stake his position or the position of his country in a risky adventure in the near or distant future. Therefore, we may rest assured that Italy will not take the offensive in disturbing the peace of Europe—nor will she enter into a war unless she is pretty sure of victory.

But Germany under Hitler is an incalculable factor,

despite the sober and cautious policy of the Reichswehr, the German Army. Nazi Germany has been dreaming dreams which can be fulfilled only through the arbitrament of war. Moreover, the economic crisis whithin Germany has been growing so acute that many observers opine that the day is not far off when she may have to launch on a war abroad, in order to stave off discontent at home. To understand the future of Germany, we shall have to probe a little deeper.

Since the Great War there has been a French hegemony on the Continent. Not content with crushing Germany, France erected a diplomatic wall around Germany through alliances with Poland and with the Little Entente—the succession states, Czechoslovakia, Jugoslavia and Roumania. She followed this up by establishing cordial relations with Turkey which was formerly within the German orbit of influence. Germany looked on helplessly while she was thus diplomatically isolated from the civilized world. Her only reply to this policy of encirclement was the Treaty of Repallo with Soviet Russia.

French hegemony in post-war Europe has been anathema to Germany whose influence on the Continent had been paramount since the Franco-Prussian War of 1870, resulting in the ignominious defeat of. France. Since then, Germany had been expanding in several directions. Outside Europe she went in for colonial expansion. In the sphere of trade she bid fair to be a rival to Great Britain and the U. S. A. She built a powerful navy which was looked upon with suspicion by Britain, She brought Austria, Bulgaria and Turkey within her sphere of influence and planned the Berlin-Baghdad Railway which was regarded as a thrust at Britain's Eastern possessions. But the war smashed all these achievements and aspirations and for a decade Germany lay in the slough of despair, while her thinkers began to philosophise about the decline of the West and Spengler wrote his *Untergang des Abend-Landes.* Then came the new awakening through the emergence of the Nationalist-Socialist or Nazi Party.

The political doctrine of the Nazi Party can be summed up in one phrase—'Drang natch Osten'— or 'Drive to the East.' The doctrine was first propounded by Muller von den Bruck in his book, *Das dritte Reich,* or 'the Third Empire.' He did not live to see the establishment of the third Reich under Hitler in 1933. for he committed suicide in 1925 in a fit of despair. His idea was, however. taken up by Hitler and amplified in his (Hitler's) book *Mein Kampf,* or "My Struggle," which he wrote in prison in 1923. The essence of the above doctrine is that Germany should give up the idea of being a naval or colonial power. She should remain a Continental Power and her expansion should take place on the Continent—towards the East. It was pre-War Germany's greatest blunder to go in for colonial expansion and thereby come into conflict with Great Britain.

The new social philosophy of the Nazis, as expounded by Hitler, advocates the purification and strengthening of the German race through elimination of Jewish influence and a return to the soil. "Blut und Boden," or "Blood and Soil," is the new slogan for the German people. In foreign policy, the Nazis advocate the unification of all German-speaking peoples and the acquisition eastwards of more elbow-room for the prolifiic German race. In practical politics, the above objectives amount to the annexation (1) of Austria, (2) of Memel which she has lost to Lithuania, (3) of Danzig which has been made a free city under the League of Nations, (4) of the German-speaking part of Czechoslovakia with a population of 3½ millions, (5) of the Polish Corridor and the Silesian coal-fields which she has lost to Poland, (6) of the grain-producing lands of Soviet Ukraine and (7) posssibly also of the German-speaking parts of Switzerland, Italian Tyrol and other adjoining countries.

Since no country will oblige Germany by handing over any of the above territories, it goes without saying that she can realize her political objectives only through war and bloodshed. Germany herself is fully alive to this fact and that is why she has been rearming at a terrific rate on sea, land and air. Having repudiated the military clauses of the Treaty of Versailles in March, 1935: and having occupied the Rhineland in March, 1936, Germany has recovered her self-respect and her full national status as an independent State. Her continued rearmanent under these circumstances can have but one meaning—*viz.*, preparation for war. Her rearmanent has driven the last nail in the coffin of international disarmament and in sheer panic the whole of Europe is now engaged in rearming. When such frantic preparations for war are going on all round, the slightest incident may one day light an international conflagration.

It now remains for us to consider to what extreme Germany will go in achieving her aim. At what stage will she go in for war and with whom ?

Political prophecy is always a difficult job—but one thing is certain. Germany has not forgotten the lessons of her last defeat. Hers was not a military defeat, but an enonomic one. And it was the British Navy which was primarily responsible for starving her to submission. It is therefore certain that Germany will not enter into a war if she knows that Britain will be against her. In 1914, Germany foolishly enough did not believe till the last moment that Britain would take up the gauntlet on behalf of Belgium and France. It is now generally admitted by historians that if Britain had made her intentions known to Germany beforehand, the latter would probably have kept aloof from the Austro-Serbian conflict and thereby averted—or at least postponed—the World War.

Though in his book, *Mein Kampf*, Hitler asked for a final show-down with France, Germany's foreign policy has been modified since the Nazis assumed the reins of office. Germany no longer wants to get back Alsace-Lorraine from France or Eupen-Malmady from Belgium. In other words. Germany does not demand a revision of the frontiers in Western Europe. The reason for this is not far to seek. Germany knows quite well that an attack on France or Belgium or Holland will bring Britain into the arena at once and there would probably be a repetition of the last war, Germany has therefore been continually offering to sign a Western Pact which would guarantee the *status quo* in Western Europe. For a large number of British politicians this offer is a tempting one, because it removes once for all any possible threat to British interests. Germany while making this offer has been striving hard to drive a bargain at the international counter, her demand being that Britain and France should cease to interest themselves in Central and Eastern Europe so that Germany may have a free hand in rearranging the map of that part of the world.

Germany is now preparing in three directions. Firstly, she is going in for an all-round rearmament. Secondly, she is trying to make herself self-sufficient as regards the supply of food and basic raw-materials. (This is provision against a future economic blockade). This work was started last year in accordance with Germany's Four-year Plan. Thirdly, she is trying to persuade the Western Powers to agree to neutrality in the event of a war in Central or Eastern Europe. Until all these preparations are complete, it is extremely doubtful if Germany will voluntarily launch on a war.

To win over Britain to an attitude of neutrality, Germany has launched on a large-scale propaganda in that country and she has already attained a fair measure of success. In this effort, Germany has exploited the general hatred of Communism which can be found among the richer and middle classes in Britain. The Franco-Soviet Pact has come handy and the Nazis continually emphasise that for Britain to be tied up with France means fighting a war in Eastern Europe on the side of Soviet Russia, though Britain has no interests in that zone. Alongside of this, the Nazis pledge themselves not to harm British interests in any quarter of the globe. As a result of this endeavour, is an influential pro-Nazi group in Great Britain— supporters in the House of Lords, in the City of ndon and generally among the ruling classes and the fighting forces. There are supporters even among the Labourites, though they are attracted by different reasons. It is generally believed that Montagu Norman, Governor of the Bank of England, Premier Nevile Chamberlain and Sir Robert Vanisttart, the strong man in the Foreign Office, are all pro-Nazi. It is even averred that Nevile Chamberlain has inherited his pro-German attitude from his father, Joseph Chamberlain, who more than forty years ago wanted to enter into an alliance with Germany.

It is too early to say if Britain's foreign policy will ultimately follow a straight line or if it will continue to wobble, as it has often done in the past. At the present moment, British public opinion is terribly confused. Firstly, there is the pro-Nazi group, referred to above. who want a Western pact and no commitments in Central and Eastern Europe. Secondly, there is the anti-German Conservative Party represented by Winston Churchill who are distrustful of the Nazis and apprehend that when Germany is once supreme in Europe, she will challenge British interests abroad. They point out in this connection that Britain has nothing to fear from France and that outside Europe, British and French colonial interests are everywhere bound up together. Thirdly, there are the Socialists and Communists who on ideological grounds are anti-German and pro-French in their general attitude.

In the midst of this confusion, the British Foreign Office, despite Anthony Eden, is following a defiinte policy *viz.*, to persuade France to give up her interests in Central and Eastern Europe. The aim of Vanisttart's policy is to force Germany to be and to remain a European Continental Power. That is why Britain has acquiesced in German rearmanent, made the Naval Agreement with Germany in June, 1935, advised France to ignore German military occupation of the Rhineland in March, 1936, warned France not to help the Spanish Government though she was clearly entitled to do so under International Law. It is further alleged by those who are in a position to know diplomatic secrets that the British Foreign Office encouraged Poland in 1933 to come to terms with the Nazi Government. (The German-Polish Non-Aggression Pact was adopted the next year). It also encourged Belgium to break the alliance with France and return to neutrality and Jugoslavia to make friends with Italy and Germany, against the advice of France. It further encouraged the pro-Nazi Henlein Party in Czechoslovakia and intrigued for breaking, or at least slackening, the bonds of the Little Entente (Czechoslovakia, Jugoslavia, and Roumania) and of the Balkan Entente (Jugoslavia, Roumania, Greece and Turkey) which are under French influence.

It would not be improper to conlude from the above facts that the British Foreign Office has been secretly working contra France, at least in Europe, and French hegemony on the Continent is distasteful to Whitehall. Perhaps because of this, French politicians of the right were greatly annoyed with Great Britain and Laval proceeded to make alliances with Italy and Soviet Russia, independently of Britain. In fact, Laval's foreign policy might, from one point of view, be regarded as anti-British. But French politicians of the left follow blindly the policy of the British Foreign Office, believing that France and Britain should hold together through thick and thin.

At present the German Foreign Office is playing an

aggressive role, while France is busy trying to counteract the former's moves and activities. Outside Britain, the Nazis have been remarkably successful in Belgium. A pro-Nazi Party (the Rexists) has come into existance in Belgium and Nazi propaganda is active among the Flemish speaking people of Belgium. The Belgium Government has broken away from the alliance with France and will in future adopt an attitude of neutrality in the event of war in Central or Eastern Europe. The treaty of Rapallo with Soviet Russia has virtually lapsed since the Nazis came to power in 1933, but as if to compensate Germany for that, the Nazi Government entered into a Non-Aggression pact with Poland. This Pact served to undermine greatly French influence in Poland. Last year, France made gigantic efforts to recover her influence in Poland and a number of visits took place on both sides. But it seems probable that the Franco-Polish Alliance will never become a living force again and that in future Poland will follow an independent foreign policy—that is, a policy of neutrality in the event of a Franco-German or Russo-German conflict.

In addition to the above activities, Germany is now exceedingly busy in trying to weaken France by slackening the bonds of the Little Entente and Balkan Entente and by getting a foothold in Spanish territory. With the help of several alliances and friendly contacts, the position of France today is exceedingly strong and as long as this position continues, she will never agree to withdraw her interest in Central and Eastern Europe. She will continue to insist—as Litvinov, the Soviet Foreign Minister, also does—that peace is indivisible and that there should be one European Pact to guarantee collective security to all the states under the aegis of the League of Nations. Failing this, besides the Western Pact, there should be another Pact to guarantee peace in Central and Eastern Europe. To this, Germany does not agree and will not agree.

France has fortified herself with military alliances with Czechoslovakia and Soviet Russia. The two latter powers have also a military alliancebetween themselves. Consequently, these three powers will always be found together in the event of an international emergency. Czechoslovakia has an understanding with the other Little Entente powers, Jugoslavia and Roumania. And Jugoslgvia and Roumania have an understanding with Greece and Turkey through the Balkan Entente. Germany hopes that by weaning away Jugoslavia and Roumania, she will isolate Czechoslovakia in Central Europe—for help from Russia can reach Czechoslovakia only through Roumania or through Poland. Poland is no longer a problem to Germany because of the non-aggression pact. Germany is trying to bring Austria under her influence through the instrumentaility of Italy. Through Britain, she is trying to persuade France that, as military factor, Soviet Russia is not of much consequence and that France should give the go-by to the military clauses of the Franco-Soviet Pact. The recent execution of eight Army Generals in Russia has given a handle to the capitalist powers and they are carrying on a terrific propaganda to the effect that the Soviet military machine is reeking with indiscipline and connot be relied on in the event of war. Last but not least, Germany is trying her level best to obtain a foothold in Spanish territory, so that in the event of war with France she could stab her in the back by cutting off her communications with North Africa, from where France always obtains large supplies of men and materials, when war breaks out in Europe. Germany hopes that by weakening France on all sides and by putting pressure on her through the British Foreign Office, she will ultimately make her agree to a Western pact, giving Germany a free hand in Central and Eastern Europe. If France does not agree to this and if she ultimately goes to war with Germany on the side of Soviet Russia, she will find herself considerably weakened compared to what she was in 1914.

But will France fall in with Germany's plans? Ostensibly not. For Britain it is immaterial who dominates the Continent—France or Germany—for Britain's interests lie outside Europe. But France cannot so easily give up her hegemony in Europe for, unlike Britain, she is a Continental Power, besides being a Colonial Power. Moreover, France is fighting not merely for power and prestige, but also for her national safety. She has not forgotten the tragic [illegible] of 1870. Her population is stationary and is about two-thirds of that of Germany, whose population is still growing. Consequently, France has a genuine horror of German invasion, while Britain has not, as long as the German Navy keeps to the prescribed limits of the Anglo-German Naval Agreement. To crown everything, there is in France, a deep distrust of German aims and aspirations which has been accentuated by violent denunciations of France in Hitler's book, *Mein Kampf.* As a writer has put it succinctly, in France the right hates Germany, the left hates Hitler. In these circumstances, it is extremely doubtful if France will ever give up her allies and alliances in Central and Eastern Europe as long as the violently nationalistic Nazi Party remains in power.

The issue of the Spanish Civil War is hanging in the balance and it is too early to say how far German diplomacy will succeed there. But in Central and Eastern Europe it has made considerable headway. In Roumania, the King and the Cabinet are, on the whole, pro-German and the Francophile ex-Foreign minister, Titulescu, has lost considerable influence. There is an anti-Semitic pro-Nazi Party, the Iron Guard, led by Codreanu, which is behind the Government. In Jugoslavia, the Premier Stoyadinovitch is pro-Nazi, as also his Government, while the royal family is under British influence. In Greece, the Premier, General Metaxas, who has made himself the Dictator, is undoubtedly under German influence. And Greece is important to Germany, because should the Russian Fleet in the Black Sea enter the Mediterranean through the Dardanelles, it could be attacked from a base in the Grecian Islands. Then Hungary and Bulgaria, being 'Have-not' powers, are expected to line up with Germany, if they see any chance of having their national grievances redressed thereby. Thus it appears that Germany has stolen a march over France throughout the Balkan Peninsula and she has been throwing out commercial baits in profusion.

But in international politics there is no finality. France is following on the heels of Germany everywhere. It is difficult to predict how long the Governments of of Metaxas in Greece or Stoyadinovitch in Jugoslavia will last. The pro-French party in Roumania, though out of power for the time being, is not negligible and the Balkan temperament is proverbially changeable. Moreover, Germany finds pitted against herself, one of the finest diplomats of modern Europe, President Eduard Benes of Czechoslovakia.

The scene is changing from day to day and political forecasts are anything but easy. One thing is certain. If war comes, it will come as the result of a German challenge to the *status quo* in Central and Eastern Europe. But will it come ? The answer rests primarily with Britain. Germany will not repeat the errors of 1914 and will not go into a war, if she knows that Britain will be against her. She might be trapped into it as she was in 1914, thinking that Britain would keep out of it. If France and Britain agree to be neutral in a conflict in Central or Eastern Europe, war will break out in Europe, as sure as the sun rises in the East, the moment Germany is ready for it. Even if France lines up with Soviet Russia, with Britain remaining neutral, there may be war, though the upshot of it will be doubtful.

At the present moment, two scenes need watching —Spain and the Balkans. If Franco wins, it will be a victory for Italy and Germany and will mean the end of British hegemony in the Mediterranean and dark days ahead of France, if war should break out on the Continent. In the Balkans, if Germany succeeds in isolating Jugoslavia and Roumania from Czechoslovakia, she will in the event of war, be able to occupy Prague in six hours and overrun Czechosiovakia within a few days. But the bigger problem will remain—Russia. The Russian Colossus has often proved to be an engima. It baffled Napoleon—the conqueror of Europe. Will it baffle Hitler ?

VII

IMPRESSIONS OF VIENNA

Subhas Bose's Letter from Vienna. *May 23, 1933.*

" Since I wrote last week, there has been a slight improvement in the condition of Mr. V. J. Patel. He is still very weak. Attempts to move about have aggravated his condition, so that he has been ordered complete rest. He will have to remain in a sanatorium in Vienna for some time yet, after which he may be going to some watering place in Czechoslovakia. The pain is less acute than before, though it comes on regularly. I am able to take walks now. The British Government have at last allowed me to go to Germany so that I may undergo treatment at a sanatorium in the Black Forest as recommended by Bob Neumdun. I shall, however, stay in Veinna for a few weeks till I feel somewhat stronger than now. Last week Vienna celebrated the 25th Anniversary of the Victory over the Turks. In 1683, the Turks, who had overrun the whole of Europe were for the first time stopped near Vienna. That proved the turning point in the onward march of the Turks and they could not make any further advance. The Austrian Fascists and the German Fascists both wanted to celebrate this event, the former being the supporters of the Government and the latter their opponents. Some leader of the Nazi movement in Germany came to Vienna to take part in the anniversay function but the Government prohibited processions through the Town on the occasion. The German Leaders were politely told on behalf of the Austrian Government that their visit to Vienna was not welcome. The Nazis were however, allowed to hold a meeting on the 13th May. The next as a contrast to the Nazi celebration, the *Heim Wehr*, had their celebration. orty thousand men from all parts of Austria arrived Vienna in special trains to take part in the meeting id the procession that had been announced. They sembled at Schon-brunu, the former summer palace of e Emperor, and from there they marched into the own. Forty thousand men in the uniform of the *Heim ehr* Party took 2½ hours to march past. At the end the march, a mammoth meeting was held, which was ldressed by Leaders of the *Heim Wehr* volunteers, and e Prime Minister Chancellor Dr. Dalfuss. The National ocialists tried a counter-demonstration when the *Heim ehr* were marching by—by shouting "Heil Hitler" in ply to the shouts of "Heil Starhemburg" which were ised by the supporters of the *Heim Wehr*. But the ational Socialists (Nazis) were dispersed by the police. id many arrests were made.

From the incidents of the 13th and 14th May, it ems as if the present Government supported by the *eim Wehr* Party intend to fight the National-Socialists (Nazis). The *Heim Wehr* demonstration, while celebrating the victory of the Viennese over the Turks—incidentally showed the public that the present Government are not weak, but they have their "Storm Troops" in the *Heim Wehr* Volunteers.

What will the present tension in Austria ultimately lead to? The *Heim Wehr* objective is a restoration of the Hapsburg Monarchy in Austria. The Nazi objective is a union with Germany. It is said that the former have the moral support of Italy while the latter have the moral support of Germany. Between these two parties—the Social Democrats, who are the common enemy of both are playing a watching game. The Social Democrats represent over sixty percent of the electorate in Vienna, but their following is less strong in the country. The *Heim Wehr* has a poor following in Vienna itself, but a fairly good following in the country as a whole. The Nazis who as a party are the latest to arrive in the field are everywhere increasing their following particularly after the victory of Hitler in Germany. They claim that if there is an election today they will increase their strength considerably and may become the largest single party. But it is difficult to be correct in one's estimate in the present uncertain state of things. The social Democrats on the other hand say that they will be able to maintain their present strength in the event of an election, and that any gains the Nazis may make, will be at the expense of other parties. The fast of Mahatma Gandhi has been causing anxiety to all Indians abroad. The latest news goes to show that he has been standing the strain of the fast fairly well on the whole. We hope, and pray that till the end, he will stand the ordeal we l, and that there will not be any permanent injury to his health. Thanks to the Municipal Authorities, during the last fortnight, I have had the opportunity of visiting some of the Municipal institutions that have been set up in Vienna during the last twelve years under the inspiration of the Social Democratic party. They have been endeavouring to convert the Municipality into a poor Man's Corporation by taxing luxuries, amusements, etc,, and without incurring loans, as is done elsewhere, they have provided housing accommodation for two hundred thousand people. Besides this, they have done wonderful work for medical relief, education, children's welfare, and health of population. Most of the public utilities in Vienna like electricity, gas, etc., are municipalised. Here you see socialism in practice and it is an object lesson to all those who are interested in civic problems and in Municipal progress.

Apart from Municipal endeavour, the efforts made by private initiative on co-operative lines to improve the amenities of life are note-worthy. The other day I was invited to a flower-show organised by the "Small Gardeners Association." I was surprised to see the progress made by the small gardners in rearing different kinds of flowers, which formerly, only the rich people could afford to rear. There was also a demonstration of different methods of decorating window-fronts etc., with creepers, and flowers in a way, which is within the reach of the poor.

The attempt being made in this way to bring culture and beauty within the reach of the poor, is really praiseworthy. I find from the papers that the relatives of those, who have been transported to the Andamans have organised an association for looking after the welfare of the transported prisoners. This is just as it should be. I have no doubt that the full weight of the public opinion will be behind an association of this kind;

Civil Disobedience Movement

"I hope that the political workers in India will ponder seriously over the situation created by the suspension of the civil disobedience movement, and chalk out the lines of our future work. There is no doubt that the only alternative left to us is to rally together all the radical elements in the country into a definite party with a definite programme and plan of action. There is no doubt that in the near future a great attempt will be made by all modrerate elements in the country to start an era of co-operation with the bureaucracy. In the face of this, if the radical elements do not organise themselves into a party, they will run the risk of being wiped out of existence.

On the 19th April. I wrote to friends in India, drawing their attention to the necessity of organising an Indian Branch of the International Society of Authors, Journalists, etc., known popularly in Europe as the P. E. N. (Poets, Editors, Novelists etc.,) club. I am glad to read in the Indian papers of the 2nd and 3rd May that an Indian Branch of the P. E. N. club is going to be started in India soon. This organisation serves to bring together the intellectuals of all lands, and is of great value in public life—both national and international. I was pained to find on reading the literature of this organisation that India was not represented on this organisation inspite of her contribution to world literature in recent years—though our Poet Tagore had been made an Honorary member of the P.E.N. club in London. At present the annual Congress of the P. E. N. is being held in Scotland. I hope the Indian Branch of the P. E. N. Club will soon send an invitation requesting that the P. E. N. Congress in 1933 be held in India. I am sure this proposal will be supported by many countries in Europe, if Indians who are known outside India, back this invitation.

VIII

A VISIT TO BERLIN

Letter from Veinnia. *12-4-33*

This morning I read the following note in the "London Times" of the 10th April sent by the Delhi correspondent of the 'Times' on the 9th April. "The newspapers give prominence to a statement, which Mr. Gandhi is supposed to have made to the Viceroy, and which was first quoted in the 'Bombay Chronicle' In it Mr. Gandhi is reported as saying, "If peaceful condition for the evolution of independence were possible, I would use influence with my friends of the Congress to ask them to agree to a suspension of strife and to the operation after examination of the Provincial constitutions as in my opinion, they may be truer test of the real transference of power."

Nothing is known in Government circles in Delhi of any such statement having been made by Mr. Gandhi to the Viceroy. "I hope that the news published above is not correct; for there is no possibility that in the immediate future the British Cabinet or the British Parliament will concede the national demands of India. Throughout the world, forces of reaction and of conservation are now getting the upper hand, and this will continue for some time.

Europe is today passing through an unsettled condition, both economically, and politically. On the one hand, there is the economic crisis. which has hit hard practically every country in the world. On the other hand, there are political factors, largely the result of the Treaty of Versailles, which are contributing to the general unrest, and unstability. Smaller nations in the Middle and Eastern Europe are suffering from this double shock more than the bigger nations. In Austria, for example, there is the economic crisis. Then there is the political crisis, because of the tug of war between different parties. The present Government of the Austrian Federal republic is supported by the Christian party, the Agrarian party, and the *Heim Wehr* (or Austrian Fascist Party). Nevertheless, the biggest party is the Social Democratic party who are out of power in the Federal Government. The Nazi party are growing in influence since Hitler came into power in Germany, and they are looking forward to the union between Germany and Austria. The Austrian Fascist Party (Heim-Wehr) on the other hand would like to see the restoration of Hapsburg Monarchy in Austria. In this tangle of parties and conflict of policies who can tell what is going to happen in the near or distant future?

A few days ago, an artist from Ceylon Mr. Surya Sena gave a demonstration of Singhalese and Indian music in Viennia. Mr. Sena was accompanised by his wife, who is also an excellent musician. The performance was enjoyed and appreciated by the Viennese public A few days later, the Hindusthan Academis Association of Viennia were at home to Mr. and Mrs. Sena and a number of distinguished Viennese ladies and gentlemen like Mr. and Mrs. Rene Fulop Miller and Dr. David Bach were invited on the occasion. A further demonstration was given by the artists, and a pleasant evening was spent on the occesion.

(2)

Impressions of Berlin

" In connection with my visit to Berlin and reception by the Mayor (Ober burger meister) of that city, I feel it my duty to communicate to you and the corporation what I was able to see of the Municipal administration there.

Though Berlin is situated on a flat country, and is therefore denied the panoramic advantages of Viennia, and Prague, it is compensated to some extent by being supplied with beautiful lakes, which have been fully utilized for bathing, rowing, and other sports. As a city it is by common consent one of the cleanest, and (probably the cleanest) in Europe,—and this has been possible only because the citizens heartily co-operate with the civil authorities by observing the rules of cleanliness. Though the population is over four and nearly five millions, there is not much congestion as would be naturally expected. This is because the city is a comparatively modern one, and at the time of planning, it was spread out over a large area. In view of the large, population of the city, the supply of such amenities as water, gas, and electricity is made not from station, but from several stations in different parts of the city. Public utilities, including transport services are owned and managed by the municipality.

" From the point of view of the problems of Calcutta I was specially interested in the work of four departments —namely, water, sewage, roads, and electricity. For water supply I found that the big lakes near Berlin had been tapped and in addition, they were using a lot of underground water obtained by pumping as we do in our tube-wells. I was told that there were in all 13 water-supply stations in the city. Regarding Sewage disposal, I was interested to find that they did not have only one outlet for the city, but many. In big stations outside the city, treatment of sewage on modern lines including the activated sledge process, was going on. The efluent, as well as the sledge derived from treatment were being made use for agricultural purpose. It was highly instructive to see how such a large city could dispose of its sewage without discharging into a river or the sea. From the sewage works, they were obtaining 8,000 cubic metres of gas every day. I was told they were getting methun gas CH_4. Berlin has uptodate laboratories for experimenting with road surfaces. I was glad to visit some of them, and see the work going on there. After visiting the laboratories I went out to see some of the roads that had been recently made. I found that they were making mostly asphalted surfaces on concrete beds. It was costing them eleven marks (one mark, one rupee roughly) per square-metre for making the concrete bed, and the asphalt layer and this included the cost of repairs for five years. I also visited the public baths (particularly the public bath in Warnses) and also the principal hospitale of the city. I was greatly interested to see the home for mentally defective boys and girls, and the home for cripples, and observed the uptodate method of looking after and educating them.

For the supply of electricity there are atleast seven stations. I visited some of the biggest ones. In the boilers of the electricity, there are atleast seven stations. I visited some of the biggest ones. In the boilers of the electricity stations, they had not only stoker-firing but also coal-dust-firing and I was told that they were making use of coal-dust on a large scale, as they found it to be advantageous.

Altogether my visit was exceedingly interesting and instructive to me. It was very good of the mayor to make special arrangements enabling me to visit the different places. Von Hane was deputed to accompany me. The Berlin Municipality, I was assured, will gladly help Calcutta in my civic problem, whenever they are desired to do so.

IMPRESSIONS OF EGYPT

There are few cities so fascinating as Cairo, the capital of Modern Egypt. Nursed by the Nile and guarded by the towering Pyramids, this city with its pleasing climate, luxuriant vegetation, lovely streets and picturesque buildings, has an unceasing attraction for the foreigner. But how few of those who repeatedly pass in and out of the Suez canal have been to Cairo.

Thanks to the arrangements made by the Lloyd Triestino Company, we could leave M. N. Victoria at Suez, drive by car to Cairo, spend a useful day there and catch the boat again at Port Said. By 9 P. M., on the 16th January, 1935, we were at Suez. The ship anchored at a great distance from the shore and we had to cross over in a ferry. It was a moonlit night. The vast expanse of water was brightened by the rays of the silvery moon. All around us were gleaming the lights of the town of Suez and of Port Tewfik with their starry reflection dancing in the bosom of the sea. Passing the customs barrier, we got into the car which was to carry us to Cairo. Soon the town was past and we were in the heart of the desert. rushing northwards. A companion of ours was expecting some adventure at the hands of desert Beduins, but he was disappointed. There was peace all along the way—endless sand on both sides—the road running straight ahead and the pale moon shedding its lustre from the canopy of heaven. It was past midnight when we reached Cairo. In the stillness of the night, the brilliantly-lighted streets of Cairo with their stately buildings looked enchanting.

The next morning we made our trip to the Pyramids. The air was cold and a biting wind was blowing as we crossed the Nile and rushed to where the world-famous Pyramids were silhouetted against the morning sky. Soon we arrived at their foot and began to gaze upwards. So these were the monuments of stone that had fired the imagination of even a soldier like Napoleon. The French Emperor had drawn up his troops near them and had stirred up their tired limbs by reminding them that 5,000 years were looking down upon them. The appeal had worked like magic and the Mamelukes had been scattered like dust before the wind. Round the Pyramids we walked and in-and-out of the several excavations, wondering all the time what the Pyramids had to teach us. Yes, we also could feel an inspiration. Standing before those towering giants against the background of the endless and dreary desert, one could realize the majesty of man and the immortality of the soul. The authors of those edifices had defied time. They had enshrined themselves in stone and whoever had any inwardness of perception, could hold communion with them.

Near the Pyramids was the Sphinx with its

riddle. One massive work of stone, the searching eyes gazing at the rising sun—what idea did the Sphinx embody ? One of the guides ventured an explanation. The ancient Egyptians worshipped the sun-god and the Sphinx was either a symbol of the sun or a representative of sun-worship. But who knew ? The soul that had built the Sphinx did not speak and the riddle remained unsolved. A little bird was sitting motionless on the head of the Sphinx. "That is the soul of the Sphinx," said a guide, to tickle our phantasy, "That comes every morning to greet him." Looking more closely at the face of the Sphinx, we found that the nose had been blown off. That was another problem, we thought. But the guides were not to be daunted. "It was a cannon-ball of the Emperor Napoleon that did the havoc," said one of them. Connecting Napoleon with the Pyramids, we were prepared to be convinced. But another guide protested. "It was the Arab iconoclasts who had done it," said he, "to spite the ancient Egyptians."

We left the Sphinx more puzzled than ever and turned to the Pyramids. "Do you want to climb to the top of the Pyramids ?" asked one guide. "There is a man who can run up to the top and descend in eight minutes, Sir," he continued. Thinking that it was a further trick for emptying our pockets, we declined, saying that that did not interest us. Instead, we sought to explore the interior of the biggest of the Pyramids. That was no difficult task. The narrow passage leading up to the big hall in the heart the Pyramid was lighted with electricity. Only our backs were aching at the time we reached the hall—the effect of continuous bending while we were climbing the steps. The total height of the Pyramid was more than 450 feet and the hall was situated almost half-way. The mummies of the ancient kings used to be stored here, but the hall was now empty, the mummies having been removed to the museums. There was another and smaller hall to a lower level, where the mummies of the queens used to be stored.

The Pyramids of Geza, where there is the Sphinx, are about nine miles from Cairo. There are nine Pyramids in all—three big and six small ones. The big ones are in perfect condition—only the alabaster-coating having come off at many places. There is another group of Pyramids at a greater distance from Cairo, about twenty miles, near the ancient city of Memphis, and some statues of the ancient Egyptian kings are to be found there.

No less interesting than the Pyramids is the Museum of Antiquities in Cairo which is a store-house of all the finds in different parts of Egypt. Within this Museum the most interesting section is that which contains the finds of the tomb of Tutankhamen at Luxor in Upper Egypt. It is not possible to do justice to them in the course of one or two visits. At every step, one is left wondering at the high level of art and civilization which the ancient Egyptians attained at a period which must be at least as old as 2,000 B. C. The works of art look as fresh as if they had been constructed only yesterday and apart from the excellence of their workmanship, what simply appeals the imagination of man is, how they have been so effectively preserved as to defy the ravages of time.

As compared with Egypt, India also can boast of a very ancient culture and civilization, but one must admit that we have not been able to preserve what we constructed, owing to our comparative inefficiency in the art of preservation. Moreover, I do not think that we developed the material side of life—the arts and crafts—as much as the ancient Egyptians did. Our emphasis was not on civilization but on culture; not on the material side of life but on the intellectual and spiritual. Therein, we had our advantages, as well as disadvantages. Owing to our superior thought power, we could hold our own against invaders from outside, even when we were vanquished physically for the time being—and in course of time we could also absorb the outsider, while the ancient Egyptians went down before the Arab invaders and disappeared altogether.

On the other hand, emphasis on the intellectual and spiritual side, caused us to neglect the development of science and left us comparatively weak on the material and physical side of life. The glorious periods of our history were, when we were able to strike the golden mean between the demands of spirit and of matter, of the soul and of the body—and thereby progress simultaneously on both fronts. Owing to the inter-relation between the soul and the body, the neglect of the body not only weakens a nation physically, but in the long run, weakens it spiritually as well. India at the present moment appears to be suffering not merely from physical weakness but from spiritual exhaustion as well —the inevitable result of our neglecting one aspect of life. And if we are to come to our own once again, we have to advance simultaneously on both fronts.

To return to our narrative. The morning excursions over, we devoted the afternoon to sight-seeing within the city. Cairo is full of mosques and tombs and much of ancient history lies embedded therein. Each mosque has its own beauty and its own story to tell. Sometimes, one is brought face to face with scenes of Biblical interest as well, but how far they are real, one cannot tell. For instance, inside the big Citadel (the old fort of Cairo) the guide showed me a very deep well which he said was the well of Joseph. One of the most interesting spots in Cairo is the Citadel from where one can have a magnificent view of the whole city. The palace of Mohammad Ali, from where this view is obtained is unfortunately in a neglected condition now. The guide showed us the room where Mohammad Ali is supposed to have invited the Mamelukes to dinner and afterwards taken them unawares and massacred them, only one of the Mamelukes escaping with his life. Outside this palace is the mosque of Mohmmad Ali which fortunately is now being renovated at considerable cost. The mosque of Sultan Hassan, the Blue Mosque, the tomb of the Mamelukes, the Al-Azhar University—are some of the other places of interest which draw the foreigner.

Having seen something of old Egypt, our thoughts naturally turned to Modern Egypt. Modern Cairo was a fine city and one could not but admire it. But the modern palace of the king was by no means an imposing structure. Even the barracks of the British troops looked more attractive. Egypt, we were told, had a king but a rude reminder came when we eyed the Union Jack proudly floating in the wind on the top of the British barracks in the heart of the town and also in the Citadel. Independence indeed!

But what about the people of Modern Egypt? I had heard of the Nationalist party of Egypt—called the Wafd Party which was once so brilliantly led by Syed Zaghlul Pasha of revered memory, who has left an able successor in Mustapha El-Nahas Pasha. A visit to Cairo would of course be meaningless without an interview with the great nationalist leader. The time at my disposal was short but I was lucky enough to have the desired interview. Mustapha El-Nahas Pasha was accompanied by two of his ablest colleagues, Mr. M. F. Nokrashy and Mr. Makram Ebeid, when I met him. We had a very interesting talk. I was anxious to know something about Egypt at first hand—while they were anxious to know about India. I was glad to learn that under the Premiership of Nessim Pasha, the rule of ordinance had ended in Egypt. The nationalists could once again breathe freely. On the 8th and 9th January, 1935, they had a Congress of the Wafd Party in Cairo attended by over 30,000 people which had proved to be an unparalleled success. Elections to the Parliament were expected to be held shortly and Wafd Party was confident of sweeping the polls. Altogether, the situation looked very hopeful for the Nationalists and the leaders were in high spirits.

Turning to India Mustapha El-Nahas Pasha first inquired about the health of Mahatma Gandhi. He said that when the Mahatma was returning to India in 1931, he had sent his Secretary to Port Said to invite him to Cairo and he had arranged a meeting in his own house of the prominent members of his party. But unfortunately the Mahatma could not come. Our talk next turned to the Hindu-Muslim question, and Mustapha condemned the action of those communalists, who were acting against the best interest of Indian Nationalism. He enquired one by one, as to who among the Muslim leaders were working with the Nationalist party and who were on the side of the Government. He said that in Egypt, the Muslims had come to a perfect understandiug with the Egyptian Christians (called Coopts) and both the communities were working hand-in-hand for the uplift of Egypt. He hoped that before long samething would happen in India. In conclusion, I assured Mustapha that we Indians were following the fortunes of the Egyptian people with the greatest interest and our whole-hearted sympathy was with them in their struggle for freedom. In return, he conveyed the warmest sympathy of the Egyptian people for the Indians in their National fight for freedom.

After a busy day spent in Cairo, we left by train for Port Said to catch our boat there. In the train we had several Egyptian fellow-passengers and as some of them spoke English (French is, on the whole, more popular in Egypt than English) we soon fell into a conversation. We wanted to find out how the man in the street looked upon the nationalist Wafd Party. One of the passengers —a Coopt who was a government servant, was at first chary of committing himself. But when he found that we were dependable, he became more frank. He spoke very highly of the Egyptian leaders and said, among other things, that all Egyptians, whether Muslims or Christians, wore the Tarboosh or Fez Cap, because it was the national head-dress of the Egyptian people, (till then I had always regarded the Fez Cap as a symbol of Islam).

By 11 p. m. we were on board our ship. Within an hour she set sail. At the entrance to the Mediterranean sea, we passed the statue of the French Engineer, Lesseps who had constructed the Suez canal and we were soon on the high seas. The lights of Port Said grew dimmer and dimmer as the waves began to grow in volume. When morning dawned, the ship was rolling and most of us were sick.

X

MY IMPRESSIONS OF ABYSSINIA

The Secret of Abyssinia and its Lesson.

The fate of Abyssinia is now in the melting pot. The outlook for her is exceedingly gloomy. But whatever happens in that part of Africa, the lesson of Abyssinia will remain as a legacy for humanity.

It is this that in the 20th century a nation can hope to be free only if it is strong, from a physical and military point of view, and is able to acquire all the knowledge which modern science can impart.

The Orient has succumbed bit by bit to the physical encroachment of the Occident, because it has wrapt itself up in self-complacency and lived in the divine contentment for some centuries and because it has refused to keep abreast of the march of human and scientific progress, especially in the art of warfare. India and Burma along with other Oriental countries, have suffered for this reason. Countries like Japan, Turkey, and Persia are still alive because they were able to modernize themselves in time.

Like the rest of the Orient, Japan, too, at one time, wanted to live in peaceful isolation. But the booming of the American Cannon burst upon her ears as a mighty challenge. She would either have to enter the arena of world-economics and world-politics as a strong and modernized nation or go down before the West. She chose the former alternative, bestirred herself in time and during the space of 50 years, emerged as a strong and modernized nation. By the time that a serious challenge to her independent existence came from a Western power, she was prepared. And her timely preparation saved her. In this hard world, only the fittest can survive.

Abyssinia is now a new problem. During the latter half of the 19th century, the Imperialist nations of Europe—Britian, France, and Italy—began to cast their eyes on her. All of them tried to grab that potentially rich country—but were baffled not only by the brave and warlike inhabitants but also by the mountainous and impassable nature of the country. One cannot forget the abortive military exploits of Lord Napier of Magdala in Abyssinia (Magdala is situated in the heart of Abyssinia) or the over-throw of Europe or Theodore by the British in 1868. Failing to partition Abyssinia among themselves—as the rest of Africa had been partitioned—they took possession of all the surrounding tracts, cutting off Abyssinia from the sea. Thus a reference to the map will show that Abyssinia is surrounded by Sudan (British), Kenya (British) Italian Somaliland, British Somaliland, French Somaliland, and Eritrea (Italian).

The liberation and unification of Italy took place in

1861—rather late in the day—while the unification of Germany took place in 1870. By that time the available colonial world had been practically divided up by the other Imperialist European powers. Hence we find that among the Imperialist have-nots, are Italy, and Germany. Germany, under Bismark, looked forward to some territories in South-West Africa—while Italy cast eyes on Abyssinia and her surroundings.

Italian penetration of Africa began in the eighties of the last century, when Abyssinia was not unified. The Northern part was ruled over by Emperor John and the Southern part by Emperor Menelik, while some other parts were virtually independent. The population of Abyssinia at that time was anything but homogenous either from the ethnic or from the religious point of view. The death of Emperor John in 1889 during a war with the Dervish rebels, paved the way for the unification of Abyssinia under Emperor Menelik. Menelik who was crowned as "Negus Nagest" (King of Kings) was great as a soldier and as a statesman. Under his leadership the great fight with the Italians took place, culminating in the complete annihilation of the Italian forces at Adowa in 1896. Since then Adowa has been remembered by the Italians as a defeat which has to be avenged.

Since 1896, Abyssinia has had a respite for nearly 40 years. If she had been able to strengthen and modernize her people within this period—as the Japanese did, then she would probably have survived.

But she has unfortunately failed to do so and hence she is doomed. The fault does not lie with the supreme rulers of Abyssinia, who have been partiotic, able and statesmanlike, but with the population. The present Emperor, for example, has shown proofs of wonderful diplomacy and statesmanship throughout the present crisis—such as one would expect in a first class British politician. But dynastic and tribal jealousies unfortunately exist (the desertion of the Emperor's son-in-law, who is a descendent of Emperor John, to the Italian which was announced in the press on the 12th Oct., is an example of dynastic jealousy). The people are mostly illiterate and slavery still exists as an institution. Last but not least, the glorious victory of Adowa has lulled the brave Abyssinians into a false sense of security. This sense of security will prove to be their ruin on the field of battle where they will realize only too late that the Italians of 1935 are not the Italians of 1896 and that the art of warfare has advanced with rapid strides since they overthrew the Italians at Adowa.

Having failed to subjugate Abyssinia by force of arms, the Imperialist powers commenced diplomatic intrigue from the beginning of this century. The story is told by the *New Leader* of London in its issue of the 23rd August 1935 (to annotate this story I shall only add that Abyssinia was admitted into the League of Nations in September 1923, inspite of the objection of the British Government).

Partition Planned

Before this British had recognized Abyssinia as an Italian sphere of influence, but the defeat of Italy was seized by Britian as an opportunity to state her own claim. In 1906, the three Imperialist powers—Britian, France, and Italy—signed a treaty which foreshadowed the partition of Abyssinia between them. The Treaty contained the usual hypocritical formula about guaranteeing the integrity of Abyssinia, but in fact, gave Britian the right to regulate the head-waters of the Nile, made Italy paramount in Western Abyssinia, and put France in authority over her railway zone.

Buying out Italy

The next stage in this story of Imperialist robbery came with the beginning of the world war. By Treaty Italy was allied with Germany and Austria, but France and Britian bought her off. They signed a secret Treaty under which Italian Imperialism was promised that the Frontiers of her East African colonies should be extended at the expense of Abyssinia.

After the war Britian wanted to make sure of her control of the Nile by building a barrage in Lake Tsana. Italy offered to support this claim ifBritian in returnwould recognise Italy's exclusive economic influence in Western Abyssinia. But British turned the offer down. She was afraid of antagonizing France and believed that she was powerful enough to win through without Italian support. She self-righteously told Italy that the claim to exclusive Italian influence would be a violation of the Treaty of 1896 which had acknowledged the integrity of Abyssinia.

Six years later the position changed. The Abyssinian government had resisted Britian's demands, and the British Government wanted Italian support. Britian forgot all about the promise to maintain the integrity of Abyssinia in the Treaty of 1906. She forgot all about the righteous indignation of her in 1919. She agreed to recognize Italy's claim to the whole of the Western Abyssinia as a " sphere of influence."

Then an unexpected rebuff took place. The Abyssinian Government rejected the agreement between Britian and Italy and threatened to expose this Imperialist design before the League......Baffled, Britian tried new tactics. It offered Abyssinia the bribe of a corridor of 600 square miles of territory through British Somaliland to the Coast, The British Government was so sure that this offer would be accepted that maps were published in 1926 making the Port of Zelia as an Abyssinia territory. To the surprise of the British Imperialists the Abyssinians rejected the offer. They were not to be bribed out of their independence."

To continue the story, in 1928, Italy and Abyssinia entered into a Treaty of Friendship providing for arbitration in all disputes for a period of 20 years. A further agreement was signed at the same time whereby Abyssinia was granted a free zone at the port of

Assab in Italian Eritrea. It is clear that upto this time the two countries were friendly to each other. Thereafter a sudden change took place in the foreign policy of Abyssinia. As technical experts, political advisers and military officers, nationals of other European countries, like Belgium, France, Britian and Sweden were brought in and Italians were carefully excluded. When the year 1934 opened, Italian influence on the Abyssinian Government was practically nothing, while British influence was in the ascendent. Moreover it was talked about that the British Government had come to a separate and secret understanding with the Abyssinian Government with regard to the waters of Lake Tsana—without the knowledge and support of Italy. As a counter-move, Mussolini came to an understanding with Laval and the Franco-Italian Pact was signed which gave Italy a free hand in Abyssinia.

In all the writings that have so far appeared in the press, one rarely finds an answer to the question as to why Mussolini decided to launch his Abyssinian campaign just at this moment. Two reasons account for this. Firstly, Mussolini felt that British influence was rapidly growing in Abyssinia as it was growing on the other side of the Red Sea in Arabia, and if it went on uninterrupted, then Italian influence would be eliminated from Abyssinia altogether. Secondly, Mussolini felt that he would get a respite of two or three years before a European war broke out and that was the only opportunity for Italy to launch the Abyssinian campaign. In fact, historically the Abyssinian campaign stands towards the coming European war in the same relation as the Tripoly and Balkan wars of 1911-1913 towards the Great War of 1914-18.

The question that one must now ask is the issue that is involved in the Abyssinian conflict. To answer the question, I must once again turn to the *New Leader* of London of the 23rd August:

"Abyssinia is the last independent state in the continent of Africa. The rest of the vast territoires of Africa have already been divided up between the Imperialist powers. Britian has seized the greatest share of the Swag. Italy is determined to get the last prize before any other Imperialist power bags it.

There are four Imperialist Powers which have interests in Abyssinia.

British capitalists are very concerned because Abyssinia contains at Lake Tsana the head-waters of the Blue Nile, which irrigates the cotton plantations of the Sudan and the Egypt. British financiers are concerned because they have control of the bank of Abyssinia, which is a subsidiary of the Bank of Egypt.

French Capitalist-Imperialism controls the only railway which runs from the French Port of Jibuti to the Abyssinian Captial, Addis Ababa.

Japanese Capitalist-Imperialism is concerned because it owns large tracts of land where raw cotton is cultivated, and because it has a practical monopoly of the

Abyssinian market in manufactured cotton goods.

Italian Capitalist-Imperialism is concerned because it controls the administration of the Posts and Telegraphs. Let no one imagine that the British and the French and Japanese Governments are now objecting to the Italian demands because of love of Abyssinia or any championship of human rights or passion for peace.

"Put bluntly, this is a case of thieves falling out. The British, French, and Japanese Governments object to Mussolini collaring the lot."

When the British Government first realized that Mussolini was not playing a game of bluff, they adopted a bellicose attitude. The *Morning Post*, which is the organ of generals. admirals, and armed services, reflected this spirit and wrote in its leading article of the 22nd August:

"Abyssinia is to be the test of our mettle. If we suffer humiliations meekly, is it not to be inferred that something more substantial can be tried on us a little later? The idea, it seems, is being cultivated in certain quarters abroad that the British Empire is only waiting to be carved up by other races whose destiny lies in the future. The sooner that idea is destroyed, the better it will be for the tranquility of the world. It is time we made it plain to all and sundry that the British Empire is neither for sale, nor to be had for the asking.

Simultaneously, war preparations were launched by

the British Government. About these war preparations the *New Leader* wrote on the 30th August :

"Since these weighty talks the public has been still more disturbed by reports that the war office has decided to send a second Battalion of soldiers to the Sudan, to increase its military forces at Malta and Aden, to send a strong contingent of the Indian army to strengthen the British Legation Guard in the Abyssinian Capital, and to prepare the Mediterranean fleet for service.

Remarkable Circular

One highly significant paragraph got into the press and was then hushed up. Last week the Sub-post-masters throughout Britian received a document headed "Partial or General Mobilization." It read as follows :

"Acceptance of Telegrams without pre-payment. In view of the present emergency, all inland or overseas telegrams on war office service should be accepted for despatch without pre-payment, if duly certified by a military officer or a permanent civil servant employed by the War office."

The authorities have explained that this circular was sent out in error. Apparently, 32,000 of these forms (numbered C18149) were printed last month by the stationery office; but it was not the intention to use them at once. The fact that they had been prepared is sufficiently alarming."

In the same issue, the *New Leader* explains the motives behind these war preparations :—

" What is the explanation of these developments ? The fear that Italy would obtain control of the head-waters of the Bule Nile at Lake Tsana in Abyssinia, and thus be able to destroy the irrigation of the British cotton-fields in the Sudan and Egypt: the danger that Italian domination of Abyssinia would enable it to bottle up the Suez canal, control the Red Sea and command the Sea-route to India, were sufficient reasons for grave anxiety among British Imperialists.

But a further danger to British Imperialism developed :

Mussolini has been indicating that he sees no reasons' why the British domination of the Eastern Mediterra- should continue. Mussolini has threatened the *status quo* in the Eastern Mediterranean and in the North-East Africa. In plain words, he menaces the very heart of the lines of communication of British Imperialism to the Near East to India and to Australia.

It is a realization of this ambitious purpose of Italy that has led the national government and British Imperialist generally to determine to use every means to stop Mussolini. The enthusiasm for the League of Nations does not arise from a love of Peace or a desire to champion Abyssinia. The British Imperialists are hiding their concern behind these righteous aims in order to win the support of opinion which is devoted to the League and to the cause of the Peace. It is actually using enthusiasm for peace to prepare the British people for Imperialist War."

There was such a wave of sympathy for Abyssinia everywhere that at first very few people realized, except probably in France, that the real motives which inspired the war Party in Great Britian were purely Imperialistic. France was sceptical of the New Fangled love of Britain for the League of nations which Italy was flouting, because she was still sore over the Anglo-German Naval agreement which had been contracted without French knowledge and approval and which had served to legalize the illegal-re-armament of Germany in defiance of the Treaty of Versailles. The French sceptics pointed out in their defence that Britain had remained quite passive, when Japan had defied the League and attacked China in Manchuria and when Bolvia and Paraguay had gone to war though both were members of the League.

I shall now proceed to show that when Britain was all but prepared to plunge into another war with all her dependencies behind her—something like a miracle happened. Suddenly the shadow of Hitler appeared on the distant Horizon and served to paralyse the outstretched arms of Great Britain ready to strike at Italy.

One feels lost in admiration at the diplomacy of British politicians in mobilizing public opinion in Great Britain, and abroad in favour of their anti-Italian policy. In 1914, the slogan had been "Save Belgium," in 1935, the slogan was: "Save the League of Nation." Even the British Labour Party and the British Communist Party fell in line with the national (conservative) Government of Great Britain. Only a small group of Independent labour party men led by Mexton, Fenner Brockway and McGovern had the courage and honesty to stand out and proclaim from the house-tops that it was going to be another Imperialist war in which the British workers had no interest whatsoever. But the efforts of the Independent Labour Party were drowned in the chorus of approval which greeted the Government With this truly over-whelming national behind him, Sir Samuel Hoare, the Foreign Secretary, spoke to Italy and to the world with a firm voice from the rostrum of the League at Geneva.

I shall leave it to students of politics to answer this as to how and why the British Labour Party and the British Communist Party gave the go by to their traditional peace-policy in this crisis and lined up behind the Baldwin—Hoare Government. It was certainly a triumph for Conservative diplomacy.

While Britain was making her war-like preparations, Italy was not idle. A virulent anti-British campaign was conducted by the entire Italian press and the Italian Dictator openly proclaimed that he was simply following France and Britain in their Colonial compaigns and was prepared for all emergencies if he met with inference from any quarter. Was it due to puffed-up vanity that Italy the creation of 1861—was prepared to cross swords with Almighty Great Britain? I think not. Italy was conscious that the development of air-power during the last decade had completely altered the old values in war and that her superior air-force combind with the small but thoroughly efficient modern many had placed her at a superior tactical advantage in the Mediterranean Sea as compared with Britain.

In spite of what the Italians may claim there is little doubt that Britain with the support of her large Empire, would in the long run have defeated Italy. But on the other, hand it is quite certain that the Italian air force—one of the most efficient in the world and by common consent. superior to that of Great Britain today —would have done irreparable damage to the British Navy. Britain would, in consequence, have emerged out of a victorious war, far weaker, than she is today. And with a crippled Navy she would have to face the gigantic re-armament of Nazi Germany.

A small group of Imperialist-strategists began to urge that the distant rumblings now heard in Memel constituted a greater menace to Great Britain than Italian exploits in Abyssinia. This warning was confirmed and reiterated by French Politicians of all shades of opinion for whom the only concern now is how to prepare for the future German menace. Ultimately the British cabinet realized that for them, discretion was the better part of valour. The reason is that though Hitler has been following a sincerely pro-British policy and has no intention of assuming the aggression on Germany's Western Front, and though all his objectives are on the Eastern Southern Front *e.g.*, in Memel, Austria, Czechoslovakia, etc. Most British politicians are suspicious of re-armed Germany. They feel that even if Germany has today no intentions of fighting England or even France, as soon as Germany attempts to expand to the East and to South, a situation may arise when both France and England may be drawn into a war with her, if they are to prevent German hegemony in Europe. In such a contingency, with a crippled Navy, Great Britain will be at a serious disadvantage as compared with Germany. Already the German Air-force is superior to that of the entire British Empire and with conscription in force the German land forces will soon become superior to those of the British Empire.

The only hope of maintaining a balance of fighting Power in favour of Britian for a future emergency lies in preserving and enlarging the present naval strength of Great Britain.

While these calculations and considerations were being carefully deliberated upon in Great Britain, Italy announced that if she was thwarted by France and Britain in her Abyssinian policy she would completely withdraw from the politics of Central Europe, and give Hitler a free hand. The effect was remarkable and sabre-rattling ceased. Thus Hitler by the re-armament policy frightened France and Britain into maintaining the peace in Europe in 1935.

As a confirmation of this statement one may refer

to the recent speech of the British Premier Mr. Baldwin, at the recent Conservative Party Conference at Bournemouth. Mr. Baldwin said :—

"But I want to say to you that recent events have confirmed in my own mind doubts and anxieties which have been present to me and my colleagues for some time past. We have as you know, since the War done more in the way of practical disarmament......than any other country.........We cannot pursue that path longer The whole perspective on the Continent has been altered in the past year or two by the re-arming of Germany. I have no reason to believe in hostile intentions........... But I cannot be blind to the fact that the presence of another Great Nation armed alters the perspective of Europe in the fulfilment of obligations under the League of Nations. I cannot conceal from myself that some day the fulfilment of these obligations may mean that the nations who are fulfiling them may have to maintain by force of arms the Covenant of the League."

It is probable that another factor also served to cool official enthusiasm for a fight with Italy—namely, public opinion within the British Empire. On this point, the *Daily Mail* (Paris Edition) wrote on the 26th September in its leading article :—

Some of our bloodthirsty Pacifist journals have now started printing articles which *suggest that the* Dominions would willingly support sanctions even though war followed. The attitude of the peoples of the

Dominions to the League of Nations in the present dispute is a matter of the First importance; and it is vital for the people of Great Britain to know whether the application of sanctions to Italy—were such a dangerous step possible—would split the Empire and gravely accentuate differences within it.

On an examination of the evidence the answer seems to be in the affirmative—that war following the application of the sanctions would divide Empire opinion seriously and produce such discontent among large sections of the population in the Dominions as to aggravate all the difficulties oversea.

The oldest of the Great Dominions, Canada, has always been uneasy as to the obligations of the Covenant. In 1924, she opposed any extension of her liabilities under the League on the ground that she was remote from Europe.

That attitude her people have generally upheld. In his broadcast of Sept. 6, Mr. Bennett, the Canadian Prime Minister, declared that it was the duty of the Government, "by all just and honourable means to see that Canada is kept out of trouble....We will not be embroiled in any foreign quarrel"....

As for Australia, Mr. Lyons, her prime Minister, has promised close co-operation' with the British Government. A very different line has been taken by Mr. Forde, the leader of the Federal Labour Party, who has proclaimed the policy of that formidable organisation to be " a firm refusal to participate in any external war." In new South Wales the Party has passed a resolution demanding that Australia should declare her neutrality at Geneva and recall her representative there, if the League's action brings war....

In South Africa, General Smuts has stated that the Union " stands to the Covenant in letter and in spirit "........The South African Defence Minister, Mr. Pirow views conditions quite differently from General Smuts. On September 15, he told a public meeting : " I am certain in any case that South Africa has no intention of firing a shot.........whatever happens we will not shoot! There is practical confimation of this feeling in the fact that South African farmers are anxious to get orders for the supply of meat to the Italian Armies in East Africa and Abyssinia.

In view of these declarations, there is a distinct likelihood that certain of the Dominions might hold aloof and sever their connections with the League were the impossible realized by some wild freak of chance, and all the status composing the League induced to vote for sanctions. Surely our League enthusiasts must realize that it is not fair, in such conditions, to create difference and sow disunion within the Empire.

The latest News from Anstralia goes to show that opinion there sharply divided on the question of sanctions against Italy, which may lead to war. The *Times* (London) of the 12th October said that by " 27 votes to 21, the House of Representative today rejected the attempt by Mr. Beasley, the Lang Labour Leader, to induce Parliament to declare Australian neutrality and refusal to endorse sanctions against Italy".

Wtth regard to the situation in Palestine which is under British Mandate the *Times* of the 12th Oct wrote as follows :—

"It is alleged that pro-Italian political sympathies are chiefly held by the Partisans of Haj Amin Effendi-el Husseini, the Mufti of Jerusalem and since the out-break of the Ethiopian dispute the Mufti's newspaper Jawia El Arabiya has published pro-Italian articles, while its rival which supports the Nashashibi party, has revealed the existence of a letter purporting to have come from the Emir Shekib Arslam to the Mufti, commending his Eminence's pro-Italian activities. During the last few weeks there have been frequent comments in the Arab Press in general on the wisdom of exploiting the present international confusion in unity with other Arab peoples for the purpose of throwing off the bonds of the Mandate. (Amir Shehib Arslam is the exiled Syrian nationalist leader who lives in Geneva).

Among the Jews, the Revisionist party, or new Zionists, are on the side of Italy. Their newspaper *Hayarden* is alone among Jewish newspapers in Palestine in reporting the events of the Italo-Ethiopian dispute in the Pro-Italian colours."

So far Egypt is concerned, it is quite clear that the

Leaders while not openly opposing British policy towards Italy, are pressing for a recognition of the full independence of Egypt, if Egyptian sympathy and support are to be secured for Great Britian. How far they will be able to drive the bargain home. depends on the international situation. If the international situation gradnally quietens then it is doubtful if the Egyptian leaders will obtain any substantial success. But in any case it seems likely that they will have some success. Already the continental papers have announced that with British support capitulations will be abolished in Egypt. That means that Egyptian courts will have full power to try foreigners and this will constitute a step towards Egypt's independence in the domain of public law.

In Great Britain, public opinion as a whole is behind the government in its policy of sanctions against Italy. Nevertheless the members of the cabinet are closely atching the situation. It is not true to say that the present cabinet have decided for an early election only because they think that the present occasion is favourable from the electioneering point of view. They also want to feel the pulse of the nation and see how far they can go in the direction of enforcing "sanction" against Italy. Meanwhile, the Independent labour Party, which has thronghout followed a bold and consistent policy on the present issue, has summoned a national conference of all working class organisations, opposed to sanctions and war and has issued the following manifesto :—

"The Labour Party, the Trade Union Congress and the Communist Party in supporting the imposition of sanctions by the national government and the League of Nations, are in fact lining up workers behind the policy which whould be used for British Imperialism. The Independent Labour Party warns workers that economic and financial sanctions are likely to develop into war. Full preparations have been made for a naval blockade of Italy. The Policy of the government should be resisted now." (The *Times*, 10th October 1935).

The *Times* of the same date gives the news that a private meeting of about 50 Conservative M. Ps led by Mr. L. S. Amery will be held to consider the present international situation and the danger of Great Britain becoming involved in the war between Italy and Abyssinia, because in their opinion the effective application of sanctions will lead to war. We have now to watch and see what effect is produced on the British Cabinet by this joint pressure from the Right and the Left.

And Now About India.

According to their practice of having no interest in international affairs the Congress Leaders seem to be without a policy on this all-important question. True, there has been a large volume of sympathy for Aby ssinia among the public at large—but this sympathy was immediately exploited by the British Government instead of being harnessed by the Leaders of the people. As a result, Indian Troops were rushed to Addis Ababa. Why was this done ? When questioned in the Council of State about this, the Political Secretary to the Government of India replied, " that troops had been sent to Addis Ababa with a view to protect Indians and other British subjects. Are the Indian people really so naive that they can be taken in by such a statement ? Abyssinia, still, being an independent country, neither Indian nor British troops can go there to protect Indians. The fact is—as stated in England,—that as a result of a special representation—the Abyssinian government allowed an extra guard for the British Legation as a special concession (ordinarily this guard should be provided by the Abyssinian government). The question now is why the extra guard was taken all the way from India. There were British troops near at hand across; the frontier of Abyssinia *e. g.*, in Kenya, in Sudan, in Egypt and in British Somaliland. Why they were not sent to Addis Ababa ? The reason is clear. Indian troops were sent with the idea of comming Indian support to British policy in Abyssinia and on the other hand, to remind Italy that the vast resources of India are behind Great Britian.

It is now an open secret that during the months of August and September we were within an inch of a European War. And but for the menace of a re-armed

Germany, the war would have broken out and India would have been dragged into it, as in 1914, before Indian leaders realized where they stood. The only difference would have been that Italy would have taken the place of Germany and Abyssinia of Belgium. Only a fool would accept the statement of the commander-in-cheif before the Central Legislature that before India gets entangled into a war, we shall be given sufficient notice of it. In the present case If war had broken out in Europe, Great Britain would have emerged victorious, thanks to the resources of India—but Abyssinia would have shared the fate of Plestine and India would have continued enslaved as before. It is to be greatly regretted that the spokesman of Great Britian at Geneva, with an unabashed impudence, mentioned Britain's treatment of India as an agreement to prove her (Britain's) moral superiority over Italy—not withstanding the fact that while he spoke, bombs were raining over the heads of women and children of the Frontier Province and the Indian Government was forging fresh letters for the Indian people in the shape of the Criminal Law Amendment Act.

It is strage that Italy has been conducting a virulent and persistent compaign against the other Imperialist powers hoping thereby to secure mitigation of the wrong that she is doing to Abyssinia. Her semi-official spokesman Signor Gayda writes, for example, in the italian Press :—

"The committee of thirteen is wrong when affirming that the Abyssinian aggression cannot be taken into consideration by the League because Italy has not denounced them at Geneva before. France has not dnounced the actions which provoked her campaign in Morocco; nor has England informed Geneva of the obscure situation which has been created on the North-Western Frontier of India where British Troops have fought against free populations not subject to her rule (The *Times*, 7th October).

This persistent campaign is now finding an echo in some European countries *e. g.*, the offical organ of the Polish Government, the Gazette Polska. wrote the other day :--

"Why does Great Britain herself, ruthless in the use of force against the coloured races, so energetically oppose Indian plans in connection with Abyssinia?"

Among the Governments of Europe, Austria and Hungary who come under the Italian orbit of influence, have openly announced at Geneva that they are opposed to sanctions against Italy. Germany being out of the League, has not yet declared her attitude towards the question of sanctions but will probably follow the policy most conducive to her own national interests—present and future. Even in countries that are officially supporting the League in the matter of sanctions against Italy, there is great deal of scepticism about the much-vaunted disinterestedness of Great Britian, as is evident from the Tone of the Press: For instance, I read in the continental press the other day that Abyssinia has placed a very large order for clothing with Lancashire's firms—the biggest order that Lancashire has received from abroad for years. Likewise, I read that the British are consolidating and extending their colonial possessions near Aden as a counter-blast to the growth of Italian power and influence on the other side of the Red sea.

Now What About the Future?

Since French policy is dominating Continental politics, including the League of Nations it appears pretty certain that two things will happen. Firstly in order to maintain outwardly the prestige of the League of Nations which means in actual practice, the prestige of the big powers, France and England, some collective move will be taken in the form of economic sanctions. Mussolini himself has prepared the way for this by stating openly in his speech on the 2nd October that he will put up with conomic sanctions, however inconvenient. Secondly, no military measures will be adopted against Italy, nor will such offective sanctions be adopted as will frustrate Italian objectives in Abyssinia. Mussolini has said in so many words that such a move will be treated by him as a casus belli. Moreover Italy has openly hinted that if she is thwarted in Abyssinia, she will by way of retaliation, withdraw from Central Europe and give Germany a free hand there. Nevertheless, one would be too optimistic to say that the war danger is off. The British Navy remains concentrated in the Mediteranean and Britian has so far refused to comply with Italy's request for its withdrawl, Besides this, it is asserted by radical newspapers in Britain that the despatch of troops and war material to the potential war-zone is going on. It is clear that Great Britain has climbed down with great reluctance and has not yet given up the war-spirit. She is however, trying to cloak her retreat with the slogan of "collective action."

They say that every dark cloud has its silver lining. So it is in the case of Abyssinia. Abyssinia will go down fighting, but she will stir the conscience of the world. On the one hand, throughout the World of coloured races there will be new consciousness. The consciusness will herald the dawn of a new life among the suppressed nations. All Imperialists are feeling uneasy about this phenomenon and General Smuts gave expression to it in one of his recent speeches. On the other hand, thinking men in the Imperialist countries have begun to ask themselves if the system of colonization is at all a justiflable one. Prof. Harold Laski once in a letter to the *Manchester Guardian* suggested for example, that all the African colonies of Great Britain should be handed over to the League of Nations. Of late, Mr. Lansbury has made a passionate appeal for pooling together all the raw materials of the world for the common benefit of mankind. And last but not least even the diehard Sir Samuel Hoare was forced to say at Geneva that he welcomed an investigation somewhat in the direction of the proposals of Mr. Lansbury. So even in the Imperialists 'haves' have begun to feel a prick of conscience.

There are two ways in which Imperialism may come to an end—either through an overthrow by an anti-Imperialist agency or through an internecine struggle among Imperialists themselves. If the second course is furthered by the growth of Italian Imperialism, then Abyssinia will not have suffered in vain."

"Since my last communication dated the 8th October, I have received a full report of the speech of the Premier, Mr. Baldwin, at the recent conservative party conference at Bournemouth, which confirms my analysis of the international situation. Mr. Baldwin said: "But I want to say to you, that recent events have confirmed in my own mind doubts and anxieties which have been present to me, and my colleagues for sometimes past. We have as you know, since the war done more in the way of practical disarmament than any other country. We cannot pursue that path any longer. The whole perspective in the continent has been altered in the past year or two, by the rearming of Germany. I have no reason to believe in hostile intentions.........but I cannot be blind to the fact that the presence of another great nation armed alters the perspective of Europe in the fulfilment of obligations under the League of Nations. I cannot conceal from myself that some day the fulfilment of those obligations may mean that the nations who are fulfilling them may have to maintain by force of arms, the comment of the League."

French Diplomacy

From this utterenee, nothing can be more clear than the fact that the British Government apprehended the possibility of a war in the not distant future, and that they do not trust Nazi Germany at all, inspite of the sincerely pro-British policy of the Hitler Government. The triumph of French diplomacy during the last few weeks consists in stirring up this apprehension about the future war in the minds of the British politicians to such an extent as to paralyse all aggressive movements against Italy; for which Great Britain was preparing on her own initiative and account through a concentration of the British fleet in the Mediterranean sea. It is now a known fact that while Great Britain was from the beginning determined to go to any length to prevent Italian expansion in Central Africa, France was anxious to allow Italy, a free hand in Abyssiania so that she (Italy) might in future play a role in European politics on the side of France, and against Germany.

A Somersault.

For several days, the future of Eurore was vailed in a mist of uncertainty because one did not know whether British diplomacy would prevail or French. Then all of a sudden British policy turned a somersault. Sir Samuel Hoare, forgetting his strong speech at

Geneva, sent a personal and friendly message to the Italian Dictator, and an official assurance was communicated by the British Government that the concentration of the British fleet in the Mediterranean had no hostile intentions against Italy. The climax came, when Mr Baldwin in his conciliatory Bournemouth speech said "I am confident therefore, that I am voicing the sentiments of the whole country in appealing to Italy, even at this hour, to refrain from action, which will render the task of the Council more arduous" (*Times*, 5th Oct. 1935) so, for the time being at least Laval's policy got the better of Hoare's.

Dictatorships

The question that one may ask is what those "Recent Aments" are, which induced the British Cabinet to change its mind. Mr. Baldwin has himself given some hint on this point. He said "We have one other thing to remember in connection with the League of Nations, another pregnant fact that we have in Europe today a new feature. We know historically that however pacific, the early steps of such forms of Government may be, and their intention, we know but too well, that tendency has shown itself later to divert attention from domestic difficulties to external adventures" One has only to note the present economic crisis and food shortage in Germany, reminiscent of conditions during the last war, and the acute tension between Germany and Lithuania over Memel, as also the French allegation that the German Rhineland is no longer a demilitarised zone, as required by the treaty of Versailles, in order to apply the necessary annotation to this part of Mr. Baldwin's speech. It is noteworthy that the only reply to Mr. Baldwin's speech came form Her Hitler, who asserted that most wars were due to democracies, and not dictatorships and that Germany has no necessity for launching on a war for diverting attention from internal troubles. Nevertheless, the fact remains, as I stated in my last communication that it is the menace of rearmed Germany constituting in the eyes of France and England a greater though future danger which has forced these two countries to capitulate temporarily at least before the lesser evil of an Italian conquest of Abyssinia.

League's Prestige

Now that French policy is dominating continental policies, including the League of Nations, it appears certain that two things will happen. Firstly, in order to maintain outwardly the prestige of the League of Nations which means in actual practice, the prestige of the big powers, France and England, save collective move, will be taken in the form of economic sanctions. Mussolini Himself has prepared the way for this by stating openly in his speech on the 2nd October that he will put up with economic sanctions, however inconvenient.

Secondly, no military measures will be adopted

against Italy, nor will such effective sanctions be adopted against Italy, nor will such effective sanctions be adopted as will frustrate Italian objectives in Abyssinia. Mussolini has said in so many words that such a move will be treated by him as a *causes belli.* Moreover, Italy has openly hinted that if she is thawarted in Abyssinia, she will by way of retaliation, withdraw from Central Europe, and give Hitler a free hand.

India's Interest

Apart from the fate of unhappy Abyssinia, what interests India in this crisis, is the future policy of Great Britian. While it is true that Great Britain has climbed down a great deal before Mussolini, she has done so with Great reluctance. She is now trying to cloak her retreat by the slogan of "Collective Action," forgetting for the present that at an earlier stage, she had been preparing for individual action against Italy. It was Britian preparing for individual action that she found it necessary to ask the French Government officially if the French Navy would come to her assistance in the event of an Italian attack on the British Navy in the Mediterranean. However, one should not go so far as to say that the danger of a wider conflagaration is off. The British Navy remains concentrated in the Mediterranean and Britain has so far refused to comply with Italy's request for its withdrawl.

Secret of Early Election

The radical organs in Britain like the "New Leader" of the Independent Labour Party have been publishing facts about the regular despatch of troops, and war-material to the potential war-zone as during the Great War. Conservative politicians in Great Britain are now anxiously watching the situation at home and abroad with a view to determining their future policy and action. It is not true to say that the present cabinet have decided for an early election only because they think that the present occasion is favourable from the electioneering point of view. They also want to feel the pulse of the nation, and see how far they can go in the direction of enforcing sanctions against Italy. Meanwhile, the Independent Labour Party which has throughout followed a bold and consistent policy on the present issues, has summoned a national conference of all working class organisations, opposed to sanctions and war and has issued the following manifesto.

"The Labour Party, the Trades Union Congress, and the Communist party in supporting the imposition of the sanctions by the National Government and the League of Nations are in fact lining up workers, behind the policy which would be used for British Imperialism. The Independent Lahour Party warns that economic and financial sanctions are likely to develop into war. The war policy of the Government should be resisted now" (*Times*, 10th Oct. 1935).

'Times' of the same date gives the news that a private meeting of about 50 conservative M. P's led by Mr. L. S. Amery will be held to consider the present international situation, and the danger of Great Britain becoming involved in the war between Italy, and Abyssinia, because in their opinion the effective application of sanctions will lead to war. We have now to watch and see, what effect is produced on the British Cabinet by this joint pressure from the Right, and the Left.

Imperialist Powers

It is strange that Italy has been conducting a virulent and persistent campaign against the other Imperialist powers hoping thereby to secure mitigation of the wrong when re-affirming that the Abyssinian aggression cannot be taken into consideration by the League because Italy has not denounced them at Geneva before. France has not denounced the actions which provoked her campaign in Morrocco, nor has England informed Geneva of the obscure situation which has been against free populations, not subject to her rule.

Why Britain ?

This persistent campaign is now finding an echo in some European countries *e. g.*, official organ of the Polish Government. "The Gazetta Polska," wrote the otherday : "Why does Great Britain herself always ruthless in the use of force against the coloured races so energetically oppose Italian plans in connection with Abyssinia ? Among the Governments of Europe, Austria, and Hungary, who came under the Italian orbit of influence have openly announced at Geneva that they are opposed to sanctions against Italy. Germany being out of the League, has not yet declared her attitude towards the question of sanctions, but will probably follow the policy most conducive to her own international interests, present and future.

Secret of Disinterestedness

Even in countries that are officially supporting the League in the matter of sanctions against Italy there is a great deal of scepticism about the much lamented disinterestedness of Great Britain. As is evident from the tone of Abbyssinia, she has placed a very large order for clothing with Lanchashire firms—the biggest order that Lancashire has received from abroad for years. Likewise I read that the British are consolidating and extending their colonial possessions near Aden as a counter-blast to the growth of Italian power and influence on the other side of the Red Sea.

Egypt's Demand

While Europe is now trying to evolve some form of sanctions, which will save the prestige of the League, but will not drive Mussolini to desperation, Egyptian politicians are trying hard to drive a bargain with Great Britain. If the international situation quietens down, it is doubtful, if they will have any substancial success. Nevertheless, they are sure to gain something for their country *i. e.*, the papers have already announced that with the approval of Britain, capitulations will be abolished in Egypt. The existence of capitulations, whereby foreigners in Egypt cannot be tried by Egyptian courts is humiliating to the self-respect of a poeple, who have been demanding full independence, and it goes without saying that the abolition of capitulations will be warmly welcomed throughout Egypt.

XI

"IMRESSIONS OF BRITAIN"

Being asked what impression he had formed of the British people's attitude towards India, Mr. Bose said, that he had found a great deal of ignorance in Great Britain, about Indian affairs. Nevertheless, he found among a section of British public. interest in and sympathy for India's struggle for independence. But it did not appear to him that this section had much influence with the ruling classes.

" Mr. Bose had the impression that even outstanding politicians were not well-informed about Indian effairs. The information that they had come usually from official sources or from correspondents of British newspapers in India, who did not always, represent the true facts of the situation.

Continental Politics

"Referring to continental politics, specially as regards the possibility of war, Mr. Bose thought that the danger of a war in Europe, in the near future was much less to-day than it was twelve months ago. Two factors he said, accounted for this, first the experience in Spain had opened the eyes of every nation to the horrors of modern war, and though every country was arming, none felt prepared to go in for war. Secondly, the attitude of Germany was much more sober at present, than it was before, because she felt that she would not have a free hand in Central and Eastern Europe.

" Mr. Bose's own view was that if there was a European war, it would be in Central Europe in the first place with possible extension to the East, and later repercussions in the west. In Central Europe, he found the people this year more confident of Peace being maintained than they were last-year. For all these reasons, he was inclined to think that there was no immediate danger of war in Europe.

Problem of Detenus

Questioned about his opinion on the Bengal Government action in dealing with the detenus' problem, Mr. Bose said that while he was glad that some steps had been taken in the direction of releasing the detenus, he must say that what the Government had done uptill now, fell far short of public expectations. He added, " We shall, of course, continue the agitation to secure not only the release of the detenus, but of all political prisoners. As to what steps we will actually take will be determined, only after I meet Mahatmaji, members of the Working Committee and my colleagues in Bengal.

Jinnah-Jawaharlal Talks

Being pressed to offer his comments on the proposed Jinnah-Jawaharlal talks, Mr. Bose said, that he was not in a position at the present moment to enter into the merits of the Jinnah-Parshad Formula, on which the talks between Pandit Jawaharlal and Mr. Jinnah were proposed to be conducted. Nevertheless, he would like to say it quite clearly, that he would welcome discussions between Pandit Nehru, and Mr. Jinnah for a communal settlement, which might lead to some favourable result and he believed that was also the view of the public.

Question of Federation,

Referring to the question of Federation and the Congress attitude to that, Mr. Bose said, he did not know, what the Congress decision would be, but personally, he thought that the Congress might have resort to all possible methods within the iimits of non-violent non-co-operation to frustrate the Federal Scheme. The attitude of British statement in regard to India seemed that they wanted quiet in India. They seemed to think that if somehow the federal part of the constitution could be put into operation, they could justify themselves that Indian prolbem was solved once for all.

He added that in his speeches, press interviews, and private conversations in England, he made it perfectly clear that there was no possibility for the Congress drifting towards the possibility of accepting the federation, as it did in the matter of accepting offices in provinces.

Further discussing the Federal issue, Mr. Bose said that he was not opposed to the ideal of Federation on principle because he believed that the constitution of

India would ultimately be that of a Federal republic. But he was opposed to the Federal scheme as embodied in the Government of India Act, 1935.

Congress Ministries

Detailing his impression of British public opinion on the working of Congress ministries, Mr. Bose said that British publicmen seemed to be satisfied with the attitude and work of the Congress ministries. They did not make any secret of the fact that they apprehended friction between the Governors and Ministers. There again, Mr. Bose had to point out to them that though on surface everything appeared to be smooth, there was in reality a certain amount of friction varying from province to province, between the Congress ministries on the one side and the Governors, and higher services on the other. Mr. Bose further pointed out that there was even a possibility of this friction leading to a crisis any moment. There was no doubt that Congress ministries would not continue in office, unless they felt that they were doing something substantial for the benefit of the country. Concluding Mr. Bose said, that there was no apprehension of Congress ministries being gradually hypnotised by the bureaucracy.

Situation in Far East

Making a passing reference to the situation in the Far East vis-a-vas, the attitude of European countries, Mr. Bose said, that England and France will naturally be on the side of China, while Italy and Germany will favour Japan."

XII

INDIA IN THE WORLD AFFAIRS

The World Economic Conference has been meeting in London, and as usual India is being represented not by elected representatives but by nominees of the British Government. Whether the world benefits from the Conference or not, it is certain, India will not gain anything. The position of the British Government seems to be an anamalous one. On the one hand, they along with other nations are talking of a tariff truce, and on the other hand, they are raising the tariff on Japanese textile imports into India. The Indian delegation to the Congress of International Chambers of Commerce in Vienna strongly opposed the idea of tariff truce so far as India is concerned, since the Indian Industries need protective tariff. The Congress in Vienna was meant to be a prelude to the World Economic Conference, but in the case of India, this is not so. India has no voice in sheltering her delegation to the World Economic Conference. Consequently, the views expressed, and maintained so firmly by the Indian delegation at the Vienna Congress will not be heard within the precincts of the London Economic Conference and the Indian Delegation to the London Conference, will in all probability, sing and dance to the tune of the British delegation. In the circumstances, what could be done? In my humble opinion, a memorandum, should have been published embodying the real views of the Indian people on all economic questions. and this memorandum should have been published embodying the real views of the Indian people on all economic questions, and this memorandum should have been distributed and broadcast among all members of the London Conference. It is also possible that some members of the Conference could have officially brought to the notice of the entire Conference, the real views of India on economic questions. But who is to organise this? Evidently, it is the duty of the Indian National Congress but the Congress is hardly alive to the necessity of International propaganda and whatever propaganda is done directly or indirectly by Congressmen is not of the effective sort, At present, the major portion of the propaganda about India that is carried on in Europe, and in America, is conducted by the pacifist missionaries, and the feminist organisations, All honour is due to them for making the voice of India heard in other lands. At the same time, one must confess that unless and until politicians and economists are interested in India, the present method of propaganda will not bring us much benefit. Politics today is largely, if not wholly, influenced by economists. Consequently, if India desires effective propaganda in other countries, she must take more interest in international economics.

Some of the Indian papers, which arrived here this week, contained the information that a special session of the Congress was being contemplated. This news was however, contradicted by other papers. I do not know what programme the Congress will adopt, if it should meet now, but in any case. I am firmly of the opinion that the Congress should have a foreign department, and the task of this department should be to see that India is adequately represented at all International Conferences and Congresses. Innumerable international Conferences dealing with all sorts of subjects meet in different parts of Europe and America throughout the year, but India is hardly represented at any of these. The result is that we are not able to keep abreast of the modern world in the different departments of human progress. Of these International Conferences, the most important are those that deal with economics. I know that it will be difficult at first to get the real representatives of the Indian people to represent India at these conferences, but, if we go agitating inside, and outside India, we shall be able to carry our point ultimately. England will no doubt, try to treat India, as a province of England, in the selection of Indian representatives but since India is a member of the League of Nations, she has got a strong case for insisting that her representatives should be the representatives of the people, and not the nominees of the Government. The other day, I was explaining to a member of a Social Democratic here, why the All-India Trade Union Congress had been boycotting the annual

Last week's papers brought the news that some politcal prisoners had died of hunger-strike in the Andaman islands. Considering the magnitude of the calamity, it dees not appear from the papers that the public have given sufficient importance, or attention to this matter. The formation of the Andaman prisoners' relief committee was a most timely one, and the full weight of public opinion in India should be behind the committee in the work that they have undertaken. The question is certainly an All-India one, and the whole country should-take up the question with the same degree of interest and enthusiasm.

During the last few years, to the outside world. India was a political problem. In other words, the outside world looked upon India, as fighting for her freedom, but of late there has been a change. India has now become a social problem. In other words, the outside India now thinks of India, as a country, teeming with untouchables in which different castes are eternally at war with one another. There is hardly one foreigneer who has not asked me how India can hope to get her freedom, when she has so many internal divisions Of course, I have replied saying that the impression that they have got from the papers is not correct, and the castes are equally interested in securing freedom for India. Nevertheless, I have felt that this impression is the result of continuous propaganda carried on in the European Press and we in India have ourselves helped this propaganda by sidetracking the national movement, and converting it into a social movement for the abolition of untouchability. The fact that India's greatest leader has fasted, and has risked his life for the removal of untouchability has naturally helped to create an exagerated notion in the Western mind of our social differences and divisions. In short, the effect on the European mind of Mahatma Gandhi's fast has not in my humble opinion, been to India's advantage.

Viennese institutions continue to interest me. This morning I had occasion to visit the national library (which is the state library of Austria). The Director of the Art Section of the library, while showing me round, brought some Indian paintings and asked me if I could interpret them. In one series there were the ten incarnations of Vishnu. Another painting represented shree Krishana lifting Gobardhangre. The Director was delighted to have the interpretation. He said that he was engaged in the writing of a book on the Theatres of the world, and asked me if I could help him by supplying some pictures and scenes from modern India theatres. If any friends from India could supply pictures displaying the modern India theatre, I shall gladly hand them over to the Director who would welcome them.

India Abroad

I think it was the late Deshbandhu C. R. Das, who first opened my eyes to the necessity of making India known in other countries. The occasion for this was the drafting of a new scheme of work for the Swaraj

Party which the late Deshbandhu and the late Pandit Motilal Nehru launched at Allahabad in February 1923. Discussions regarding the new scheme of work had begun as early as April 1922, when we were all in prison. There were two items in the Deshbandhu's scheme on which he was personally very keen, but which did not evoke much enthusiasm at the time, because public attention was drawn towards the capture of legislatures and local bodies. These two items were—Indian propaganda in foreign countries and the organisation of a pan-Asiatic League.

Several years elapsed before my interest in the question of Indian propaganda abroad was once again stirred up. Early in 1928, when I was in Calcutta, I was interviewed by an American journalist (I forget his name at the moment). In the course of our conversation he described in vivid colours how China had managed to capture the imagination of the whole civilized world. According to him, India should also contrive to put herself before the world's eye. How that could be done, was the question of method for Indians to decide but the need was an imperative one in India's own interest.

Two other factors have helped to deepen my conviction that Indian propaganda abroad is absolutely necessary for India's progress—(my experience in Europe during the last two years and (2) my study of History. During the last two years I have travelled through many.

countries in Europe. Everywhere there is a colossal ignorance about India—but at the same time there is a general feeling of sympathy for, and interest in, India. This sympathy can easily be enlarged and developed, if necessary steps are taken from our side. But while we are quite indifferent to this question, missionaries and other "civilizing agencies" are not inactive. For several decades they have painted India as a land where widows are burnt, girls are married at the age of 5 or 6 and people are virtually acquainted with the art of dressing. I remember vividly that when I was in England in 1920, I was one day passing a lecture-hall in front of which there was a pictorial advertisement of a lecture to be delivered by a missionary about India. In that advertisement, there were pictures of some half-naked men and women of the blackest complexion, possessing the ugliest features. Ostensibly the lecturer wanted to raise funds for his "civilizing" work in India and was therefore painting India in this light, without the slightest compunction. Towards the end of 1938, a German journalist who claimed to have visited India recently, wrote in a Munich paper that she had seen widows being burnt in India and dead bodies lying uncared for in the streets of Bombay. Recently in a Vienna pictorial paper (*Wiener Bilder*, dated the 30th June) a picture of a dead body covered with insects was printed and there was a footnote saying that it was the corpse of a "Sadhu" which could not be removed for several days because of the Hindu belief that the dead body of a "Sadhu" should not be removed by ordinary men. What surprises me is the careful selection of pictures about India made by propagandists in Europe with a view to depicting India in the worst colours possible. This is as much true of pictorial magazines as of films. Regarding the anti-Indian propaganda conducted by films like "India Speaks" and "Bengali"—there has been some exposure in India already and I need not dilate on it. But I am afraid there has not been sufficient exposure of the mischief which is being done by the film "Everybody loves Music," in which Mahatma Gandhi appears in his own dress dancing with a European Girl.

If this sort of propaganda goes on in other countries, is it to be wondered at that Indian should be *called* "Balckie"—as it happens sometimes in England—or as "Neger" (Negro)—as is the experience sometimes in Germany? In such circumstances, what should be our reaction? The first and easier course would be to shut our eyes, quietly pocket the humiliation and remain silent. The other and more difficult course would be to start our own propaganda. I remember talking to a Turkish Diplomat in 1933 on the question of foreign propaganda. I complained that there was no literature on modern Turkey meant for foreigneers, written by Turks themselves. By way of self-defence, he said, that the Turks did not believe in propaganda (this is not wholly true because the Turks also are beginning their propaganda). I doubt if any other country in this age of propaganda, would have attempted to justify its lack of propaganda. In any case so far as Europe is concerned, propaganda is now regarded as one of the normal and legitimate activities of a Government. Of the European countries, England and Russia are pastmasters in the art of propaganda,—with Italy and Germany coming next Of the Asiatic countries, China is at present most active in her foreign propaganda. The New world has generally been indifferent to propaganda in the Old world. But I believe that the League of Nations is now helping to bridge the Atlantic Ocean. In 1934, when I was in Geneva, I happened to come into touch with a number of South Americans and I realized that even the South American States were anxious to carry on propaganda in Europe.

I said towards the beginning that two factors helped to deepen my conviction that Indian propaganda abroad was absolutely necessary for our national advancement: (1) My experiences in Europe, and (2) my study of History. Regarding the second, I may say that the study of the history of those countries that have won their freedom in recent years will reveal the importance of this work. I hope my readers are aware of the extensive propaganda conducted in the United States of America by the Sinn Fein Party in 1920 and 1921. The Party sent their best man—no less a man than their President, Mr. De. Valera—to organise and conduct this propaganda. The Party had also centres of propaganda on the Continent. The most important and interesting example of foreign propaganda is, however, furnished by the Czech leaders. For 20 years, Dr. Masaryk, Dr. Benes and others carried on a steady and sustained propaganda in different countries, especially England, France, and the United States. Only after two decades could the harvest be reaped—and it will now be admitted on all hands that without the sympathy and support of England, France, and the United States. Czechoslovakia would not have come into existence as an independent state.

It is not the enslaved countries alone that carry on a systematic propaganda. Even independent countries have now taken to it. Countries like Hungary in Europe and China in Asia that have a national grievance set store by foreign propaganda. Hungary today hopes to secure a peaceful revision of her present frontiers which have been defined by the Treaty of Trianon, which she regards as unjust and iniquitous. She is therefore, spending large sums of money for winning international sympathy and support for her cause. China has recently launched an extensive scheme of propaganda in Europe with Geneva as her Headquarters. There they have taken a Villa and fitted up a Chinese library for the use of all those who desire to study anything about China. The society publishes literature in French and English for propagating Chinese culture in Europe. They have taken another house in Geneva where they have periodic exhibitions. In 1934 they had an exhibition of adults' paintings which was a great success. After the Geneva's Exhibition, the pictures were sent to other European capitals and similar exhibitions were held there. In April 1935, when I visited Geneva again, they were holding an exhibition of children's paintings and I was informed that the exhibition would be sent round to other European capitals in succession.

Any one visiting such an exhibition would come back with an impression that the Chinese are a highly gifted and cultured people. In November 1935, an art exhibition was held in Burlington House in London and a ship-load of Chinese art treasures is being brought to London for the purpose. I cannot help remarking in this connection that through her steady and continued propaganda, China has been able to win sympathy of the whole civilized world. This was evident during the Sino-Japanese dispute over Manchukuo, when China won the support of the League of Nations, in spite of the best efforts of Japan. That China was not able to utilize fully this hard-won support was due to her military weakness. Nevertheless the Chinese people have realized the value of propaganda so much that they have now launched an extensive scheme. Though this scheme is backed by the Nanking Government, a large portion of the funds comes from private individuals.

Even independent countries that have no national grievance devote much attention and money to foreign propaganda. They generally have a twofold aim, cultural and commercial. They desire, on the one hand, to make their culture known to other countries and on the other to develope more trade with them. The propaganda conducted by the British is, in my opinion, more effective than that of other countries, because it is more natural and scientific. The British method of propaganda is roughly as follows :—

(*i*) News agencies like * * * carry on a subtle propaganda in favour of Great Britian through the manipulation of everyday news.

(*ii*) Britishers make it a point to attend every International Congress which is held in any part of the world.

(*iii*) In every country, special societies exist for developing friendly relations with that country. For example in Vienna there is a society called the Anglo-Austrian Friends. Similar organisations exist in every country in Europe and America and all these societies have corresponding organisations in Great Britian.

(*iv*) A large number of Britishers representing different walks of life go abroad every year to lecture on different aspects of British culture. In this work, British artists play an important role.

(*v*) Foreigners and foreign students are invited to visit Great Britian. In some cases foreign students are given scholarships.

(*vi*) There are numerous international societies like the Quakers, the all-Peoples Association, etc., which have their headquarters in London and branches all over Europe —through whose medium a very subtle propaganda is carried on in favour of Great Britian, These societies generally have a stock of English books in their libraries.

(*vii*) In almost every important city of Europe there is an English-speaking club. These clubs are invariably centres of propaganda.

(*viii*) Books, etc., about Great Britain are published in every language.

The above propaganda is carried on mostly by non-official agencies, in addition to the official propaganda conducted through Embassies and Consulates. British propaganda is not obstructive and people for whom it is meant, hardly realize that a conscious propaganda is going on. Where it is moreover as in the case of Miss Mayo's " Mother India " for the film " Bengali "—it is conducted through the medium of a third party, so that no one can say that Britishers are behind it. As compared with this, German propaganda is crude and obtrusive and it therefore sometimes defeats its own purpose.

During the last two years I have realized from time to time how very sensitive the British people are to any propaganda that is not in keeping with their requirements. One would ordinarily expect such a powerful nation as the British to be quite indifferent to what other people may think or say about them. But the exact contrary is the case. Here I am reminded of the extraordinary step taken by the British Ambassador in Belgrade in June 1934, in requesting the Foreign office to stop the Yugo-Slavian papers from publishing interviews with me. I am also reminded of the wrath of Sir Walter Smiles, M. P. over a speech that I made in Geneva in September 1933 (Sir Walter Smiles wanted that I should be put in prison on my return to India because of this speech. When I asked him to correct my mis-statements that I might have made therein, he did not reply). Because of her ultra-sensitiveness to foreign opinion, Great Britain is now taking steps to strengthen her propaganda abroad. Recently a society, called the "British Council of Relations with Foreign Countries" has been started with H. R. H. the Prince of Wales as its patron, for carrying on pro-British propaganda in other countries. Addressing his Royal Highness on the 2nd July 1935, the Chairman, Lord Tyrell, said that the society has been started at the instance of the foreign office and with the active collaboration of five Government departments—while the Government Treasury had made a grant of £6,000. The *Daily Telegraph* of London, while giving its whole-hearted support to this endeavour wrote on the 3rd July as follows :—

"Now France and Italy each budget one million pounds a year for national propaganda and prestige. Japan has recently budgeted one hundred thousand pounds for similar purposes during the coming year and the vast resources of the German Ministry of propaganda are being expended outside the Reich no less than within. Funds on a much larger scale than £ 6,000 though not necessarily Government funds, are necessary if we are to take similar interest in making ourselves known."

Coming to India, the question is—what should we do ? I am sorry to say in this connection that among the older generation I find a complete lack of appreciation of the utility of Indian propaganda abroad. The opinion expressed by Mr. Bhulabhai Desai and the Editor of *Indian Social Reformer* are typical of what the older generation think. The views of the Congress president, Sjt. Rajendra Parsad, are somewhat more progressive. He welcomes such propaganda, but regrets that the Congress does not possess sufficient means to undertake this work. One is, therefore, left with the feeling that the older generation regard this work as a superfluous luxury and not as an indispensable necessity. If they had regarded it a necessity, they would certainly have procured funds for it.

Of the Indian leaders, the late Sjt. Vithalbhai Patel was the only one who had a full appreciation of the utility of foreign propaganda and a clear conception as to how it should be carried on. It is no exaggeration to say that in the cause of this propaganda he laid down his precious life. It was his American tour, in the course of which he delivered 85 speeches, in three months, that damaged beyond repair his already broken health. At the end of this campaign and after mature deliberation with American friends of India, he returned with the conviction that the Indian National Congress should have a permanent representative in the United States. This suggestion was duly conveyed to Mahatma Gandhi. The Late Sjt. Vithalbhai Patel was of opinion that for our propaganda work, we should have our Headquarters in Geneva with branches all over Europe and America, One such branch he was able to start during his lifetime in Dublin, under the name of the Indo-Irish League. His journey to Geneva about a month before his sad and premature death, was for the purpose of preparing the ground for a centre there—but fate prevented him from accomplishing this work.

If foreign propaganda be necessary for independent countries as well as for those who fight for their freedom with arms—it is an absolute necessity for countries like India that have discarded the method of physical force and armed revolution. To such a peaceful and constitutional acitivity, the British Government, too, can have no objection. We have every right to mobilize world-sympathy on our side in an open and peaceful manner and the British Government have indirectly recognised this right by sponsoring India's membership of the League of Nations, which implies that India has all the rights of a full-fledged nation.

There may be a feeling in certain quarters that foreign propaganda must in all probability be something of a secret or revolutionary or anti-British in character. But such an impression, if it exists anywhere, is altogether without foundation. Propaganda, by its very nature, must be open and above board and propaganda methods are inherently opposed to secret and revolutionary methods. Moreover, this propaganda should not be anti-British but only pro-Indian. I have had some experience of propaganda in Europe and I am definitely of opinion that the moment we attempt anti-British propaganda, we shall defeat our purpose. The British have a vast machinery for their propaganda—including Embassies, Consulates, and numerous non-official associations with which they can counteract our activities. Moreover, if we begin to attack the British, we shall lose sympathy, instead of gaining it. On the other hand, as long as we carry on pro-Indian propaganda, our appeal will be irresistible. And if the British try to thwart our legitimate propaganda, they will automatically put themselves in the wrong and forfeit sympathy everywhere.

In my opinion, Indian propaganda abroad should have the following objectives :—

(1) To counteract false propaganda about India.

(2) To enlighten the world about the true conditions obtaining in India today.

(3) To acquint the world with the positive achievements of the Indian people in every sphere of human activity.

The last objective is the most important, because if we can give the world a good idea of our culture and civilization, we shall automatically dispel false notions regarding the Indian people, raise the status of India in the eyes of the civilized world and obtain sympathy everywhere.

To accomplish this threefold purpose, the following steps among others may be taken :—

(1) Indians should be induced to attend every International Congress.

(2) Articles about India should be written in foreign newspapers and journals.

(3) Books about India should be published in the different languages of Europe and America.

(4) There should be at least one well-equipped library in some central place in Europe to which reference could be made by all those who are interested in India.

(5) Prominent Indians representing different aspects of Indian culture should regularly travel abroad.

(6) Films about India should be exhibited abroad.

(7) Lectures on India with the help of magic lantern slides should be organised in foreign countries.

(8) Foreign scholars should be invited to India and they should be helped to make contact with the best type of Indians.

(9) In every country, mixed societies of Indians and Nationals of that country, should be organised for developing closer cuttural relations with India. Every such society should have a corresponding organization in India. An instance of the first is the Indo-Czecho-Slovakian Society.

(10) Such mixed societies should also be formed everywhere for fostering closer commercial relations between India and other countries. (An instance of this is the Indian-Central European Society of Vienna). Corresponding organisations should be started in India.

(11) Mixed Chamber of Commerce (*e.g.*, Indo-Czecho-Slovak Chamber of Commerce, Indo-Italian Chamber of Commerce, Indo-Austrian Chamber of Commerce, etc.) should be organized in every important capital. Corresponding Chambers of Commerce should be started in India. Such mixed Chambers of Commerce exist in every European country. India alone has not yet realized the importance of this.

(12) Regular assistance should be given to such bodies as the International Committee for India in Geneva which have so far been working independently.

There are several organizations of this sort in Europe and America. Some sort of co-ordination should be established among such societies.

The impression that has been created in many circles all over the world, as a result of prolonged hostile propaganda is that we are an uncivilized people—that our women are enslaved and that we are not a nation, as our society is seething with dissentions. Can we shut ourselves up in a room and remain indifferent to what the world thinks of us ? We cannot. For good or for ill, we are forced by mordern circumstances to share the common life of humanity. We cannot therefore be indifferent to what the outside world thinks of us. Moreover, we can see with our own eyes what other nations are achieving through a course of systematic propaganda. History further teaches us that for enslaved and suppressed nations—especially for those that eschew the path of violence—the sympathy of the civilized world is absolutely necessary and in order to win that sympathy propaganda has to be undertaken. Distinguished Indians like Swami Vivekanand, Dr. Rabindernath Tagore, and Mahatma Gandhi have in the past done a certain amount of propaganda abroad and their work has been supplemented by foreign friends of India. As a result of this, India still has a reputation for an ancient culture and civilization. But if we are to make further progress, it is indispensably necessary that a systematic propaganda, backed by the Indian people, should be undertaken. There are Indians abroad who are determined to do this work with the limited resources at their disposal. The only question is whether the Indian National Congress will take charge of this all-important work and do it in a more effective and efficient manner.

XIII

ANTI-INDIAN PROPAGANDA IN EUROPE

Mr. Bose's protest Letter to Archbishop

Vienna (By air Mail)

Sj. Subhas Chander Bose has lodged a formal protest with the Archbishop of Vienna in connection with the exhibition of the anti-Indian film entitled " ***BENGALI*** *" in the different cinema houses in Vienna.*

" To His Eminence the Archbishop of Vienna,
Cardinal D. Innitzer.

Your Eminence :—I am taking the liberty of addressing your Eminence partly because the subject on which I am writing is of interest and concern to your Eminence and partly because there is unfortunately no one at present in Vienna better qualified to take up this matter on behalf of and in the name of India.

The subject on which I am writing is the film " BENGALI " which is now being shown in different cinema houses in Vienna under the title of " A sensational film from mysterious India." This film does grave unjustice to India and the Indian people and has outraged the feelings of all Indians who have happened to see it or hear of it.

If there had been an Indian Embassy in Vienna to represent India and Indian interests, undoubtedly the matter would have been officially taken up by that Embassy. But in the absence of any such institution in Vienna, I feel called upon to take up this matter by virtue of the position that I hold in the social and public life of my country as one of the leaders of the Indian nationalist movement and also as a former Mayor of the first City in India.

Your Eminence, I am aware, has been taking a most prominent step and also the leading part in a movement in Austria for purifying the films and it is therefore in the fitness of things that this matter should be brought to the notice of your Eminence in the first instance.

"It will be apparent to any one who has seen the film "Bengali" that it represents the species of very skilful propaganda on behalf of the British Imperialism India. In view of the movement that is going on now India for the attainment of India's birthright and freedom and also in view of the sympathy that this movement has drawn in many parts of the world to give such a piece of propaganda is from the British point of view very timely. We Indians have no concern with any positive propaganda that may be carried on behalf of the Great Britain, but we certainly resent the fact that that propaganda should be carried on by the sacrifice of India's interests and of India's reputation as a land of ancient culture and civilization.

I shall now proceed to lay before your Eminence the main points on which our Indian feelings, as true sense of our home-land, have been out raged :—

(*i*) The Hero Mohd. Khan who has been put up to represent India (as against Colonel Stone who has been put to represent Great Britian) has been depicted as a particularly brutal, cruel and inhuman type of man.

(*ii*) The representation of torture inflicted on British officers under the orders of Mohd. Khan is most outrageous and objectionable and brings Indians into hatred and contempt in the eyes of all objective spectators. I fail to understand how such scenes can be shown to the cultured audience of Vienna.

(*iii*) The film further tries to make out that the Indians are a race of cowards because the very sight of pigs makes them collapse. All this is entirely false.

(*iv*) The film tries to make out that the British are in India to protect 300 million Indians. We have no objection to the British claim that they have conquered India but we certainly resent their claim that they are acting for India's interest or they are in India for protecting India.

In conclusion, I beg your Eminence to be so good as to take up this matter at once and take steps to prohibit the exhibition of this film in Austria. If this is not possible atonce, the least that could be done, would be to announce at the beginning of the film that the Indians regard this film as a false representation of their character and morality and strongly resent the outrageous and objectionable nature of the scenes displayed. Such a procedure has been adopted in the past when films have been shown in Vienna which did injustice to a particular nationality.

What I am thus submitting to your Eminence, would, I think also, be welcome to every true and patriotic Austrian abroad, namely—to protect his homeland and home-country against calumny and slander.

May I be permitted to express to your Eminence my deepest respect and in advance my gratitude for your Eminence's discernment and comprehension of your feelings.

I have the honour to be,
Yours faithfully,
(Sd.) S. C. Bose
Former General Secy. Indian National Congress and former Mayor of CALCUTTA.

XIV

NEED FOR FOREIGN PROPAGANDA

(1)

London (By air mail). Sj. Subhas Chander Bose has issued the following statement regarding the foreign propaganda on behalf of India :—

" My attention has been drawn to a statement made by the Congress President Sj. Rajendra Parshad and by Mr. Bhulabhai Desai regarding Indian propaganda in America, and other countries. For an efficient propaganda two things are necessary :—(1) accredited representatives and (2) necessary funds. It is superfluous to say that the larger the funds, the more effective can be the propaganda. Nevertheless, much useful work can be done without large funds if only we have the will to work. As a matter of fact, there are many Indians in Europe and America who have been doing useful propaganda, some in their individual capacity, and others in the name of certain organisations started by them without grant from the Indian National Congress. If some of them could be nominated by the Indian National Congress as its representatives abroad—then even without any extra funds they could render greater service to their country. The late Mr. Vithalbhai Patel of revered memory, always used to say that if he could have spoken in the name of the Congress, his work abroad would have been much more effective. And that is also the experience of lesser people like myself. If the only difficulty confronting the Congress is lack of funds, will the Congress at least authorise me (and other workers like myself) to work and speak in the name of the Congress. In that case even without any financial grant from the Congress, we should render greater service to our country and give a better account of ourselves. I am putting a straight question to the Congress President and I beg of him to give me a straight answer.

In this connection I may say atonce that our differences if any, over internal questions should not stand in the way of our joining hands in our external propaganda. Whatever views we may hold on internal questions, the moment we face the outside world, our cause is one and our programme of work is one. That programme of work may be described roughly as follows :—

(*i*) to counteract false propaganda about India.

(*ii*) to acquaint the world with real conditions, political and economic, obtaining in India's fight for Swaraj.

(*iii*) to acquaint the world with the positive achievements of the Indian people in the domain of philosophy, art and science, and culture in general.

Regarding the legacy of the late Mr. V. J. Pacel, all that I shall say at this stage, is that though the probate was granted nine months ago (or more) the money is still lying in the hands of the executors and much useful time is being wasted.

(2)

Madras (By mail). Mr. Subhas Chander Bose in a communication addressed to a local journalist writes from Karlsbad under the date 26th July, 1935 as follows :—

"Your letter of the 30th May reached me on the 21st June. I regret the delay in replying to it.

I came here about a month ago and am taking a course of Karlsbad treatment. I have been making slow but steady progress.

My views on foreign propaganda are, I think, well-known to you in this matter. I had only one supporter among the Congress leaders, the late Mr. V. J. Patel. The majority of the Congress leaders of today consider it unnecessary. A few consider it a useful luxury. You may ask why ? I shall explain.

There are two ways of winning our freedom—by force or through non-violence. If you rely entirely on physical force, you may dispense with the sympathy or support given by other nations, provided you feel sufficiently strong to fight your own battle. If your method is one of non-violence, as in our case, you have to rely on world opinion. And there can be no doubt about it. Without the pressure of world opinion you can never win your freedom even if you carry on satyagrah till eternity. In order to retain her Empire, England has to keep up her prestige internationally, and has to get the backing of world opinion. I wonder how many of our Congressmen realise the elaborate measures adopted by the powerful British Empire and the sums of money spent annually in order to keep a continuous pro-British propaganda throughout the world. If it is necessary for the British to cultivate world opinion in order to maintain her position, how much more necessary it is for us to cultivate world opnion in order to win our freedom. Britian has convinced Europe that in India she is doing the work of Europe and is not pursuing her selfish ends. Therefore you will find that wherever there is a discriminatory legislation in India in favour of a Britisher, it is extended to all Europeans. We have to undo this influence through our own patient and persistent propaganda.

Hence, I regard foreign propaganda as an integral part of our scheme of work. In recent years no country has been able to dispense with international sympathy in its struggle for liberty, though the method was one of physical force. If money can be found for Charkha and anti-untouchability campaign, it can also be found for foreign propaganda. What is lacking today is not money —but the will and desire. The moment Congress leaders realize that foreign propaganda is essentially necessary for the success of our movement, money will be forthcoming. How do political parties in Europe find money for their foreign propaganda ?

When the late Mr. V. J. Patel was in America, he had long talks on this matter with Dr. Holmes and other American friends of India. They all agreed that the Indian National Congress should have representation in America. This request of the American friends of India was sent to Mahatma Gandhi through the Late Mr. V. J. Patel. The latter could not unfortunately deliver this message to Mahatma Gandhi personally and before his sad and unexpected death he charged me to have it conveyed to Mahatma Gandhi. After his death it was duly sent by me to Mahatma Gandhi but nothing came out of it. The result is that there is no one in America with authority, who could mobilize the large volume of sympathy for India that exists there. It will not do to say that the Congress has no money for fereign propaganda. Though money is one of the requirements for this work, it is not the only one. There are people in Europe and in America who have been trying to serve the country's cause in their indivdual capacity or through organisations started by them mithout any monetary grant from the Congress. And they will continue to work whatever the attitude of the Congress may be. Will the Congress utilize their services and give them the stamp of authority ?

XV

INDIA AND THE LEAGUE OF NATIONS

Geneva White Elephant

Karlsbad July 29 (By air mail)

(1)

Sj. Subhas Chander Bose who has been convalescing here since his discharge from the sanitarium of his recent intestinal operation, has sent the following press-note urging India's withdrawl of membership from the League of Nations

There is an institution in Geneva called the League of Nations of which we hear much but unfortunately know little, though every year poor India has to pour out the sum of 1,666,205 gold Francs towards its upkeep.

The income of the League of Nations is spent in maintaining the (1) organs of the League (2) the international labour office at Geneva (3) The permanent court of international justice at the Hague ; in arranging for all the conferences and commissions under the auspices of the League and for the construction of the new palatial Headquarters at Geneva.

The organs of the League are :—(1) The Assembly which consists of representatives of States members of the League. (2) The Council which consists of representatives of the principal Allied and associated powers, together with representatives of four other members of the League. (3) the Secreatariat which is a very big body with various sections *viz*, (*a*) Minorities. (*b*) Mandates (*c*) Opium Traffic and Social questions. (*d*) Disarmament (*e*) Legal (*f*) Information (*g*) Financial and economic intelligence service (*h*) Economic relations (*i*) Communication and transit (*j*) Health (*k*) Intellectual co-operation and (*l*) Political.

Reference should also be made to the Auxiliary organisations which have been created under resolutions of the League Assembly or the League Council.

The League of nations is maintained by the contributions made by States members of the League according to a scale adopted by the League Assembly. This scale is revised at intervals. The present scale was adopted in 1925. According to it. India has to pay 55 units of contributions. China 46 units. France 79 units. Italy 60 units, Spain 40 units, U. S. S. R. 79 units. One unit is equivalent to 30. 224 gold Francs—so that India's contribution comes to 1,662.205 gold Francs. as stated above. In 1934 India's contribution was reduced from 55 to 35 units.

published some time ago, that Great Britain's contribution per annum towards the upkeep of the League is less than the total amount drawn annually by British officials and employees of the League as salary.

Compared with this, what does India get out of the League? The advantages that she gets are practically nil, because India is invariably represented at meetings either by Britishers or by de-nationalised Indians. And as far the Secretariat, there are two ill-paid Indians at the League Headquarters and three or four ill-paid Indians at the International labour office in Geneva. Up till now there was no Indian at the Court of International Justice at the Hague. Only recently have I seen in the papers a proposal to appoint Sir Tej Bahadur Sapru to a vacant seat.

In the light of the above facts, I ask my countrymen if it is worthwhile for India to waste her meagre resources in maintaining this Geneva White Elephant.

Other countries have set an example to India. Costa Rica, a Central American State, withdrew from the League on December 24th 1924; Brazil withdrew on June 14th 1926, Japan withdrew on March 27th 1933 and last but not least, Germany withdrew on Oct. 14th 1933. All these countries are flourishing without the help of the League.

Will the members of the Legislative Assembly take up this question at the next meeting of the Assembly? If so, they may ask the Government of India to ask the

Secretary General of the League to furnish the following information :—

The contribution made by each State member of the League. (2) The total number of officials and employees belonging to each nationality that is a member of the League. who work in the different organisations, International labour office and Court of Justice. (3) The total amount drawn as salary each year by the above officials and employees belonging to each nationality, that is a State member of the League.

There is one other fact which I shall mention before I close. The delegations that are sent by the different governments to Geneva from time to time always use their influence with the Secretary General in order to better the lot of their own nationals at Geneva. This does not happen in the case of the Indian employees, because the Indian delegation to Geneva do not consider it necessary to bother their heads about the fate of Indian employees there.

(2)

League's Refusal to supply Information to Mr. Bose

Karlsbad (By air mail). With reference to the press-note recently issued by Sj. Subhas Chander Bose through the United Press on India and the League of Nations, an interesting correspondence passed between Sj. Subhas Chander Bose and Director of the Information Section of the League of Nations. In releasing the same for publication Sj. S. C. Base makes the following observations :—

" Since I wrote to the Indian press about the League of Nations and the futility of India remaining a member of it, some correspondence has passed between me and the Director of the Information Section of the League of Nations. I am issuing for publication a copy of this correspondence. It will be clear therefrom that the League Secretariate is unwilling to disclose information for the use of the public which is nevertheless available to the Government concerned. Such attitude is most astounding because the League of Nations was brought into existence for abolishing secrecy in public affairs. However, it is clear from the Director's letters that much of the information that I asked for is in the possession of the Government of India. Consequently, if questions are put by Assembly members, the required information should be forthcoming atonce.

" In connection with the India's contribution for the upkeep of the League, it would be interesting to know what contribution if any, has been paid by the Indian States up till now. It is common knowledge that since the treaty of Versailles in 1919, Indian Princes or their nominees have always formed a part of the delegation nominated by the British Government to represent India. This year also the delegation to annual Assembly of the League contains a nominee of the Indian Princes. It would therefore be desirable for the Assembly members to ask the Government of India pointedly what contribution if any has been paid by the Indian Princes uptill now. In case any such payment has been made so far, the Assembly members should demand that the Indian Princes should pay to the Govenment of India their share together with all arrears in view of the representation they have enjoyed so far.

Kurhans Konigin Alexendera,
Karlsbad (Czechoslovakia)
The 3rd August, 1935.

To

The Director of the Information Bureau,
League of Nations, Geneva.

Dear Sir,

I shall be greatly obliged if you kindly could furnish me with the following information which is necessary for my own use as well as for the use of friends in India who are members of the Indian Legislative Assembly :—

(*i*) The total number of officials of all grades in the service of the League of Nations in its different departments *viz.*, League Secretariate, International Labour Office, permanent Court of International Justice etc.

(*ii*) The total number of such officials belonging to each country who is a member of League of Nations.

(*iii*) The total amonnt drawn as salary per annum by such officials belonging to each country who is a member of League of Nations.

(*iv*) The total income and expenditure per annum of each country who is a member of the League of Nations.

(*v*) The present value of Franc in terms of English Currency.

(*vi*) What are the various factors that are considered by the League Assembly in determining the annual contribution to the League of Nations of each state member.

(*vii*) The official position, length of service, qualifications and salary to each Indian who is in the service of League of Nations in any of its departments.

If for any reason full or accurate information on any of the above heads is not forthcoming, will you be so good as to give me as much information as is available.

Thanking you in anticipation.

Yours faithfully,
(Sd.) Subhas Chander Bose
President,
National Congress Committee,
Bengal and Ex-Mayor of
Calcutta.

League of Nations,
Geneva, Dt. August 22, 1935.

Mr. Subhas Chander Bose,
Kurhaus Konigin Alexandera,
Karlsbad, (Czechoslovakia)

Dear Sir,

With reference to your enquiry of the 3rd August, I have been asked by the Director of the Information Section to tell you that the League of Nations Secretariate is not in a position to reply to the different querries in your note. The States members of the League of Nations are regularly informed of the total number of officials in the Service of League, nationality of these officials, details regarding their salaries etc. The documents which furnish these details are however, confidential and are available only for the governments belonging to the League of Nations.

I have pleasure in sending you the complementary copy of "Essential factors about the League of Nations." This publication gives a general survey of the structure of the League organisation, contains a table of the States members of the League and their annual contribution (which are assessed on the National Budgets).

About 15 gold Francs are equivalent to £. 1 at present.

Believe me.

Your faithfully,
(Sd.) Illegible.
P. P. Director information Sec.

Kurhans Konigin Alexendera
Karlsbad, (Czechoslovakia)
Dt. 80th August, 1985.

The Director,
Information Section,
League of Nations, Geneva.

Dear Sir,

I thank you for your letter of the 22nd August in reply to my enquiry of the 3rd August but I must say that I am extremely surprised at the contents of your letter. I had the impression that the League of Nations had come into existence for abolishing secrecy in public affairs. I fail to understand how information on the points mentioned in my letter could be available to the Government concerned but should be withheld by you from the public belonging to those States that are members of the League of Nations.

I thank you for the booklet you have sent and of which I already possessed a copy. It is because this booklet does not furnish information that I want that I had to write and trouble you for required information.

May I again request you to be so good as to furnish me with as much information on the points I have mentioned as you possess.

Thanking you.

Yours faithfully,
(Sd.) Subhas Chander Bose.

XVI

REUTER'S PROPAGANDA TACTICS

My attention has been drawn to an air mail message sent by Reuter from Belgrade on the 9th June, which has been reproduced in the Yugoslav Press. The message runs thus :—

"The State Censor has intervened to prevent articles by Mr. Subhas Chander Bose, being published in the Yugoslav press. Mr. Bose, who has been touring Europe, lecturing, and writing about the Indian Nationalist cause recently arrived at Belgrade from Sofia, and contrasts the attitude of the Yugoslav authorities unfavourable with that of Bulgarians, and Roumanians, who gave him a most cordial reception."

The fact is that my reception at the hands of the Municipal and State authorities at Belgrade, the capital of Yugoslavia, was as cordial as that I had received at Budapest (Hungary) Bucharest (Roumania) and Sofia (Bulgaria). The only difference was that the press in Belgrade was not as hospitable as the press in Budapest, Bucharest, and Sofia

"In Hungary, Roumania, and Bulgaria, in connection with my visit the press gave prominence to India's struggle for freedom. The same thing would normally have happened at Belgrade, but for the intervention of the British Ambassador. Soon after my arrival the most prominent paper of Belgrade, the 'Politika' sent a representative to interview me. I had to give a long interview, so varied and numerous were the questions I was asked. Later I was invited to visit the office, and printing press of the 'Politika.' The representative of 'Politika' told me that the Editor would be very glad to publish a nationalist account of India's struggle as given by me—because a few days earlier, the Nawab of Rampur who had visited Belgrade had given an interview to say that the people of India were satisfied under British rule and that conditions in India under British rule were ideal.

"Later at night, the 'Politika' office rang me up to say, that they were sorry to inform me that the interview in question had been held up by the foreign office —after it had been approved by the Editor for publication. The next morning I made enquiries at the foreign office, and also from friends whom I had come to know at Belgrade—and I was informed that the British Ambassador had made repeated requests to the foreign office to withold any interviews that I may give to any of the Belgrade papers. For reasons best known to them, the Foreign office was not able to refuse the request of the British Ambassador, and so the Belgrade papers were not able to publish any interviews, though they were anxious to do so. I have nothing to complain about the reception I received at Belgrade nor about the attitude of the

Belgrade Press. I was very glad to be able to rouse interest about India among the public through my visit to Belgrade. My only complaint is against the British Ambassador, who intervened in the matter, and that in a secret manner. It interested me greatly to hear that I had been described by him as undesirable.

"Reuter's message gives the impression that my interview, (not article) was withheld because I had criticised the Yugoslav authorities. This is absolutely false. The interview was withheld only because it was regarded as 'anti-British by the British Ambassador. This incident gives some idea of the difficulties that are thrown in our way, by our rulers, when we try to make India's voice heard in foreign countries, where there is genuine interest in, and sympathy for India."

INDIA AND CHINA

Ever since the Japanese aggression in China began last year, the Indian National Congress has repeatedly expressed its sympathy for the Chinese people in their struggle for freedom and peace. Apart from resolutions of sympathy being passed, pro-Chinese demonstrations were held all over the country. A sum of Rs. 8,000/- (eight thousand) was also collected and is now in the hands of the All-India Congress Committee office. The Working Committee of Congress, at its last meeting in Bombay, decided to send an Ambulance unit with the doctors to China for demonstrating our solidarity with the Chinese people, instead of sending only monetary relief. The committee also appointed a sub-committee consisting of Dr. Jiveraj Mehta, Dr. Sunil Chander, B.Sc. Dr. R. M. Lohia, Shri G.P. Hutheesing for the ambulance unit together with the doctors. The sub-committee held a meeting in Bombay on the 24th instant, and decided to send a fully-equipped motor car Ambulance to China and a batch of four qualified doctors, preferably experienced surgeons. One year's expenses were worked out and it was found that a sum of rupees thirty thousand was needed for the Medical Mission. Since we have only rupees eight thousand in hand, we shall have to collect a further sum of rupees twenty-two thousand.

Applications from qualified medical men who would like to join the Medical Mission to China are invited. Applicants should preferably be Surgeons with some experience and should undertake to serve for at least one year. They should send in their applications to the Secretary, Foreign Department, All-India Congress Committee, Allahabad, with a copy to the Secretary of the China sub-committee, Mr. G P. Hutheesing of Gulshan Villa, Qamar Park, Werden Road, Bombay. The expenses of equipment, board and lodging in China together with a small pocket allowance will be provided for the doctors but no salary will be paid.

In order to demonstrate once again our deep sympathy for the Chinese people in their hour of trial, I request all Congress organisations in the country to observe the 12th June 1938, as an All-India Chinese Day Meetings and Processions should be held on that day and a serious endeavour should be made to collect funds for our Medical Mission. If the necessary efforts are made it should not be difficult to collect the entire amount of rupees twenty-two thousand by that date In this connection I also appeal to firms dealing in Medical stores and appliances which are badly needed in China today and help in kind will not be less welcome to the distressed and injured Chinese people than assistance in cash.

In conclusion, I may remind my countrymen that it is essential that our proposed medical aid should reach China as early as possible. We should therefore, get ready to give a send-off to our Medical Mission by the first week of July at the very latest. The seventh of July, the day on which Japanese aggression started last year, would be an appropriate day for wishing Bon Voyage to the Indian friends of China.

XVIII

MEETING WITH A PHILOSOPHER THINKER AND A DREAMER IN GENEVA

Wednesday, the 3rd April 1935. It was a bright sunny morning, and Geneva was looking at its best. In the distance, silhouetted against the clear blue sky, stood the snow-capped heights of Saleve. In front of us there lay the picturesque lake of Geneva with the stately buildings mirrored in its glassy bosom. I was out on a pilgrimage. Ever since I had landed in Europe, two years ago, I had been longing to meet that great man and thinker—that great friend of India, and of Indian culture—Mon. Romain Rolland. Circumstances had prevented our meeting in 1933 and again in 1934, but the third attempt was going to succeed. I was in high spirits but occasionally a thrill of anxiety and doubt passed within me. Would I be inspired by this man or would I return disappointed? Would this great dreamer and idealist appreciate the hard facts of life—the practical difficulties that beset the path of the fighter in every age and clime?

Above all, would he read what fate had written on the walls of India's history?

What heartened me, however, were inspiring words in his letter of the 22nd February......"But we men of thought must each of us fight against the temptation that befalls us in moments of fatigue and unsettledness, of repairing to a world beyond the battle called either God or Art or Freedom of the spirit or those distant regions of the mystic soul. For fight we must, as our duty, lies on this side of the ocean—on the battle-ground of men."

For full two hours we drove along the circuitous route which skirts the lake of Geneva. It was charming weather and while we raced along the Swiss Riviera, we enjoyed one of the finest sceneries in Switzerland. As we came to Villeneuve, the car slowed down, and ultimately came to a standstill in front of Villa Olga, the residence of the French Savant. That was indeed a beauty-spot. Sheltered by an encircling row of hills, the house commanded a magnificent view of the lake. All around us there was peace, beauty and grandeur. It was indeed a fit place for a hermitage.

As I rang the bell, the door was opened by a lady of short stature but with an exceedingly sympathetic and lively face. This was Madame Romain Rolland. Hardly had she greeted me than another door opened in front of us and there emerged a tall figure with a pale countenance and with wonderful penetrating eyes. Yes, this was a face I had seen in many a picture before—a face that seemed to be burdened with the sorrow of humanity. There was something exquisitely sad in that pallid face—but it was not an expression of defeatism. For no sooner did he begin to speak than colour rushed to his white cheeks—the eyes glowed with a light that was uncommon and the words that he poured forth were pregnant with life and hope.

The usual greetings and the preliminary inquiries about India and Indian friends were soon over and we dropped into a serious conversation. Mon. Rolland could—or did not—speak English and I could not speak French. So we had as interpreters, Mademoiselle Rolland and Madame Rolland. My purpose was to discuss with him the latest developments in the Indian situation and to ascertain his present views on the important problems before the world. I had, therefore, to do much of the talking at first in order to explain the Indian situation as I analysed and comprehended it.

The two cardinal principles on which the movement of the last 14 years had been based were—firstly, satyagraha or non-violent resistance and secondly, a united front of all sections of the Indian people, *e.g.*, capital and labour, and landlord and peasant. India's great hope was that the satyagraha movement would fructify, in a peaceful settlement in the following manner. Within India, the movement would gradually paralyse the civil administration of the country. Outside India, the lofty ethics of satyagraha would stir the conscience of the British people. Thus would the conflict lead to a settlement whereby India would win her freedom without striking a blow and without shedding any blood. But that hope was frustrated. Within India, the satyagraha movement no doubt created a non-violent revolution, but the higher services, both civil and military, remained unaffected and the King's Government therefore went on much as usual.

Outside India, a handful of high-minded Britishers were no doubt inspired by the ethics of Gandhi, but the British people as a whole remained quite indifferent; self-interest drowned the ethical appeal.

The failure to win freedom led to a very earnest heart-searching among the rank and file of the Indian National Congress, one section of Congress men went back to the old policy of constitutional action with the Legislatures. Mahatma Gandhi and his orthodox followers after the suspension of the Civil disobedience movement (or satyagraha), turned to a programme of social and economic uplift of the villages. But the more radical section, in their disappointment, inclined to a new ideology and plan of action and the majority of them combined to form the Congress Socilist Party.

" What would be Mon. Rolland's attitude," I asked at the end of my lengthy preface, "if the united front is broken up and a new movement is started not quite in keeping with the requirements of Gandhian satyagraha ?

He would be very sorry and disappointed, said Mon. Rolland, if Gandhi's satyagraha failed to win freedom for India. At the close of the Great War, when the whole world was sick of bloody strife and hatred, a new light had dawned on the horizon when Gandhi emerged with his new weapon of political strife. Great were the hopes that Gandhi had roused throughout the whole world.

" We find from experience," said I, " that Ghandi's method is too lofty for this materialistic world, and as a political leader, he is too straight-forward in his dealings with his opponents. We find, further, that though the British are not wanted in India, with the help of superior physical force, they have nevertheless been able to maintain their existence in India inspite of the inconvenience and annoyance caused by the satyagraha movement. If satyagraha ultimately fails, would Mon. Rolland like to see the national endeavour continued by other methods or would he cease taking interest in the Indian movement ?"

" The struggle must go in any case "—was the emphatic reply.

" But I know several European friends of India who have told me distinctly that their interest in the Indian freedom movement is due entirely to Gandhi's method of non-violent resistance.

Mon. Rolland did not agree with them at all. He would be sorry, if satyagraha failed. But if it really did then the hard facts of life would have to be faced and he would like to see the movement conducted on other lines.

That was the answer nearest to my heart. He then was an idealist, who did not build castles in the air but who had his feet planted on *terra firma*.

" There are people in Europe," I said, " who say that just as in Russia there were two successive revolutions—a bourgeoise democratic revolution and a socialist revolution—so also in India there will be two successive revolutions—a national democratic revolution and a social revolution. In my opinion, however, the fight for political freedom will have to be conducted simultaneously with the fight for socio-economic emancipation. The party that will bring political freedom to India will be the party that will also put into effect the entire programme of socio-economic reconstruction. What is Mon. Rolland's opinion on the point?

He found it difficult to express a definite opinion because he was not aware of all the facts of the Indian situation.

"What would be Mon. Rolland's attitude," I continued," if the united front policy of the Indian National Congress fails to win freedom for India and a radical party emerges which identifies itself with the interests of the peasants and the workers?"

Mon. Rolland was clearly of opinion that the time had come for the Congress to take a definite stand on the economic issues. "I have already written to Gandhi," said he, "that he should make up his mind on this question."

Explaining his attitude in the event of a schism within the Indian National Congress, he continued, "I am not interested in choosing between two political parties or between two generations. What is of interest and of value to me is a higher question. To me political parties do not count; what really counts is the great cause that transcends them—the cause of the workers of

We talked at length of Mahatma Gandhi and his tactics. I ventured the remark that the Mahatma would not take a definite stand on the economic issues. Whether on political, or social or economic questions, he was temperamentally a believer in 'the golden mean.' I then referred to what the younger generation regarded as some of the defects in his leadership and tactics, namely, his incorrigible habit of putting all the cards on the table, his opposition to the policy of social boycott of political opponents, his hope of a change of heart on the part of the British Government, etc. It did not afford us any satisfaction I said, to oppose him or even criticise him—when he had done more for his country than anyone else in recent history and had raised India considerably in the estimation of the whole world. But we loved our country more than any personality.

I asked Mon. Rolland if he would be good enough to put in a nutshell the main principles for which he had stood and fought all his life. "Those fundamental principles," he said, "are (1) internationalism (including equal rights for all races without distinction), (2) Justice for the exploited workers—implying thereby that we should fight for a society in which there will be no exploiters and no exploited—but all will be workers for the entire community, (3) freedom for all suppressed nationalities and (4) equal rights for women as for men." And he proceeded to amplify some of these points.

As our conversation was drawing to a close, I remarked that the views he had expressed that afternoon, would cause surprise in many quarters since they appeared to be a recent development in his thought-life. This remark worked like an electric button and set in motion a whole train of thought. Mon. Rolland spoke of the acute mental agony he had passed through since the end of the war in trying to revise his social ideas and his entire ideology. "The combat within myself," he said, "extended over a very wide field and the problem of non-violence was only a part of it. I have not decided against non-violence but I have decided that non-violence cannot be the central pivot of our entire social activity. It can be one of its means—one of its proposed forms still subject to experiment."

Continuing he said, "The primary objective of all our endeavours should be the establishment of another social order, more just and more human.* * * If we do not do so, it will mean the end of society." Then referring to the methods of activity, he said, "My own task has been for several years to try and unite the forces againet the old order that is enslaving and exploiting humanity. This has been my role in the World's Congress of all political parties against War and Fascism, which was held in Amsterdam in 1932 and in the permanent committees appointed by that Congress. I still believe that there is in non-violence a strong, though latent, revolutionary power which can and ought to be used."

I interrupted him at this stage to ask him how the world at large could know of his present ideas. To this he replied, "My social creed of these fifteen years has been expounded in two volumes of articles which have been just published. In the first one "Quinze ans de Combat" (Fifteen years of Combat), Editions Rieder, Boulevard St. Germain 108, Paris VI—I have spoken of my inner fight and the evolution of my social ideas. In the second book 'Par la Revolution la Pais' (By way of Revolution to Peace) Editions sociales Inter-nationales 24, Rue Racini Paris, VI, I have dealt with questions concerning war, peace, non-violence and the co-ordination of their efforts in fighting the old social order." Continuing he said that some of his friends had refused to recognize all that he had written, preferring to accept only those portions with which they agreed, These two volumes would, however, be a faithful record of the evolution of his thought.

Our conversation did not end without a discussion of the much-apprehended and much-talked of war in Europe. "For suppressed peoples and nationalities," I remarked, "war is not an unmixed evil." "But for Europe war will be the greatest disaster," said he. "It may even mean the end of civilization. And for Russia, peace is absolutely necessary if she is to complete her programme of social reconstruction.

Before I took leave of my host, I expressed my deep gratitude for his kindness, and my great satisfaction at what he had conveyed to me. I valued so greatly his sympathy for India; and her cause, that it had filled me with anxiety and fear whenever I had tried to imagine what his reaction would be towards the latest developments in the Indian situation.

The sun was still shining on the blue waters of the lake of Geneva as I emerged out of Villa Olga. Around me there stood the snow-covered mountains. The air was pregnant with joy and it infected me. A heavy load had been lifted off my mind. I felt convinced that this great thinker and artist would stand for India and her freedom whatever might be her immediate future or her future line of action. And with that conviction I returned to Geneva a happy man.

XIX

AN INTERESING PERSONALITY IN ROUMANIA

During my recent visit to Roumania, I came across in Bucharest a very interesting personality. He is Dr. Narsingh-Mulgand, a Lt. Col. in medical department of the Roumanian army. I became so interested in him that I obtained from him the particulars of his early life which I am now writing for the information of my countrymen.

A Maharashtrian by birth, his home was in Taluka Bhuvangir, sixty miles from Hyderabed city in Deccan. He had his early education in Bombay and after matriculating, he went over to Calcutta.

In Calcutta he joined the Scottish Churches College and studied for the F. A. Examination. Simultaneously, he studied at the National Medical Collge of Dr. S. K. Mullick. Among the teachers at latter college were Dr. S. K. Mullick, Dr. Y. M. Bose, Dr. B. C. Ghosh, and Dr. M. D. Dass. He duly passed the F. A. Examination, and the M. G. P. S. Examination from the National Medical College. In 1912, he went over to London and took the M. R. C. S. Diploma.

About this time the Turko-Balkan War broke out and Dr. Mulgund volunteered for service in the Red ed subject. With the help of his two friends and through the strength of his war services he was able to become a naturalized subject long before the usual term. Soon after this he obtained a job as an assistant in the Eye-clinic, attached to the University Hospital. He then passed the State Examination in Roumania. After passing his examination he was able to obtain an appointment as a sub-Lieutenant in the medical department of the Roumanian army.

This was in April 1915. On August 15, 1916, Roumania declared war against Germany. In 1917, Dr. Mulgund became a Lieutenant and in 1918, a Captain. In 1926, he became a Major and in May, 1934, a few days before I came to Bucharest, he became a Lt. Colonel.

Dr. Mulgund, or rather Lt. Col. Mulgund, is one of the best Eye-specialists in Roumania. From 1919 to 1922, he was chief of the Eye-Hospital in Oradia and from 1922 to 1928 he was an Eye-specialist attached to the Military Hospital in Burcharest. During my stay in Bucharest he was asked by the War Minister to open a new Eye Hospital for the benefit of the army.

Lt. Col. Mulgund married a Roumanian lady, and they have two children, both of them girls. They are a happy family. He is quite well known in Bucharest and even before I met him I came to hear of him, from several Roumanian friends. During my stay at Bucharest, I had the pleasure of spending much of my time with him. From the way he used to be accosted by the Roumanian gentry and military officers, whenever we went out together, one could see, that he was not only well-known there, but much esteemed also.

Though he has been away from India, and though he is now a Rumanian subject, he has not forgotten his own language. Besides Marathi, he can speak Hindi fairly well and still retains a fair knowledge of Sanskrit. He is very fond of quoting Sanskrit maxims and verses from the Gita. It was a very great pleasure and honour to meet Lt. Col. Mulgund in Bucharest and I have no doubt that those of my countrymen who read this, will be equally pleased and interested. Lt. Col. Mulgund lives at Strada Canzasi, 14, Bucharest.

Missing Page

SIDELIGHTS FROM VEINNA

(1)

"Since my last letter, the X-ray, and other tests have expressed a definite opinion about my abdominal trouble. They have discarded the theory of duodenal ulcer, and have opined that the pain in the abdomen is due to gall-bladder trouble—Cholecystities as they say. I have already written about the abnormality found in both the lungs. The doctors have expressed the opinion that for treatment of gall-bladder trouble, it is not necessary to go to a sanatorium at first—but that I should live in or near Veinna so that my progress *or otherwise could be watched from day to day.* They think that in 3 or 4 days time there will be an improvement in my condition. If they are satisfied with my progress, they will then advise my removal to a health resort or sanatorium. Since the 11th instant, when I came to this sanatorium, there has been a change in my condition—partly for the better, and partly for the worse, My temperature is running at a lower level than before, but I have lost a kilogram in weight, which is equal to 2 lbs. Besides this, the pain in the abdomen has increased considerably, much to my discomfort. I am still confined to bed, and all exercise is banned. I thought it advisable to give the doctors here a chance, and have therefore, placed myself under their treatment, since the 16th March, when they declared their final diagnosis of my abdominal trouble. Though the treatment for Cholecystitics in many cases is removal of the gall-bladder by operation, my doctors do not advice operation now—partly because of my weak condition, and partly because they want to give their own treatment a trial. But whether I improve under their treatment or not, in either case, the possibility of an operation still exists. If I improve under their treatment here, be in a position to decide the future line of treatment. From my experience, since sailing from Bombay, I am afraid that my progress will be much slower than I had anticipated. My only hope is, that if the present diagnosis is right, and if I improve under treatment, my digestion and appetite may so improve in consequence that my subsequent recovery may be expedited.

The publication of the white paper in London, within the last week, has been responsible for bringing the representatives of the *Teutar* and some of the London newspapers to me. I do not know, if my statements to them have reached the Indian papers.

Among the distinguished Vieneze citizens who have been good enough to visit me is Herr Rene-Fullop Miller and Frau Mrs. Flau-Miller. Herr F. Miller is a most amiable gentleman and one of those highly cultured souls, whose universalism knows no national boundaries. He has won international fame as a thinker, art critic, and author. Frau Faloop Miller is a great admirer of Shri Aurobindo Ghose and an ardent friend of my friend Sj. Dilip Kumar Roy, who is now at Pondichery. Frau Miller has been exceedingly good to me, and frequently visits me in this hospital. This week an international conference on India is to be held at Geneva, on the 3rd March. Friends of India in foreign countries will participate in this conference and Madame Horup of Denmark is the Hon. Secretary of this conference. She visited India in 1931, and was an eyewitness of the lathi-charge on Independence Day in Calcutta in January 1931.

After the Gandhi-Irwin Truce, she interviewed me in Bombay; where both of us had gone to meet Mahatma Gandhi. I had forgotton all this, but she has written to me reminding me of her experiences in India. Some friends requested me to attend the conference, but as it is impossible, I had to content myself with sending a message. Continental Europe is now passing through exciting times, and Austria is feeling the shock along with other countries. In Austria a tussle seems to be going on between Social Democrats, and the Fascists. I think that those of our countrymen, who travel to Europe, and back would be well-advised to try the Italian boats. I am sure they will get better service, attention and food than in other boats.

(2)

On the eve of Departure for Vienna

"It is difficult to express any categorical opinion based on the meagre information in my possession, as I am naturally not in touch with recent developments in the country. Neverthless, I can sense the general atmosphere. There is no doubt that at present we are passing through a political slump, and therefore the most important problem for us is to keep up the enthusiasm of the public. We have been suffering from another piece of misfortune, in as much as political giants are leaving us one by one, the latest, incident being the sad and untimely death of Mr. Abyankar, whom I can rightly call the Lion of Nagpur. His death has created another void in the public life, which will be difficult if not impossible to fill in."

Regarding the decision of the Congress to enter the legislatures, Mr. Subhas Bose said, "We have to guard against the possible danger of being deluded by the hope that our parliamentary activities can by themselves carry us to any distance towards the goal of Swaraj. If we only have the backing of the public, the agitation in the legislatures can be of any use, and we should not allow ourselves to be drawn too much to the legislatures."

Communal Award Controversy

As regards the Communal Award Controversy Mr. Bose said "I believe in unity based on national principles only. Any unity, which is achieved after surrendering our national principles is too illusive to be of any benefit to the nation. I oppose the Communal Award, and it is too bad for India as a whole. I cannot think of any Indian Nationalist to whatsoever community, he may belong, who cannot but in his heart of hearts oppose the pernicions Award. India that we can built on the basis of the Award is a divided India."

J. P. C. Report

Regarding concerted action by all parties against the Joint Committee Report Mr. Bose said "I have no faith in all party conferences. Though the Congress did its best to co-operate with the liberals over the question of the Simon Commission, the Congress was left in the lurch by the liberals, when the Round Table Conference was appointed. Therefore, there was really no concerted action.' I am all for real concerted action, but not a mere all parties conference. If as a result of another attempt to co-operate with other parties, there is a danger of the Congress being left in the lurch, it would be much better for the Congress to plough a lone furrow. For the same reason, I have no faith whatsoever in the proposed Constituent Assembly. The responsibility for producing a constitution for India devolves entirely on those who are going to fight for India's freedom."

Congress Executive

Regarding his opinion on Gandhiji's retirement from politics, Mr. Bose said. "I do not think Gandhiji's retirement is real because it is his programme that the Congress has adopted and his own orthodox followers are in entire charge of the Congress Executive. There is unfortunately no room in the Congress Executive for those who think differently regardless of sincerity or patriotism. The Congress Executive does not represent the party as a whole but it represents only the majority party in the Congress.

Regarding the Village Industries Association of Gandhijis, he said, I welcome the idea of All-India Village Industries Association of Gandhiji and I regard it as a progressive step. But village re-organisation is not possible through Khadi alone. but through a general revival of the dying village industries.

Concluding Mr. Subhas Bose said, we have to face facts. In view of the present unfortunate circumstances,

on-the only course for us is to settle down to progressive constructive work in all possible directions, spread over a number of years and simaltaneously we must do. our best to keep up the spirit in the public life."

XXI

ANALYSIS OF POLITICAL SITUATION IN INDIA

Geneva (By air mail).—Subhas Chander Bose in the course of a signed article in "Neva Zuercher Zeitung" (A Swiss Democratic daily of international repute) writes :—

"The European press knows at present very little to report on the political events in India. In general the impression prevails here that Mahatma Gandhi has completely played out. Undoubtedly Mahatma Gandhi has suffered a defeat in his fight with the British Government. When after 8 years he brought into being his great movement a second time in 1930, he placed hope in two things. In the first place he expected that he would be able to paralyse civil administration in India by passive resistence. Further he hoped that the ethical character of his movement will find such a strong echo in the conscience of the British people that a peaceful settlement of the Indian problem will come of it. But Mahatma Gandhi suffered dis-illusionment. The movement of passive resistence was mighty and conquered widely different strata of the people, but it was not strong though to paralyse the administration of British India. In spite of the great difficulties and inspite of an extensive opposition, the British Government managed to continue its administration further. The moral appeal of Mahatma Gandhi made a little impression on the conscience of the British people. These are the causes of the failure of the movement of passive resistence which he himself suspended in 1934.

The question arises what kind of actual forces are behind Mahatma Gandhi, where is the secret of his power which this slender man uses, a man who barely weighs 90 lbs., and gladly goes out in the tatters of a miserable beggar. The answer is very simple. Foremost of all, he is in his last and deepest motives absolutely selfless, he identifies himself completely with the interests of the people. Behind him stands a powerful political organisation, the Indian National Congress founded in 1885 to struggle for the political emancipation of India. Without the fame and appeal of his sacredness Mahatma Gandhi would not be so powerful as a political leader that he actually is. But without a well organised political party behind him inspite of all his popularity he would not be any danger for the British Government.

When the passive resistence movement was temporarily suspended, the tactics of the Indian National Congress changed. A group of the party resolved to participate in the activity of the parliament, the Indian Legislative Assembly, in order to carry on there a fight for Indian freedom in a constitutional and legal manner. Another group, Mahatma Gandhi himself at the head, tries first of all to improve economic condition of the country people. Mahatma Gandhi has temporarily retired from the leadership of the Nationalist party and the Indian National Congress, But his influence on the masses of people is just as great as ever. The present leaders of the party consist of men and women whom he himself has determined and the present programme of the Congress and tactics of the Congress, have his express assent. In this manner Mahatma Gandhi is even today the power behind the Congress.

In India as well as in Europe the interest is concentrated on the new reforms which the British Government has placed for approval before its parliament. The differences which have broken out between Baldwin and Churchill have absolutely no importance for India. What Baldwin wants to offer to India may be capitulation of England according to Churchill. That does not prevent even the most moderate politician in India to refuse the offer of Baldwin. Why ? The projected new reforms provide methods for Central and the Provincial Parliaments. In the Provinces Ministers responsible for the local parliament will take charge of Administrative departments but the Governor appointed by the British Government in England and responsible to it will have the power to hinder the different ministries and even to take upon himself the administration of any department. Over and above this, the officials of highest services are not placed under the control of Ministers responsible to the Provincial Parliament but will exclusively be responsible to the British Cabinet in London. At the centre of the Fedration, the Viceroy who will also remain Governor General will exercise even wider veto powers than the Governors of the Provinces. Nearly 80 per cent of the Federal budget estimates will be exempted from the sanctioning powers of the Legislative Assembly. Many departments such as Foreign, Financial and Army, are not subject to parliamentary control. Above all neither the Federal Parliament nor the Federal Government will be in a position to push through any measures likely to be against the commercial interests of England.

A Further whittling down of the effectiveness of the new constitution is attempted by an artificial limitation of the representation of the Hindus in the Parliament. The Hindus who form about three-fourths of the population are mostly behind the demands of the Indian National Congress in the Provincial Parliament; therefore the ethical and religious minorities according to the most complicated provisions of the new reforms receive a representation far beyond their numerical importance. In both Chambers of the Federal Parliament the Government wants to give the Indian princes, whom it tries to induce to participate in the Government of Federation, an extraordinarily important representation.

If the British Government conceded to the Indian people, a really substantial part of political power no doubt, an influential section of the national party would go over to the Englishmen and the party itself would thus be paralysed for a long time. Under the actual conditions the party will continue to be an uninterrupted opposition. The movement cannot be stopped by giving minorities a greater number of seats in the Parliament because with these seats no real power is attached so that their possession will not satisfy even minorities. They (Princes) are hesitating yet to join the planned federation because they fear thereby to lose the autonomy till now enjoyed by them. If they, however, follow the wishes of the Government the national democratic movement will spread inevitably into their territories which the national Congress till now leaves out all again.

There are besides other sources of political power which have nothing to do with the Congress. There is peasent organisation, a powerful trade union movement under the direction of the all-India Trade Union Congress and within the Congress itself a militant radical group which calls itself a socialist congress party (The Congress Socialist Party).

The progressively worsening economic condition of the country can in addition to the unsatisfied thirst for political liberty easily drive the country into another fight.

The introduction of the new constitution can therefore be a signal to a new popular movement. If Mahatma Gandhi still lives and is strong, as all Indians eagerly hope, he would place himself again at the head of such a battle.

XXII

NEW REFORMS IN EUROPE—AN ARTICLE

The article from the pen of Mr. J. L. Keenan, the General Manager of the Tata Iron and Steel Works of Jamshedpur, in 'The Modern Review" for December 1935, is interesting for more reasons than one. It is interesting for the digressions from the steel-making into the domain of historical research—interesting for the placid self-complacency which inspires the writer—interesting also for the many contradictions in which the article abounds.

A word about historical and sociological matters. When Mr. Keenan talks about steel-production, he is on solid ground and his self-confidence is an asset. When he digresses into the thorny domain of Ancient History or Sociology, his self-confidence becomes a handicap. Says Mr. Keenan :—" He (J. N. Tata) realized that India from the time of Manu was condemned to be a country of capitalists and slaves." (P. 705). It is a truism in Economics that capitalism is a recent growth in consequence of the advent of large-scale production. How there could have been a capitalist order at the time of Manu and after, passes my comprehension. Even 'landlordism' as we see it today in India, is a recent growth. Further, even the state in ancient times did not amass wealth—the prevalent idea being that the state (whether monarchy or a republic) should give everything to the people. A typical example of this was King Harshavardhnana. who emptied the Royal treasury once in five years.

Then Mr. Keenan goes on to say :—" We (Tata) know that in India before his time the mere name of a labourer must be expressive of contempt." (P. 705). If Mr. Keenan used the word " labourer " in the sense of artisan. he is mistaken. The artisans in the Indian village economy—whether carpenters or blacksmiths or potters—were never looked down upon with contempt. They were indispensable elements of the village economy and their relations with the rest of the village population were perfectly friendly and cordial. Labourers in the sense of industrial proletariat are an excrescence of capitalism and not an Indian phenomenon as such. If labourers (Industrial proletariat) are looked down upon in India, similar is the case in other countries. I have heard from Indian apprentices in European factories that the gulf which separates workmen from officers in European factories is very wide.

Mr. Keenan is also wrong when he goes on to say that a labourer was as a rule forbidden to accumulate wealth and though he was a slave, even if his master gave him freedom. he was still a slave." I wonder from where Mr. Keenan culled this valuable piece of information. We know, on the contrary, that in India low-born people often rose to the highest positions by dint of their personal qualities. If we investigate the past history of some of the present Maharajas and landed aristocrats, useful information can be collected in this connection. I may also point to examples like that of the alleged Kaivarta Kings of Bengal, who came from a so-called low stratum of society.

The distinction, between 'Labour of Necessity' and 'Labour of Progress' which Mr. Keenan had drawn, is artificial and if I may say so, fantastic. Even in ancient times, all labour was not labour of necessity. People did not work only for hunger, nor did they always get starvation wages. Most people worked partly because of hunger, and partly because of the pleasure in working and it is too much to say that labour in the good old days was always sweated. The huge monuments of art that still live—Mohenjodaro, Harappa, Taj Mahal, Madura, Kanarak—do they not represent labour of progress as well? It is true that industries in the old days did not pay huge dividends as they sometimes do now. But we have to remember that huge dividends are exclusively the product of the industrial revolution that is of large scale production. Moreover, this phenomenon of huge dividends can hardly be called an advantage or an achievement. Thinking men everywhere are now coming to admit that the evils resulting from industrial capitalism are due largely to the accumulation of wealth in the hands of a few and to abnormally large dividends which are gathered either at the cost of sweated labour or at the cost of the exploited consumer in colonial or semicolonial countries.

Mr. Keenan transgresses the limits of decency when he refers to President Roosevelt "assisted by a group of asinine professors" trying to find a way out of the present depression. I do not hold any brief for President Roosevelt, nor does the noble President stand in need of it. But is there anyone who can deny that the biggest experiment to end unemployment and depression that is going on in the world today outside Russia, is in the U. S. A.? I would refer the writer to the excellent treatise written by Mr. H. G. Wells, "The New American in New World." in which he discusses the American experiment and compares it with the Russian. Incidentally Mr. Wells refers therein to the question as to why President Roosevelt sought the help of some professors, whom Mr. Keenan in his self-complacency calls "asinine." Possibly what has annoyed Mr. Keenan is that President Roosevelt is laying his hands on the large dividends with a view to dividing them, in part at least, among the exploited proletariat and that he (President Roosevelt) maintains that the employers should recognize organised trade unions and treat them as equals.

Mr. Keenan is not only self-complacent, he is more. He says that "as far as making steel in India is concerned that Company (Tatas) has ended the depression in that trade and I think that Company should be proud of this fact. But let me ask Mr. Keenan what after all, "ending depression under a capitalist system" means. It means finding more markets and also sufficient capital to keep a concern going until more markets are found. The huge bounties given by the Indian people through the Government of India in the lean years helped the Company to keep going until more markets or orders could be found. That the company today is able to make more profits is due to two factors: firstly, the duties imposed on foreign specially continental steel, which make it possible for the people to patronise Tatas, and secondly the orders directly placed by the Government of India with the Tata Iron and Steel Company. It is therefore the people and the Government of India who are really responsible for ending the depression in the steel trade, if really it has ended. Mr. Keenan has not a word of thanks for either of them, though he congratulates the Company, and therefore himself, for the recent improvement.

I happen to know something about Tatas since September, 1928, and I should like to enquire if the 'ata Iron and Steel Company would have been alive oday but for the heavy state bounties which kept the Company going in the lean years and provided the fat salaries for the covenanted officers at a time when thousands of workmen were thrown into the street without employment, dole, or insurance benefit. I should, also, like to enquire if the Company would have been able to end the depression, as the General Manager claims it has done, without the aid of the heavy duties levied on imported steel and without the sympathy and support of the public and the Government of India.

The confusion of thought which the writer shows in some places is pathetic, and makes one wish that he would devote more attention to the study of economics than to history and sociology. Here is specimen of his reasoning :—"In 1929 and 1930, our monthly staff with the exception of a few whom you could count on the fingers of two hands, were 'Labourers of Progress.' The Steel Company rightly paid those " Labours of Progress' a reward for their extra effort which they had put forth.' A perusal of the above would lead one to think that the financial improvement of the Company was due to improvement in the work put forth by the employees in 1931 and after. The fact is that the financial improvement was due solely to the larger orders secured by Tatas, as explained in the previous paragraph. If one were to go round and examine one employee after another, one would not find any difference between his work in 1929-30 and his work in 1931-33. I clearly remember that in 1929 and 1930 the General Manager used to complain of lack of orders which forced him to reduce wages—to order sweeping retrenchment and to shut down certain departments of the Tata Iron and Steel Company in Jamshedpur.

The writer remarks in one place as follows : "At the present time, in my opinion, due to economic factors, the entire labour of the steel world, with the exception of the labour in the Tata Iron and Steel Company Ltd., have forgotten that they are 'Labour of Progress' and they are not 'Labour of Necessity.' There is no body in the United States of America today, in my opinion at least in the ranks of Labour, who are attempting to get out of the category of 'Labour of Necessity'............... There is no doubt that each and every one of us realises that we have had a depression from 1928 until 1933 in India. The same depression exists in other countries. The Tata Iron and Steel Company, in my estimation, is the only company in the steel trade which has advanced............"

The above statements would lead one to expect that Jamshedpur has become a paradise for steel-workers—an object lesson for steel companies in other parts of the world. But what are the facts ? Earlier in the article the writer states that American steel workers are the best paid in the world. Quoting a report of the American Iron and Steel Institute dated the 30th January 1935, the writer says :—

'American workers......earned an average of 64·7 cents an hour in November 1934......The Japanese wage-rate was 9·7 cents per hour and in India 8·6 cents per hour in 1933' (The figures for European countries are in the neighbourhood of 25 cents per hour). If the average for India is one eighth of that of the United States of America, and if the Tata Iron and Steel industry in India, I think the General Manager of Tatas should hang his head down in shame instead of indulging in meaningless bragging ?

That the writer was conscious of his Company's short comings when he first sat down to write is clear from the following remarks on p. 705—"We think we are doing good work; we brag about our hospitals; we boast about our wages paid, but do we stop to think and make a comparison between India and Europe or America? I certainly can state that we do not......We must compare the emoluments we pay our workmen with the wages that are paid in Europe."

I shall now come to the more serious charges that can be levelled against the Tata Iron and Steel Company. These charges are under the following heads :—

(1) Their attitude towards Indianization.

(2) Their inefficiency in the matter of checking wastage.

(3) Their attitude towards Labour.

I should preface my remarks under the above three heads with the statement that the Directors of Tatas always claim that theirs is a 'National' industry and on this ground they have taken the fullest advantage of the sympathy of the unsophisticated public. But I shall presently show that Tatas' concern in Jamshedpur is much less "national" than even the textile mills of the Indian industrial magnates for whom 'nationalism' or 'patriotism' is often a convenient excuse for robbing the public.

When the Steel Company was first started about 24 years ago, a large number of foreigners mostly Americans and Britians, were appointed to the higher, posts on a covenant. They were given princely salaries with princely bonus—and I know of cases in which the bonus was even higher than the salary and was independent of production or profit. If I mistake not, The General Manager draws Rs 10,000/- a month—equal to what the Governors of major provinces in India get. The public were given to understand that as soon as a sufficient number of Indians would be trained, they would take the place of the covenanted officers. This promise has not been redeemed. Between 1928 and 1931, we made repeated requests for Indianisation but without much success. The position today is that in many departments, Indians are doing the same work as covenanted foreigners but at half or one-third the total emoluments enjoyed by the latter. Moreover, during this period when I was in close contact with the General Manager, I complained that the contracts of several covenanted officers were being renewed for a further period, though there were competent Indians to take their place—but to no purpose. If an imperial investigation were made today into the number of foreigners empolyed at Jamshedpur and the emoluments they draw—the Tata Iron and Steel Company would stand condemned.

Tata Iron and Steel Company is undoubtedly a very big concern and there should be very close supervision in order to prevent wastage. But on this point, too, the situation is far from satisfactory. The Directors are all absentees and have very little knowledge of the inner working of the concern. They are all busy men with several irons in the fire and have not even the desire or leisure to know more of the working of the Jamshedpur machinery. The result is that the actual working of the vast machinery is left in the hands of foreigners who have no responsibility to anyone except the absentee Board which is entirely under their thumb. I first realized the helplessness of the Board when I had to discuss the terms of settlement on behalf of the strikers in September 1928. If on any point the General Manager said 'yes' the Board would consent. If, on the contrary, the General Manager said 'no'—it was also 'no' from the Board.

That a settlement did take place after all was due to the fact that the then General Manager, Mr. Alexander, felt disposed to welcome it. Not long after settlement, I once suggested to the chairman of the Board of Directors that he and the Board should have more contact with the workmen and for that purpose, it would be good for him to go round the works without being chaperoned by the Company's officials. The Chairman seemed agreeable to my proposal but my suggestion could not be given effect to, because the General Manager was opposed to it. Nevertheless, the Board began to realize their position, I think, because not long after that they sent one of the Directors to Jamshedpur—and later on to Calcutta—to act as a liaison officer between the Board and the Management. Since his appointment there has been some administrative tightening up in Jamshedpur. And in Calcutta and elsewhere most of the papers have been won overly the help of advertisments with the result that today one finds very little criticism of Tata Iron and Steel Company in the nationalist press. But the real trouble—*viz*, wastage and inefficiency continues.

The above-mentioned Director is an ex-I. C. S., and an able administrative—but he lacks technical knowledge without which it is impossible to force the hands of the Management. One of the results of this is that in the matter of Indianisation the progress so far made has been unsatisfactory. There are any number of covenanted officers whose places could easily be filled up by competent Indians at a much lower rate of pay. I have quoted above the average Indian wage-rate as being 8.6 cents per hour for the year 1933. But if we exclude the highly paid foreigners, there can be no doubt that the average would fall much lower.

The top-heavy administration represents, however, a small item in the wastage that has been going on in Jamshedpur. If one would go over the Stores Department and see the amount of capital lying uselessly idle there, and would also examine the annual orders that are sent out for machinery, spare parts, etc., one would have some idea of the wastage that goes on in Jamshedpur. About 7 or 8 years ago, the services of the Indian Chief Electrical Engineer—one of the most popular officers of the Company—were suddenly dispensed with and a foreigner was imported in his place. Then followed a period during which wastage took place in the Electrical Department owing to faulty and unscientific methods of handling. Fuel consumption is another important source of wastage. For a huge concern like Tata Iron and Steel Company, it is absolutely necessary to make use of the latest scientific devices for reducing fuel consumption and also to carry on continuous research in this matter. But Tata Iron and Steel Company are backward in this respect. It is because of the wastage combined with top-heavy administration that the Tata Iron and Steel Company cannot stand on its own legs and must always depend on the state for either bounties or protective duties. In a country where labour is so cheap, any well-organized steel concern should be able to maintain itself without being spoonfed by the state. There are independent concerns in Jamshedpur which buy raw materials like scrap-iron (or electrical power) from Tatas and make a profit out of their products, only because they avoid wastage and top-heavy administration.

The last—and to our purpose the most important—point to which I shall refer is the attitude of the Tata Iron and Steel Company towards labour. The first trade union was organised in Jamshedpur in 1920 and by that time so many grievances had accumulated that the years 1921-22 witnessed a serious labour-trouble there. About this time, the late Deshbandhu C. R. Das's sympathy was drawn towards the Jamshedpur workers and as long as he was alive, he gave them the fullest support. But this support was of no avail until the Swaraj Party emerged as the most powerful element in the Indian Legislative Assembly in the 1922 elections. Deshbandhu Das was joined by Mahatma Gandhi and Pandit Motilal Nehru and Tatas then found it necessary to come to terms with these nationalist leaders because the Assembly would soon consider the question of a state-bounty for Tata Iron and Steel Company. Tatas then agrred to recognise the trade union (called the Labour Association), to collect the union subscription on pay-day and generally to ameliorate the conditions of the workers. For sometime, the position of the worker saw a decided improvement but after the death of Deshbandhu things began to grow worse again.

Deshbandhu's place was taken by Mr. C. F. Andrews who kept the flag flying with the moral support of the Congress party in the Assembly—but the unsympathetic and callous behaviour of the Company's officials led to a serious strike in 1928. Since then the Company's attitude towards labour has been such as would not be worthy of a national industry but of the worst bureaucratic Government. My connection with Jamshedpur labour began in August 1928, when the strikers and their leader, Mr. Homi, put irresistble pressure on me to espouse their cause. When the Company found themselves in a very difficult situation as a result of my joining the strikers, they agreed to accept the demand of the workers but only on condition that the Company did not have to negotiate with Mr. Homi, against whom personally, they said, they had many grievances. Mr. Homi at first agreed to stand out if a settlement helpful to the workers could be arrived at thereby. But when the settlement was actually drawn up and ratified by the workers at a mass-meeting, he changed his mind and set up a new organisation to oppose the settlement.

Soon after the settlement, the Company refused to give effect to some of the important terms, as a result of which a large number of the workers went over to Mr. Homi's party. For a few months the Company refused to recognise Mr. Homi's organisation but one fine morning their tactics were changed. Their erstwhile enemy Mr. Homi was invited by the General Manager and his organisation was recognized. The old organization, Labour Association, was ignored and those who had drawn up the sellement and had stood loyally by it were left alone. After sometime the scene changed once again. Prosecution was launched against Mr. Homi under various charges and he found himself in prison; with the disappearance of Mr. Homi, his organisation became a shut-up shop.

The withdrawl of the Congress party from the Assembly in January 1930, led, to a definite stiffening of the Company's attitude towards the workers. After Mr. Homi's imprisonment, whenever a workers' meeting was held, a band of goondas armed with sticks and other weapons would appear on the scene and break up the meeting by force. In 1931, I was presiding at such a meeting which was broken up in this way and I can therefore, speak from personal experience. This situation continued for some years and even in 1934, things were so bad in Jamshedpur that during a visit to that town, Mahatma Gandhi was constrained to remark in a public meeting that he was 'grieved to learn that the issues between the employers and the employed were being settled at the point of the lathi.'

It can be alleged on behalf of the workers that since 1930, the Company has been following a ruthless policy towards them. Recognition was withdrawn from both the workers' organisations—the collection of subscriptions on pay-day was discontinued and employees connected with the trade-union movement were either victimized or transferred to places far away from Jamshedpur. In January, 1934, when the local Government officials in Jamshedpur prosecuted a gang of about 40 goondas, high officials of Tatas were found to take interest in the affair for settling the matter out of court.

The climax was reached in 1935, when the Company ..ed a notice on the Labour Association demanding arrears of rent for 4 years for the premises used by the Secrstary and by the office—though 4 years ago, a clear understanding had been arrived at between me and the Managing Director, Mr. Dalal, that the Company would waive their claim for rent. The Company thought that the Association would not be able to pay and could thereupon be ejected and since all the houses in Jamshedpur are virtually owned by the Company, the Association would cease to exist for want of a habitation. The Secretary of the Association went so far as to offer to pay rent in future and also to pay the arrears by instalments—but the Company refused to accept any compromise, proving thereby that what they really wanted was not rent, but the liquidation of the trade-union organisation in Jamshedpur.

The Company was going on merrily with their game when suddenly the Congress party decided once again to enter the Indian Legislative Assembly. The Company knew from experience that two or three M. L. As were in the habit of raising incovenient questions about their treatment of labour, and they felt it advisable to change their tactics once again. A new group called the Metal workers' Union, thereupon came into existence under the Company's patronage and the workmen in the factories were advised by the officials to join this group. This group is still in the good books of the company, and one of its principle activities is to give tea-parties to Government and Company officials and to wait on deputation on the General Manager. The object of this new policy on the part of the company is to show to critics in the Assembly and elsewhere that Tata Iron and Steel Company do not suppress all trade-union activity.

I have dealt at length on the attitude of the Company towards organised labour and shall now say a few words about their treatment of the individual workers. I have before me a printed copy of the Memorandum submitted by the Metel Workers Union (which in Jamshedpur is called a 'Company's Union') to the General Manager which contains the following remarks :—

"The service conditions of the majority of the workers employed in the Tata Iron and Steel Company are not sound as many of them are given notices of discharge, compulsory leave, etc., without sufficient consideration. For example, the workers of the old Rolling Mills who have long service with the Company and who have contributed towards bringing the Company to the present position it occupies among its sister industries, ...are laid off on compulsory leave.................

"The Company recently started a policy of employing men 'temporary' and it is interesting to note that this 'temporary' has no limited period. Cases of such men who have put in more than two years of service are not uncommon. By this, the Company is able to save a good deal by non-payment of bonuses and non-extension of privileges according to Works Service Rules, Provident Fund etc., which can be enjoyed only by permanent employees.

"Suspension of a worker from his duty extending to weeks is common. Inspite of several rulings of the management to afford a chance to the worker to defend a charge brought against him, the rules are either not followed in several cases, or prompt attention is not paid to the explanation submitted by the party................ similar remarks would apply to such other exemplary punishments such as reduction of salaries.............

"There is no regular system by which employees can get promotions and increments in their wages. For some time past it has become a policy of the Company to abolish as far as practicable higher rated posts, when vacant and lower rated men are made to undertake the the extra work without adequate compensation............

"While we appreciate the spirit of encouragement underlying the Bonus Schemes, we feel it has been restricted only to some workers. Then again a distinction has been made between Operating and Maintenance Department in respect of Departmental Bonuses..........

"The system of weekly-paid labour was introduced when the Company was in need of men to do some seasonal work. But for sometime past we find weekly labour is employed in permanent force in certain departments whose total number at Jamshedpur comes to about 5,000 (including both male an d female labour) thus forming about 20 per cent. of the total number of employees. Most of such employees have already put in service of over 5 years. Most of such weekly-paid labourers get rates varying from 5 annas to 8 annas par day. According to the following statistics showing the minimum of expenditure for a family of 5 members as shown in the Report of the Royal Commission on Labour, it will be clear that the cost of living at Jamshedpur is by far higher than that of the two places quoted—Sholapur and Ahmedabad........." (Then follows the statistics showing that the monthly expenses in Sholapur come up to Rs. 37-13-11 and in Ahmedabad to Rs. 39-5-8. But 5,000 Jamshedpur workers get a daily wage varying from 5 annas to 8 annas.

In view of the above statements made—not by hot headed agitators—but by a loyal " Company's Union," may I ask Mr. Keenan how many "Labourers of Progress' there are in Jamshedpur ? I am afraid that excluding the General Manager and the covenanted officers, very few Indian employees could be classified as 'labourers of progress.'

The only portion of the article for which I feel thankful is where the writer refers to the appalling condition of the workers in the Tata Mines. I do hope that with the sympathy of Mrs. Keenan behind him, the General Manager will be able to bring about an increase in the wages of the poor mine-workers.

The writer has evidently referred to the iron-ore mines only. But what about the coal mines ? A few years ago when I was working as the President of the Tata Collieries Labour Association I happened to look into the conditions in the Tata Coal mines. At that time some mines were being closed down, and thousands of workers were being thrown out of employment. We naturally wanted the mines to continue working, but two arguments were urged by the Company in opposition to our demand, firstly that the Company had long-term contracts with some collieries, and after taking this supply, the Company did not require an additional supply from their own mines ; and secondly, that the cost of production in the Company's mines was rather higher as compared with the prevailing market rate.

It is difficult for an outsider to understand why the company went in long term unprofitable contract and at the same time invested capital in buying collieries. Firstly, it was wrong to go in for long-term profitable contracts. Secondly, if they did go in for them they should not have bought any collieries. Thirdly, once they started working these collieries, they should not have shut them down—because it costs a lot of money to keep mines in proper order when they are not working. Fourthly, there is no reason why they should have had a top-heavy administration in the Collieries Department also—and thereby put up the cost of production. The result of all this inefficiency is that the people and the state have to pay for the sins of the company and the Indian workers have to be content with low wages.

If Tata's employees at Jamshedpur are to become 'Labourers of Progress' then the top-heavy administration has to be rectified, the covenanted officers have to be got rid of and wastage and inefficiency have to be eliminated. The paltry bonus thrown at a section of the ill-paid Indian employees for their last year's work does not appreciably alter the position of the workers in Jamshedpur, nor does it entitle the company to claim that they are better employers of labour than any other.

XXII

BENGAL OF MY DREAMS

Subhas's message......Forget quarrels,......Differences

S. S. "Ganga" March 2:—Mr. Subhas Chander Bose in the course of a press statement says :—

"For over a year, I have been exiled from my province. During this period owing to unhealthy conditions of confinement, my health completely broke down. As my condition worsened, I was shifted from one province to another. Even the prisons of Bengal so hospitable to thousands of my countrymen could shut their doors on me."

"All that I could do in the circumstances, was to silently pray in the seclusion of my cell that the Divine Mother may grant strength to our people to go through ordeal without suceumbing to weakness or demoralization and that a new Bengal may be born out of the ahes of our past sufferings.

Torn away from the realities of life through those long and dark hours, I sought refuge in contemplation. The vision of India conjured up and worshipped by our great seers from Bankim and Vivakananda to Durijendralal and Desh bandhu rose before my mind's eye to give me solace, strength and inspiration. I felt as I had never felt before that the vision of Bharatmata as she was destined to be, was the supreme reality which transcended the short-comings and imperfections of the present hour.

That vision was a treasure of which no earthly power could deprive me—it was a shrine on which I worshipped from day today.

One of the dreams that have inspired me and given a purpose to my life, is that of a great and undivided Bengal devoted to the service of India and humanity,—Bengal that is above all sects and groups and is alike of the Musalman, the Hindu, the Christian and the Buddhist. It is this Bengal—the Bengal of my dreams—the Bengal of the future still in embryo—that I worship and strive to serve in my daily iife.

To interpret this dream and to endeavour to translate it into reality is one of the passions of my life. It is a task to which we must give our very best if success is to be ours. No sacrifice is too dear—no suffering too great if we are to fulfil this mission. Friends, will you not rise to that noble height where the vision of great and undivided Bengal be the only reality before ? Remember the legacy bequeathed by our great men. Forget not that you are heirs of their dreams—the hopes of the country's future. If you are great yourselves in thought and deed—then alone will you be able to make your country great. Therefore I say with all the sincerity that I can command, forget your petty quarrels, sink your personal differences, strive to make

Bengal united and great so that in her greatness may be our highest happiness and glory, after all who dies if Bengal lives, who lives if Bengal dies?

(2)

Appeal to Bengal Congressmen

"I have been pained by the action of the members of the majority party resigning from the Executive, and abstaining from the general meeting of the B. P. C. C. It is difficult for me to judge from this distance, whether this action signifies want of confidence in me or merely an inability to work in a spirit of real comradeship with the minority party, in view of the bitterness caused by the past feuds. If it implies want of confidence in me, then it is I who should have resigned, and not they. I accepted the presidency because of the unanimous support of the B. P. C. C. members and I have no reason to retain it for one day, if that support is withdrawn. As a matter of fact, after I sailed for Europe, I worte to the Secretary B. P. C. C. offering to resign if there was objection in any quarters to having an absentee president, and I was informed in reply that the B. P. C. C. wanted me to continue in office.

"I sincerely regret that the members of the majority party have been unable to rise to the height of magnanimity I had expected of them. I have suffered as much as they have as a result of past feuds. But today there is not a trace of ill-feeling or bitterness left in my mind against my former political opponents.

On the contrary standing in the invisible presence of two of our departed leaders and witnessing the increasing demoralisation in the public life of Bengal, I feel that the least we can do is to bury the dead past and proceed to build a new future on the basis of mutual toleration, respect, and love. It has been asserted that the trouble is chiefly due to the fact that there is no leader available who can give a "Live" programme to the province. To this I can only reply that Bengal is not the only province which is suffering from want of such a leader. Indian politics today is drifting without a bold and definite lead. But that is no reason, why we should start quarrelling over un-important issues. Rather, when we are faced with a national crisis, and feel the want of an outstanding leader we should all the more forget our past feuds and our personal differences, as our rulers have repeatedly done, and unite for the sake of our common cause.

In the present circumstances, the proper procedure would be for the arbitrarfor to proceed with his mission. I earnestly hope that all sections of Congressmen, who previously accepted and put into effect the award of an outside arbitrator (who by the way never gave any lead to the province nor a "live" programme) will unhesitatingly accept, and work the award given by their own arbitrator. Let no one have an opportunity of saying in future that Bengal always looks forward to an outsider to settle her own disputes.

" In conclusion, I would like to give a friendly warning to the members of the Minority party, I expect that they will now be called upon to share the burden of office, and their responsibility will be great. If they can demonstrate by their attitude, and conduct that they are capable of that large-heartedness of which the majority party showed themselves to be lacking, they will be able to arbitrate once for all the existing party divisions in the province, and create for Bengal, a strong and united Congress party."

(8)

Bengal Affairs

" In order to close up the ranks of Congressmen in Bengal, and help the Provincial Congress Committee to put up a united front in all necessary matters the new Executive Council of the B. P. C. C. should be dissolved, and a new council should be constituted giving equal representation to the two Congress groups. No hesitation or sense of prestige should stand in the way of this step. In this connection, I implore all Congressmen in Bengal to whatever group they may belong, to stop once for all, the undesirable habit of appealing to the working committee or the A. & I. C. committee whenever they have any grievance against fellow Congressmen in the province. This deplorable habit is responsible for enabling other persons to interfere in Bengal affairs, and has helped to perpatuate or prolong our internal differences.

As soon as the B. P. C. C. Executive is reformed, steps should be taken to convene a session of the Bengal

Provincial conference at an early date with a view to considering the outstanding national problems and what steps should be taken towards their solution. Thereafter the Provincial Congress Committee should settle down to a programme of peaceful constructive work spread over a number of years.

"It will be generally admitted that the Calcutta corporation has been reponsible to a large extent for the recent squabbles within the Congress, and that the present administration of the Corporation is not such as to make us feel proud. Only if there is one strong united Congress party, can the administration of the Corporation be appreciably improved, and the interests of citizens be properly served. It is therefore, my considered opinion that if the present division among Bengal Congressmen continues the Congress should wash its hands of all responsibility at the next general election of the Calcutta Corporation to be held in March 1936. "In conclusion, I should like to say that the new Congress constitution represents a change for the worse, and is unworkable. The reduction of the strength of the Provincial and All India Congress Committee, and of the number of Congress delegates is undemocratic, and reactionary in character. The formation of autonomus boards has taken away practically all the work out of the hands of the Congress organisations. While the formation of the All-India Village Industries Association stands for a more progressive idea than that of village reorganisation through Khadi alone—and should therefore be warmly welcomeed—the compulsion in the matter of wearing Khadi etc., is a reactionary and altogether unnecessary provision. Further, the proposed change in the creed of the Congress,.which is under consideration, instead of making the people more truthful and non-violent, will open the way to greater dishonesty than exists at present. Moreover, such creeds, though they are suitable for Ashrams. are quite out of place in a political organisation, which strives to attain freedom for the masses of India."

(4)

Bengalis and Non-violence

"It is known to everybody that the Indian National Congrees stands for the attainment of Independence by peaceful means. Congress Organisations in the country have as a part of their duty been regularly carrying on the propaganda for inculcating the spirit of non-violence among the people. Taking the country as a whole, the results of this propaganda have been exceedingly satisfactory.

"Unfortunately, in Bengal, in the past there have been deviations from the path of non-violence on certain. occasions and these instances have given the Government a handle for using wide powers of constraint, and for depriving thousands of men and women of their liberty. It is a happy sign of the times that those who are most impressionable and in whose minds appeals for using violent methods could ordinarily be expected to awaken response have definitely turned away from the path of violence. This is the information not only of the public but of responsible police officials. But we cannot rest on oars. The congress has a special duty to perform in this connection since there is no other organisation in the country that can influence the massess and reach the hearts of impressionable youths. It is our bounden duty to do our utmost to prevent a possible recrudence of violent activities in future. The congress is futher in a position to undertake this task, because it fights for the Independence of the country, and always stands by the weak, the oppressed, and the exploited. We congressmen, do not condemn the desire for independence of the country as loyalists, reactionaries, and members of the anti-Terrorist societies in Bengal generally do, but we only ask our countrymen to seek the panacca for all our ills through peaceful and non-violent means. Consequently, our appeal to the masses and to the youth cannot go in vain. I therefore appeal to all congress organisations and to individual congressmen in Bengal to carry on a continuous and persistent campaign for inculcating the spirit of non-violent among the people. This is a special necessity in Bengal. This propaganda, therefore needs special emphasis and should be treated as a part of our permanent scheme of work in this province. If the rest of India, hopes to win freedom through non-violence, there is no reason why Bengal should think otherwise.

"Bengal's contribution to the non-violent non-co-operation movement has not been a mean one. And I have no doubt that our contribution will be even greater in future, if we inculcate the spirit of non-violence more strongly and deeply among the people."

(5)

Letter Regarding Bengal Politics

"The Manchester Guardian of March 1 has published the following letter of Sj. Subhas Chander Bose dated Geneva Feb. 26, 1934.

"Mr. J. C. French in your issue of Feb. 8, quotes Mr. Nalini Rajan Sarkar in support of his statement before the joint Parliamentary committee that the Calcutta corporation had 'gone bankrupt.' As I stated in my last letter, owing to the world crisis, the finances of the Calcutta corporation have suffered. Nevertheless, the year 1933-34 began with an opening balance of 66,24,000 as against a statutory requirement of Rs. 6,00,000. A reference to the report will show that the so-called deficit of which Mr. French makes so much refers to the estimated income and expenditure for the current year, leaving out of consideration, the huge opening balance, which should normally be credited on the income side. The opening balance for 1934-35 will be Rs. 53,66,000. Mr. Sarkar, in his report demanded the balancing of the recurring income and recurring expenditure every year, so that the huge opening balance could be made permanent. The estimated income of the Calcutta corporation for the current year being Rs. 2,56,83,000 the opening balance for the year represents more than 25% of the annual income. Let Mr.

French compare with this annual deficit of about 2,00,00,000 which the Bengal government has had for several years during the past decade.

With reference to the charge of teaching terrorism in the schools of the Calautta Corporation, I regret, I have not been able to find the speech which Mr. French says the Minister made on September 9, 1933 in the Bengal Council. It had been suggested that had stated that the corporation of Calcutta encouraged revolutionary ativities, and that it was an anti-government body. That was not a correct interpretation of his speech. There were good reasons to suppose, Mr. Townsend continued, that the corporation had gone out of its way to encourage disobedience to law. None had suggested that it encouraged terrorism directly.

(Calcutta Municipal Gazette September 9, 1933, page 6 of the supplement).

" I have not said anything in defence of (or against) the employment of terrorists by the Calcutta corporation for the simple reason that that charge has not been substantiated. The amending Act has not provided for the dismissal of any employee of the corporation and in my view, the government brought forward the bill because the Calcutta corporation refusal on principle to debar permanently from their services in future, all ex-political prisoners.

"The Amending Act has disqualified only those who may be convicted of an offence against the state or may be sentenced to imprisonment for a term of 3 months or more. Consequently, the 2,000 detenus' who are now in prison under the old regulation or under the recent ordinance are eligible for employment by the corporation. It may be further pointed out that while the Amending Act may disqualify certain people from Municipal, service, it does not disqualify them from election as counciller or Alderman or Mayor. According to the Amending Act, further Sir Surrender Nath Banerjee, who as Minister brought the present corporation into existance, would be disqualified for any service under the corporation, though he could become the Mayor of Calcutta. "What is more astounding to an Impartial outsider is the statement of the Minister in Bengal council to the effect that the provisions of the bill were never meant to apply to persons convicted of offences of a non-political character. The congress party cannot take the same view as Mr. French with regard to political offence, because they knew many countries in Europe, today are being ruled by ex-political prisoners —for instance Ireland, Itlay, Germany, Russia, and because they believe that inspite of all that may be happening today, no one can in the long run prevent the congress party from getting into power in India."

(6)

To The Bengal Governor

When I left Bengal in April last, I intended not to issue any statement on the situation there until I returned to active service. But as political situation there. is worsening daily and my absence has to be prolonged for reasons of health, I feel called upon to break my self-imposed silence. Four months experience has shown that Bengal has been saddled with a most reactionary ministry in the whole of India. Though none had expected anything big from Khawaja Haq ministry, I am sure nobody had bargained for profound disappointment that has now overtaken the province. After his lavish promises for solving province's *dal-bhat* problem his stentorian demand for release of detenus, and eleborate nation--building programme of his proja party people naturally expected that Mr. Fazal Haq Premier would put into practice at least a fraction of what he had professed. But little did they know that like a great American Sanant Mr. Haq believes that consistency is Hobgoblin of little minds. Throughout the world, the inaugeration of liberal regime is always heralded by an amensty for political prisoners. The Bengal, where over 2000 detenus are still in-carcerated without trial, where there are large number of convicted political prisoners many of whom have been transported to Andaman Islands and where machinery of repression is still working with full force, it is impossible to believe that there is anything in the nature of provincial autonomy.

Greatest Disappointment

Greatest disappointment has naturally been over the none-release of detenus. One can underetand the mentulity of the Governor, of the permanent officials, and of the C. I. D., who have been long accustomed to a policy, which Besmarch would have called a policy of blood and Torn". But one cannot understand the mentality of an ex-champion of the people who now seeks detention without trial, and sermonises University students to eschew politics. Truly has Mr. Fazal Haq out-heroded herod.

Our Task

"Our task in these circumstances is clear. We have to start a raging and tearing compaign all over the province to demand the release of all detenus to be followed by the release of all political prisoners including those in the Andamans, I welcome the decision to observe the 24th of July as *Detenu Day* all over Bengal. I hope that on that day meetings will held in every town and village to demand present ministry. And I want provincial congress committees to continue observing Detenus day every month on a suitable date as long as there is a single detenu left in custody. We have in this manner to create such a volume of public indignation as will bring about the fall of this ram shackle ministry.

Virtual Rulers

Before I close I would like to address a few words to His Excellency Sir John Anderson, and permanent officials, who are virtually ruling Bengal now. His Excellency in recent speech has very signifiiciently pointed out that there is no dis-agreement between him, and his ministers on questions affecting law and order. It has caused us no surprise that the present ministry has fallen in line, with repressive policy that is being pursued in Bengal for the last seven years. His Excellency has also referred to the part he played in bringing about release of political prisoners In Ireland, and has regretted that facts, and circumstances in Bengal are quite different from those in Ireland, but is it not true that in Ireland there was an open rebellion in which thousands of Britishers were killed, while in Bengal at the worst, there was a terrorist movement the victims of which did not number more than a few dozen. Sir John knows and all his permanent officials know that terrorist movement is a thing of the past. Apart from my own information I have it on the authority of more than one responsible police officials whom I met during my internment that youth of Bengal including inmates of prisons, and detention camps are thinking not in terms of terrorism, but of socialism and mass movement. What justification can there be for continued incorrection of those who according to Government were imprisoned for being connected with terrorist movement. Five years ago, before Sir John left the shores of England, he was criticised for his part in black and tan regime in Ireland, and he retorted by saying that he had also participated in handing over power to Irish people. His Excellency has had his regime in Bengal for full five years. He will now soon lay down his Governorship. Will not repeat what he did in Ireland, set free all political prisoners, and hand over power to real representatives of the people before he leaves the shores of India. As far as we congressmen are concerned, I can say with full sense of responsibility, and on behalf of congress organisations in Bengal that if government will do an act of belated justice we shall certainly respond by redoubling our efforts for inculcating spirit of none-violence among the people for in any case in her own interest and in the interest of India as a whole Bengal will have to fall in line with principle policy, and method of the Indian National Congress".

(7)

Bose Criticism of Bengal Ministry

It is difficult to read the utterence of some of the Bengal leaders, without being overcome by a feeling of annoyance and disgust. No sun dried bureaucracy of pre-reform days could have given a better exhibition of irresponsibility and vindictiveness. Sir Nazim-ud-din, the minister said the other day, the Andaman prisonars could forward their demands at the point of bayonets. I am sure that the prisoners in the Devil's island are supplied bayonets. Sir Nazim-ud-din objects to the hunger-strike. Why did he not take action during the four month he had been in office before the prisoners could even think of hunger-strike, I may say for Sir Nazim-ud-Din's edification that the pre-reform bureaucra'ic Government had times without number yielded to the demands of hunger-strikers ond this happened in my own case, when I was a prisoner in Burma. Outside India, stronger elements than this have often yeilded to the moral pressure of hunger-strike, and full-blown bureaucrat must remember the epic fast of Mahatma in 1932, which brought White Hall to a better frame of mind.

Congress Give Lead

The Governments are never tired of making concessions. Weak Governments are ultra-sensitive about their prestige and about doing justice or being generous. The Public are aware that in 1933 the Hunger-strike in the Andamans took toll of three lives. I have it on the authority of some prisoners recently released from the Andamans that their compatriots there are so devitalised that proportion of the hunger-strike will result in a large number of deaths. Moreover, as Raizada Hans Raj has recently pointed out that most of the prisoners are so strong-willed that they will rather die than give in, if a substantial concession is not made to their legitimate demands. In these circumstances only hope of averting a large-scale tragedy rests with the congress ministers. Therefore, along with the rest of the public, I earnestly appeal to them to immediately order the repatriation of the prisoners belonging to their provinces. If the other ministries do not voluntarily follow suit, they will be shamed into action before long. Only when repatriation has been ordered, can the Prisoners be requested to give up the hunger-strike.

All Bengal Andamans Prisoners Day

So far as Bengal is concerned, I called upon the Provincial congress Committee to carry on an unceasing agitation for the repatriation of the Andaman prisoners and as a step in that direction observe an all-Bengal Andamans Day within one week from today. In order to resist the demand for an Amnesty, Bengal Ministrial circles have got into the habit of asking for assurances for the non-recrudescence of political violence. No individual can give an assurance which will bind the whole of the society and a popular Government will never dream of asking for it. Now that, an official testimony, the minds of the younger generation have turned away from thoughts of violence, the Government can by its own beneficance harness their activity along peaceful channels. In a recent statement, I said that if the Government took courage and declared an amnesty, the congress organisation in Bengal would voluntarily spond by re-doubling their efforts to inculcate the spirit of non-violence among the people. Without waiting for the Government to act, I have already issued instructions to congress organisations and to individual congressmen to implement my offer and to regard propaganda for inculcating non-violence as a permanent item in our future plan of work. More than this no public organisation can do. I earnestly hope that the Bengal

Ministry will no longer stand on false prestige, but will endeavour to gather real prestige round itself by immediately ordering the release of the detenus and the repatriation of the prisoners in the Andamans as a prelude to the release of other classes of political prisoners.

'Join the Congress'

Now that the Indians have begun to realize the need for independence, it is for us to think out ways and means for the achievement of our goal. The condition of India during recent times has much deteriorated, and India that was well known for its riches, is now the home of poverty, and ignorance. The bankruptcy of British Statesmanship has been manifested during the past few years in the conquest of Abyssinnia and annexation of Austria, and parts of Czechoslovakia. This is the right time when India should give a fight to British Imperialism. Constant vigilance is the price that we have to pay for liberty. No doubt we shall have to make supreme sacrifices but this should not deter us from our path of independence. It is the duty of Indians to organise themselves under the banner of the congress, which is the only All India national organisation. I admit that there might be certain draw-backs in the Indian National Congress but it is for all of you to join your sole national organisation and purge it of all drawbacks, and short-comings. Our first step should be to become the disciplined soldiers of our motherland under the banner of the congress, and through it to carry the message of independence to those reactionaries, who are still acting as the agents of British Imperialism, and are thus proving the greatest hinderance in our way to independence.

Punjab and Bengal

Congress today controls the governments of 9 out of 11 provinces, and the differences between a congress Government, and non-congress Government can be easily seen where as the congress ministries are the agents of the congress for the service of their motherland, the non-congress ministries are the agents of the British Imperialism, who are doing everything in their power to prolong India's years of slavery. The Punjab, and Bengal are the two strongholds of British government in India, the former for its trade, and the latter for its strategic political position. Therefore a special responsibility falls upon the Punjabies in the country's next fight for independence. The Punjabies should make it clear to the British Government that Sir Sikander is not representing their views, when he goes about telling the Britishers that Punjab to a man would rally round the British banner in the event of European war—breaking out. India has no time to fight other people's battles, when it has itself to carry out her own war' against the universally condemned Federal scheme as outlined in the Govenment of India Act 1935.

The Constructive Programmes

The constructive programme should be carried out with a radical outlook, as Mr. De Valera has done in Ireland within a few years, while Mr. Cosgrave failed in

tional character, inrespective of community, caste, or creed, the muslims and also the scheduled castes in Hindu community would surely come round the congress in thousands and in lakhs. Freedom meant removal of all shackles of bondage, political economic, and social. The gospel of equal right for all had to be preached to the remotest corner, to the poor down trodden millions to create in them confidence and courage.

"No solution of the unemployment problems was possible, without attainment of true liberty in this country. The present ministry of Bengal, he said, which thrives on communalism had failed to satisfy the hungry millions, They had also unsuccessfully tried to olve the unemployment problem of the Muslims.

XXIII

POLITICAL VIEWS

Feb. 23rd. 1934.

Calcutta Feb. 20. In the course of a statement to the press, Mr. Subhas chander Bose writing from Geneva says :—

" In view of certain statements made in the British Press and reproduced thereafter in the Indian Press, which may have led to some misunderstanding of my Socio-political views, I desire to say that there has been no fundamental change in my position since I came to Europe. I ma ntain more strongly than ever that while it is imperiatively necessary that we should study all the modern movements abroad. It is equally necessary for us in India to chalk out the future lines of our progress in confirmity with our past history and our present and future requirements. The geographical and intellectual isolation which India has enjoyed for centuries should enable us to adopt a sympathetic but critical attitude towards other lands and nations.

" It is necessary for us in India to distinct clearly once for all between our internal and external policy. I am aware that the Indian National Congress has not yet developed its external policy but if we are sincere about what we talk, we shall have to do so with delay.

In the domain of our external policy, our own Socio-political view or predilections should not prejudice us against people or nations holding different views whose sympathy we may, nevertheless, be able to acquire. This is a universal cardinal principle in external. policy and it is because of this principle that to-day in Europe a Pact between Soviet Russia and Fascit Italy is not only a possibility but an accomplished fact. Therefore in our external policy we should heartily respond to any sympathy for India which we may find in any part of the world.

" In determining our internal policy it would be a fatal error to say that the choice for India lies between Communism and Fascism. No stand-point or theory in Socio-political affairs can be the last word in human wisdom. The Socio-political theories an institutions of modern nations are the product of their history, environment and needs. They are liable to change and development just as human life is. Moreover it should be remembered that some of the most interesting institutions of the present day are still experiments. Time must elapse before they could be declared to be successful and in the meantime we should not mortgage our intellect any where. My own view has always been that India's task is to work out a synthesis of all that is useful and good in the different movements that we see today. For this purpose we shall be to study with critical sympathy all the movements and experiments that are going in Europe and America. And we would be guilty of folly if we ignore any movement or experiment because of any preconceived bias or predilation.

" It shall enunciate what I consider to be the essential features of the future Indian movement. Firstly, India must be consolidated under a strong Central Government before we can hope fore internal reconstruction and security from external attack. Secondly, a strong and disciplined party must be organised before we can hope for a National Government and the entire nation must be brought under the influence and control of this party. Thirdly, this party must stand for the masses as distinct from the vested interests. It must stand for justice for all sections of the people and for freedom from Bondage of every kind—whether political, economic, or social. In order to ensure justice and freedom for all, the party must stand for the principle an equality and work for the destruction of all artificial barriers whether of religion, creed, caste. Sex or Wealth. Thus it should aim at a really Democratic state in which we shall all be equal and in which way there will be no problem...... of minorities. I would like to call this party the " SALYARE ADI SANGHA " of India.

" The immediate problem before this party will be to transform the Indian National Congress into an organ of the masses of India. Bitter experience has taught us that it is futile to expect the Congress to adopt a radical programme until we first alter the composition of that body. I disagree with the Communists when they alledge that the Congress is essentially a Bourgeois institution and is incapable of this transformation. To alter the present composition of the Congress, however, we shall have to bring into our fold the three radical groups in the country—Youths, the workers and the Peasents " and give them adequate representation. This will be possible only when the present constitution of the Congress which is based on the British model, is radically changed. One of our immediate tasks, therefore, is to organise branches of the party all over the the country and to agitate for a radical change of the present Congress constitution. Only when this done, will the Congress adopt, a radical programme and plan of action on the lines that we now contemplate.

(2)

Hunger Strike Problem

"The country should feel grateful to Mr. Mohan Lal Sexena for taking up the question of the Andaman Prisoners, grievances, with the supreme head of Government of India, and simultaneously be thankful to the latter for the courteousy shown in replying at length. It must however be regretted that behind the veneer of humanly courteousy the bureaucratic mentality still menifests itself. It is only in India that the question of voilence or non-violence is raised in classifying prisoners. Whereas in all other contries it is taken for granted that the political prisoners are those who are convicted for the most heinous crimes with the only grace that the motive underlying the crime is patriotic. Mr. Sexena has permanently and effectively pointed out in his second letter that in several countries, people occupying the highest positions were guilty of such crimes. I can only add that the heads of Government of Germany, Russia, Italy, Spain and Irish Free State, and some other countries were imprisoned for crimes much more serious than those for the vast majority of the civilian prisoners have been convicted. It may be remembered also that President Benes of Czechoslovakia, and President Kamal Ataturk of Turkey would certainly have been shot if they had been caught by any chance, when they were proclaimed rebels.

"Pilsudski, the former Polish Dictator used to commit political decoities regularly besides engaged in rebel activities. I say this to condone what the Andaman Prisoners may have done, but urge that in the changed circumstances of the country, their career should be regarded as a closed chapter.

Does the Viceroy maintain that Provincial autonomy has been granted to India. If he does, then are the provincial governments prepared to take charge of political prisoners, that is repatriate them, or to release them. If they are, then there is not the slighest excuse for the Government of India to stand in way of repatriation or release. If the Government of India still adhere to their former bureaucratic and punitive policy, they will be reducing provincial economy to a force. Today I am pleading with the government at the centre and in the provinces only because of the changed circumstances and the new constitution otherwise I would have taken it for granted that the Government would do their worst. I am exceedingly surprised and pained at the argument urged by His Excellency that yielding to the hunger-strikers would set a bad example. As I have once said already, a strong Government does not lose but actually gains in prestige by being magnanimous. Only a weak Government is afraid to be either fair or generous to its opponents. Moreover it is no use shutting once's eyes Ostrich-like to the fact that in the past the Government have yielded to the demands of the hunger-strikers time without number. as I can tell from my own experience.

This has happened whenever public opinion has stood behind the hunger-strikers. Once again Mr. Suxena has cogently remarked that if the Government relurt, it will be a case of yielding not to the hunger-strikers but to public opinion. Today the whole country stands solld, and united behind the prisoners and a Government which flouts public opinion of this character will forfeit its claim to be regarded as a civilized government.

Viceroy's Fallacies

I should now like to respectfully point out some of the fallacies in the Viceroy's letter. Regarding the health of the prisoners, the facts given by

Raizada Hansraj in his statement published not long ago. afford a crushing reply. The refrence to the death rate among the Andaman prisoners is quite irrelevant because they are young-men in the prime of life and generally posses a hardy costitution. The prisoners in Indian Jails on the other hand include aged and infirm men, drunkerds, cocain-magglers, debauchers, and the like. Consequently, it is but natural that the death rate among the Andaman politicals should be much lower than among the convicts in Indian Prisons. But the fact that the politicals are alive and have not swelled that death rate does not prove that they are healthy.

C' Class

Regarding general treatment I may inform his Excellency that C' class prisoners do not get the same rations as B' class do. The latter who are fewer in number get better food, and share it with the forma in order to avoid invidious distinction. The Anglo-Indian weeklies which are supplied to them are carefully censored and all political news are generally cut out before the papers are passed in. Regarding lighting of the cells I may say that in several Indian Jails which I have inhabited the wards for 'C' class prisoners have their lights on for the whole night and whenever we happened to be put in these wards we had to make special arrangements with the jail authorities to have the lights put out at night so that we might sleep. Consequently the permission to have lights burning till 10 P. M. does not appear to be much of a concession.

Games Facilities

Regarding the facilities for outdoor games, it has already been pointed out that there is a football ground of the size of a tennis court. I shall only add that as there is a rain for nine months in the year opportunities for outdoor games, must be few and far between.

And as regards a swimming pool, I remember that we also were provided with such a luxary in Mandalay Jail and the whole world was informed about it though it was nothing more than an enlarged reservoir for storing water such as can be found in most jails in India.

In conclusion I would earnestly request the Central and Provincial Governments to put aside all nations of prestige and to view the situation from the human point of view as a Government responsible to the people should.

The congress is doing its level best to meet the Government, half way on this question and so far as Bengal is concerned, I have already announced that all the congress organisations there have undertaken to carry on a persistent campaign for inculcating the spirit of non-violence among the people. In this tense, crisis every hour, nay every minute, is precious and the Government should therefore act at once. It is possible that in response to the appeals of the leaders the prisoners may suspend their hunger-strike without waiting for the Government of India to reconsider their decision. And if they do so, I would beseach the Central and Provincial Governments to respond with a gesture of generosity.

(3)

Congress Golden Jubillee

Mr. Subhas Bose has sent the following message in connection with the Congress Golden Jubilee celeberations.

" The Indian national Congress now completes 50 years of its existence. During this period it has grown from a small group into a country-wide organisation with ramifications from the Himalayas to Cape Comorin. It is the only organisation which stands for the Indian people as a whole. It is a unique embodiment of all our political hopes and aspirations and is the central organ of our struggle for political emancipation.

As we look to the past and the future, we are with pride and hope, pride because of the nation's past achievements and hope, because of the confidence in our ultimate victory. With feelings of pride and hope let us participate in the Jubilee celebrations of the congress.

On this auspicious occasion let us pay our respectful homage to our national Heroes who made congress what it is today. Let us pray for added strength to continue their unfinished task till the victory is achieved, and last but not the least let us devise men and measures to rectify our past errors and ensure our future success.

The Indian National congress is not a property. Its registered members only are the property of the Indian national congress. To the entire nation, I therefore appeal to make the Jubilee celeberations a success worthy of themselves and their country. Let us all renew on this memorable occasion our vow of self-immolation at the altar of India's freedom.

(4)

Inclusion of fresh Blood in Congress Cabinet

The resolution that is now before the House is one with which I am vitally concerned, and it would perhaps help the discussion if I could indicate my reaction to it. I feel greatly honoured that Pandit Jawaharlal should move a resolution requesting me to withdraw my resignation in a light-hearted manner, I should ponder deeply before coming to a decision. So I welcomed the adjournment of the debate last evening.

This resolution is in effect identical with the suggestion made informally by Mahatma Gandhi, and others during my conversations with some members of the previous working committee. Ordinarily, Mahatmaji's word is law to me, but where principles are involved, I sometimes feel unable to accept his advice or suggestion.

" When unfortunately Mahatma Gandhi has not found it possible to help us by maintaining the working committee, should we attempt to solve the problem without reference to the congress constitution. I leave it to you friends to answer the question.

Main Question

Judging from this point of view, the main question is what sort of a Cabinet is needed now and for the next few months. Last year at Haripura, I made three changes in the personnel of the previous cabinet. My own view definitely is that there should be an inclusion of fresh blood every year. To ensure continuity of policy the majority of the old members may remain. But in a vast country like India, the highest executive of the congress should not be made the close preserve of a group of individuals. A change, should, therefore, be made every year under normal circumstances.

Now what about an emergency like the present one? You know that even in countries like Great Britian, where there are well-defined political parties, a war crisis or a national emergency breaks down political barriers and at such a time there are on the same committee people, who normally regard themselves as deadly opponents and in Continental countries like France, composite Cabinets are the order of the day. Are we less patriotic than Britishers or Frenchmen that we cannot do what they can? I refuse to think that we are so inferior to them in quality. If we want a strong cabinet with a dynamic urge, it is necessary for us to put on it representatives of different shades of oppinion in the congress, giving the majority to those, who will ensure continuity of policy. If we do not allow this inclusion of fresh blood, the cabinet will lose in power and potency. If in countries like Great Britian, it is necessary to do away with party cabinets in times of war crisis, and substitute "national" cabinets. do we not feel the same necessity here. "It may be argued that such a composite cabinet will be too heterogeneous function properly ; but such Apprehension is unfounded Within the A. I. C. C., or within the congress there are different shades of opinion. But we do not have a large measure of agreement among ourselves ? Are we not all of us anti-Imperialists. who accept the present constitution, creed. and policy of the congress ? Are not all congressmen homogeneous in this sense vis-a-vas, the world outside ? I am afriad that we *sometime* give a too narrow meaning to the word Homogeneity. Let us face the fact that the congress has changed its composition to some extent since 1921. This change should be reflected in the composition of the working committee also, so that that committee may be truly representative of the general body of the congress. Further, we should not forget the latent implication of the voting at the last presidential election. Shall we not move with the times, see the writing on the wall, and adjust ourselves to it ? I do know exactly the mind of the A. I. C. C. today, but irrespectfully submit that if you desire that I should continue as President, you should be good enough to show some consideration for the views indicated above. If however, you think otherwise you should kindly release me from the responsibility of Presidentship.

Critical Times Ahead of us

Serious and critial times are ahead of us. We must pool all our resources and pull our whole. weight if we are to emerge triumphant out of external crisis that is fast overtaking us. To this arduous task I shall contribute my humble mite. What does it matter if I am not in the presidential chair. My services will be always at the disposal of the congress, and the country for what they are worth. I claim to have sufficient patriotism and sufficient sense of discipline to be able to work as an ordinary soldier in this great fight for Indians political economic emancition.

(5)

Appeal for Unity

"I am not inspired by the spirit of taking advantage of England's difficulties—nor have I any hatred for the individul Britisher. I hate Imperialism no doubt, but I know that the individual Britisher is as much a human being, as any one of us, and he is as much a prisoner of the wretched Imperialist system, as we who are slaves in our own country. It is a dictum with me that there can be no freedom and no real democracy in Great Britian until India becomes free, and the British cease to be an Imperialist nation for the sake of this common fight against British. Imperialism we should end all our petty differences, and close up our ranks. This task has become all the more imperative because today Europe is on the brink of a

Colossal war, and if this war does breakout—which God forbid,—it will soon grow into a world war surpassing all previous woe in its magnitude, as in its deadliness. If we do not have unity today, we shall miss this golden opportunity of winning Puran Swaraj at an early date..............

" I therefore appeal to you, friends to come forward and help in this task of establishing and strengthening our National Unity. Let us so conduct ourselves that even if we fail, the responsiblity for the failure will not be laid at our door. Standing on this platform I desire to declare once again that I am prepared, and I whole hartedly desire to work with all anti-Imperialist elements which have for their goal the political and economic emancipation of India. We have to build up the broadest anti-Imperialist Front under the banner of the congress. I desire also to assure all those who will work with me in future that I shall try me very best to give them a square deal.

(6)

National Flag.......Symbol of Aspiration

'It is the visible symbol of our aspirations. It is the sign of our determination to be free. The flag salutation has come to be the significant function of our gatherings. It signifies our determination and typifies the national struggle. Every free nation has its own flag and great homage is paid to it as it the visible symbol of the country's greatness and no sacrifice is thought too great for the protection of the flag. History is full of florious deeds of valliant soldiers who fought for the honour of their flag. History of our struggle also is replete with the deeds of devotion for our beloved tri-colour which we have come to love and respect. This flag of our freedom has a great inspiration in our struggles and spur to march on towards our goal. It is true that we have not yet reached our cherished goal but let me assure you that we have travelled a way towards it and we are now nearing it. Determined and eager as we are, shall soon attain it. Nothing can stop us in our onward march to freedom.

Proceeding. he referred to the Lahore Congress when Pt. Jawaharlal Nehru made the flag-hoisting a ceremonial function of the congress gathering. 'It has become almost customary to begin all our meeting and session with flag salutation ceremony. Our sacrifices have been immense to keep the honour of the flag unsullied but we have yet to make greater sacrifices and fight greater struggles before our flag of freedom can be hoisted on the pinnacle of our aspirations and raised aloft to the great heights of our cherished goal !

Continuing Mr. Bose referred to the resignation of Ministries in U. P. and Bihar. He said it is not a question that affects these two provinces only. It is a problem that faces the whole country and we shall find proper solution. You may be rest assured that the working committee will give the correct lead in this matter—a lead that will help us in our onward march to freedom, a lead that will give us more strength. It will then be your duty to follow that lead and carry out the mandate of the congress.'

Concluding he said, 'Let us renew our pledge today on this auspicious occasion to fight till we have reached our goal and never to rest till then. In this sacred spot in the presence of this mighty gathering under the visible symbol of this glorious tri-colour flying aloft let us once more vow to attain complete independence and not to tarry on the way, not to cease our fight even for a moment till Victory is ours. We shall strengthen our movement, redouble our efforts, unify our ranks so that we can give more effective battle and hasten towards our goal of Swaraj. As a reminder of this pledge, let us keep ever in mind this symbol of our freedom movement and raise our United voice to the honour of the flag. We have vowed to be free and we shall keep our vow. And let us say Victory to our flag 'Jhanda Uncha Rahe Hamara' and the whole concourse with one voice joined him.

"Message of Haripur is Sanghthan (Disciplined organisation). We have demonstrated that we are capable of iron discipline and solidarity in the face of the gravest crisis. When I accepted office, I had my apprehensions about the outcome of this congress session. Tnere were threats of internal strife and differences. But Haripura has given a different account I do not know whom to thank but I know one of those who deserve our best, is the British Government. They deserve it for creating crisis in the two provinces. It has made us realise that we are all congressmen and Indians and that our points of difference are few and far and points of agreement are many."

Speaking of the future and the need for united front, Mr. Bose said "The Federation should be combated with all the weapons in our armoury within the limits of non-violent, non-co-operation. Today it is constitutional crisis, tomorrow it may be agitation and the day after it may be compaign of civil disobedience but whatever it is, let us be determined to show united front. For our soul is one, our goal is one and our vision is one. We are one in spirit, one in ambition, one in our dreams and one in our efforts. Let us make the sacred resolve today on the banks of the river Tapti and under the canopy of the heavens to sink our differences and march shoulder to shoulder on the path to victory, the path to Swaraj (applause) India is going to be free and we all are going to play our part in making her free. I have no doubt in my mind, I see it with my own eyes. Let us believe in India's destiny and strive for India's freedom.'

(7)

Federations.

Mass civil disobedience is the very last item in our plan of action. What is wanted first of all is that we should stop the drift towards constitution-alism, which is apparent in some parts of the country, and among some sections of the people. If we can do that, we can prepare the country for a future fight. Once we create fighting mentality, our task will become easy. The fight against Federation must be waged from all sides. The congress ministers, the Provincial Assemblies. and the whole congress organisations must begin the fight, when the time comes, each in its own way. If the fight continues, and the British Government do not yield, we shall have to carry on the struggle to the stage of Satyagaraha and mass civil disobedience".

I would like to add that in my personal view, it may not be enough to wait till the British Government seeks to enforce the Fedral scheme in India. We should take the initiative, and present our demands to the British Government, as our alternative to the solution of India's problem. This will mean that even if the British Government tactfully refrains from forcing the Fedral scheme on us, we may still have to start our fight in the event of the national demand being rejected".

London Jan. 11.—India's destiny is bound up with that of the rest of humanity," declared Mr. Subhas Chander Bose at a reception in his honour at St. Pancras Town Hall, London.

Mr. Bose added that the congress had begun to realise that India's struggle for freedom, Domocracy, and socialism, was part of the world struggle extending from the East to the West through China, Spain, and Abyssinia. India could no longer regard herself isolated.

Speaking of the political situation in India, Mr. Bose said that since he had been to England, he had heard much speculation with regard to the ultimate outcome of the present experiment. Mr. Bose assured his listeners that the congress ministers would remain in office only so long as they would be serving some useful purpose in advancing the national cause. The congress executive would ensure that their ministers were always kept in proper place. If the Executive apprehended any danger they would immediately call on the ministers to lay down the office. Regarding Federation, the hope was often expressed that as the congress had drifted in to office in the Provinces, so would the congress drift into accepting Federation. Mr. Bose maintained that there was no analogy between provincial autonomy and Federation. They, at least, had some power in the provinces. He had yet to find a congressman who believed that there was anything worthwhile in the Federation.

they had lo face. Even if congress leaders failed, India herself would throw up new leaders.

The reception, which was attended by a large and representative body of Indians, was presided over by Mr. R. Palma Datt, who assured the audience that "congratulations of Imperialists in respect of working of reforms were premature as the fight remained against the existing constitution". Other speakers were Dr. Vakil, Mr. Sakir Mohamedi and Mr. J Parekh.

"India will never accept any ties with Great Britian which may be forced on her against her will. But she may contemplate friendly and cordial relations with the latter through treaty voluntarily signed by her".

He continued "I must say at the very outset that I do not know of any Indian leaders being prepared to negotiate with regard to the Federal side of the Government of India act. I had made it clear more than once that mere amendments of the Government of India Act will not meet the demands of the Indian people. What they stand for, is the substitution of the Act by a constitution framed by the Indian people through their representatives.

"The framing of such a costitution need not be such a difficult task as some may be disposed to think. To use the words of the Manchester Gaurdian, what is wanted on the British side is a radically new approach not merely to the problems of the Federation but to the problem of India as a whole. That redically new approach will consist, as suggested by the Guardian, in visualising the future in terms of self-governing India by which I mean free India. If the British Government can treat the Indian people as free nation, it should not take more than 24 hours to settle the outstanding differences between India and Great Britain. I do not say this in a light hearted manner. I am fully conscious of the many thorns in the path of Indo-British conciliation, but what I may urge is that once the Indian people acquire the status of a free nation, they or their representatives will not take long to make any adjustments which may be found necessary to establish a lasting peace and goodwill betweet the two countries.

"As I have made it clear before I am not opposed to the idea of federation as such; rather I believe that free India will have a constitution that will be federal in character. But that federation cannot grow out of the present federal scheme. It must be an entirely new constitution to replace the latter.

(8)

Congress War Resolution

Our own path is clear. We are now passing through the anti-imperialist phase of our movement. We have to rally all uncompromisingly anti-imperialist elements for the next move. The problem today is not merely to force the hands of the Congress Working Committee. That we must do. But even if we succeed therein, with Mahatma Gandhi at our helm, there will always be the danger of another Chauri Chaura, or another Harijan movement or another Gandhi-Irwin Pact. For that danger we must prepare in advance, so that we may be able to meet it successfully when the time comes.

Let the Congress committee have the leadership of the nation for all times, we have no objection to that. But a leader must lead. We still hope against hope that the Committee will soon make a move. But if they do not, then we must act. We are confident that the masses will follow no matter who gives the lead.

When Imperialism is ended, the Socialist phase of our movement will commence. Those who have power must undertake the task of post-struggle reconstruction.

XIV

FORWARD BLOC

After my release from internment in March 1937, the first meeting of the All-India Congress Committee, which I attended was at Haripura in February 1938. I noticed at Haripura that the Leftists instead of gaining in strength since the previous year, had lost ground. In my discussions with the Leftists of different shades of opinion, after the Haripura congress, I pointed out that this set back bad occurred probably because there was something wanting in the policy, and line of action hither to pursued by them.

Analysing the composition of the congress at that time, one could distinguish the following main parties or groups. There was firstly the official bloc led by S. Patel, Rajêndera Prasad, Abu-ul Kalam Azad, and others. On the Left there were three well-defined parties or groups differing in their numerical strength—the congress Socialists. the ultra-leftists and Royists. In between parties or groups, there were unorganised radical anti-imperialist elements who had a large numerical bloc, and on the other hand, for reasons of their own, did not like to join any of the existing Leftist parties or groups. It appeared to me that until and unless these radical anti-Imperialist elements were organised on a definite platform, the Leftist movement was not likely to gather further accession of strength to an appreciable degree.

It was suggested, therefore, that a new bloc should be organised within the congress on the basis of a minimum programme and that it should preferably be called the Left bloc. The existing Leftist parties would be free to join it, and unorganised radical anti-Imperialist elements would also be invited to come in. This idea appealed strongly, at first, to most of the leaders of the existing Leftists parties and it looked as if they would sponsor the proposed new move. A step forward was taken at the time of the All-India Congress Committee meeting at Delhi in September 1938, when a draft manifesto was amended by a congress socialist Leader. It was then sent out to a limited number of congressmen holding radical views for ascertaining their opinion.

Later on, opinion in the Socialist circles began to change and some prominent congress Socialist leaders openly declared themselves against the idea of forming a Left Bloc.' In view of their altered attitude the proposed move could not be launched by any existing Leftist group or groups.

The idea of a Left bloc persisted, however, and several prominent congressmen continued their efforts in this behalf. After the presidential election on January 29, 1939, an informal, gathering of radical and Leftist congressmen was held in the first week of February.

The question of a Left-bloc was discussed afresh but it was discouraged by some prominent socialist leaders. It was then felt that there was no hope of a Left-bloc being sponsored and started by any of the existing Leftist group or groups.

The enthusiastis persisted and another informal conference was held at Tripuri in 1939 to discuss the same question. Some of the prominent socialist leaders having dropped off, it was suggested that a name should be substituted for Left bloc. A draft programe was formulated and adopted provisionally. It was then decided to take the final decision when the next meeting of.the all-India congress Committee was held.

From the very beginning I was in favour of the new move, but I felt that I could best serve the public cause by keeping out of it, while maintaining a friendly attitude, as in the case of the congress Socialist party. The promoters of the Left bloc, including both socialists and non-socialists, agreed with me.

At the informal conference held in Calcutta a few days ago, it was unanimously decided that there should be no futher delay in forming a bloc within the congress for rallying all radical and anti-imperialist progressive elements on the basis of a minimum programme which would represent the greatest common measure of agreement among the radicals of all shades of opinion.

It was then alsodecided to adopt a new party namely "Forward Bloc." In place of the original proposal of a Left Bloc 'the Forward Bloc' will not be a party, as ordinarily understood. But a platform for rallying all those who accept the programme of the bloc. Besides, the unorganised radical elements in the congress members of the existing Leftist parties will be free to join the Forward Bloc. In fact, they will be warmly welcomed. It is hoped that with the progress of time, the Forward Bloc will draw into its fold all radical and socialist elements and parties in the congress.

For the last 12 Months or more, I have been pondering deeply over the problem of Left consolidation. After matured deliberation, I have come to the conclusion that the cause of the Left consolidation can be furthered only by a move like the present one If the socialist leaders decline to sponsor this venture, it is for others who believe in the idea to come forward and do so.

Stepping Stone.

The official bloc in the congress has as its organisational basis the Gandhi Seva Sangha. Now what is the organisational basis of the non-official elements in the congress? So far there is none. It is hoped that the Forward Bloc when it is fully developed, will serve as the organisational basis of all the non-official radical and Socialist elements. Only then will the Left in the congress come to its own.

It may be argued by our critics that formation of a "Forward Bloc" will cause a split in the congress and destory national unity. If the organisation of Gandhi Seva Sangha did not create split then why should the formation of the "Forward Bloc" do so. Left consolidation, will, in my view, be a stepping stone towards real national unity, which is unity of action and not unity of inaction. Without Left consolidation I do not see how we can arrive at real National Unity.

Since the birth of the congress Socialist Party in 1934, Socialist ideas have been widely propagated throughout the country. As a result of it, large masses of our people have been permeated with the ideas of anti-Imperialism democracy and Socialism. but organisational effort has not been kept pace with agitational endeavour. That is one of the reasons why though we had a majority at the Presidental election, we failed to have a majority in the All-India Congress Committee. It is no exaggeration to say that the Gandhi Seva Sangha is the only well organised and disciplined political party among Indian nationalists.

Mahatma Gandhi's Gift

The Forward bloc will function as an integral part of the congress. It will accept the present constitution of the congress, its creed, policy, and programme. It will cherish the highest respect and regard for Mahatma Gandhi's personality and have complete faith in his political doctrine of non-violent and non-co-operation, which is Mahatmaji's gift to this nation. But that will mean that the Forward Bloc will necessarily have confidence in the present High Command of the Congress. The question may also be asked as to why we are creating an internal crisis within the congress at the juncture by starting the Forward Bloc. Personally I am of the opinion that an internal crisis to day or tomorrow is inevitable in view of the uncompromising attitude of the present High Command and their failure to move with the times. We can avert the internal crisis today only by surrendering completely to them but what shall we gain by postponing the crisis through a surrender? Why put off the evil day? We are fast approaching an external crisis. It would be disastrous to have an internal crisis when the external crisis overtakes us. It will be much more desirable to face the internal crisis, now, go through it and emerge out of it before the external crisis seizes us.

Necessary and Inevitable.

It would be fatal mistake to think that a split even when it is temporary, is an unmixed evil. On the contrary, it may be urged that temporary split is sometimes necessary for the sake of political advancement. The Secession of moderates in 1918 and of the anti-non-co-opertionists in 1920 was not an unmixed evil. It was necessary and inevitable for the sake of India's political progress. To take an example from abroad, the emergence and growth of the Bolshevick Party would never have been possible but for the split in the Russian Social Democrat Party in 1903. I would, therefore, beg of my country-men not to think highly or lossely of the so called split that the Forward Bloc may responsible for. The revolt of the Swarajists at Gaya Congress in 1922 led to him mis-understand friction and even recrimination, between congressm and congressmen for sometime but ultimately congress adjusted itself to the new situation by acce ing the policy and programme of the Swarajis The same will happen in the present case. It shou not be forgotten that the Left within the Congr believes in national unity more than the Right. Tl is why the Left stands for a composit cabinet, wh the Right stands for a homogenous one. Consequent the Left within the congress will always work w the object of establishing real national unity. T present move in the matter of forming the "Forwa Bloc" at the juncture has been forced by unavoidal circumstances and by the uncompromising attitu of the High Command.

It remains for me to say what my attitu towards the Forward Bloc will be. Till recently, was of the opinion that I should keep out of t proposed Left Bloc and help in the task of Le consolidation from outside. The recent informal co ference in Calcutta decides otherwise. It unanimous resolved to request me to join the Forward Bloc a help in the task. Pondering over the matter I ha decided to join it. I shall now appeal to r countrymen to help us in the task that lies ahe of us and particularly in the work of building up the Forward Bloc.

Forward Bloc.

"There is a two-fold distinction, firstly the Forward Bloc desires to work the existing programme of the congress, not with a reformist, or moderate mentality, but with a revolutionary mentality. Secondly, it has an advanced programme of its own, which it will try, and persuade the congress to accept. This advanced programme will have as its objective the early attainment of India's Independence.

"The Forward Bloc" being platform for all anti-Imperialist radical, and progressive groups including the socialist parties, will naturally have a friendly attitude towards the existing Leftist parties or groups in the congress. It will not do anything consciously to weaken or undermine them. The Forward Bloc expects to have members from these parties or groups."

Reviewing the present position, Mr. Bose said, "There is no doubt that for some time past, we have been drifting towards constitutionalism. This tendency has been considerably accentuated since congressmen took ministrial office in several provinces.

He emphasised that "the truly gandhian spirit of non-violent non-co-operation is being smothered by the newly developed parliamentarian constitutionalist mentality—which is none other than a moderate mentality".

Declaring with the programme of his party, he said, "The two-fold task of the Forward Bloc' will consequently be firstly to instil life and revolutionary impulse into the existing programme of the congress and secondly, to prepare the country for the coming struggle through a countryside agitation, and through an advanced radical programme. This advanced programme the congress will be persuaded to accept in December, if only they do the necessary propaganda, and agitation from now. If it be found ultimately that our Parliamentary machinery is incapable of any further advance or any Forward move in the battle of freedom, we may have to discard it and we may have to fall back exclusively on a mass movement leading in to mass satyagraha.

Programme of Forward Bloc.

Mr. S. C. Bose at a meeting of journalists outlined in general, the future programme of the Forward Bloc.' He said,. it was difficult to describe in detail the exact form of the struggle, because that would depend largely on the extent of circumstances, and also the tactics of the British Government. However it may be safely predicted, he said, it will be some form of civil disobedience in which organised peasants workers, and states people will take a more prominent part than similar movements in the past.

Two aspects.

The programme of the forward Bloc will have two aspects. On the one hand, we will try to instil more life, and dynamism into the present parliamentary and extra-Parliamentary programme of the congress. This will be possible, only if we create a new revolutionary urge. Besides, we will place before the congress and the country an advanced radical programme which will have as its immediate objective the preparing of the country for the impending struggle. If we carry on propaganda activities, extensively during the next few months, it is possible, we may be able to persuade the next congress to adopt this programme, with a view to prepare the country for the struggle.

Congress volunteer corps.

Mr. Bose added: As illustrative of the point, I shall mention a few items of the programme. It will be necessary to raise and equip a congress volunteer corps on an All India basis, and develop closer, and intimate contact with other anti-imperialist organisations, such as Kisan Sabhas, Trade Union congress, Youth League, and Students Movements, if we want to mobilize all available revolutionary energy of the nation. In organising the Forward Bloc we intend taking practical steps towards the establishing of closer relationship between the congress, and the states peoples movement. We are of definite opinion that a sub-committee of the congress should formulate a comprehensive programme for helping and guiding the peoples movement in the six hundred and odd states. This plan should be given effect to simultaneously all over the country.

Hindu Muslim Question.

" Apart from this we should devote our attention to minority problems particularly Hindu-Muslim Question. Inspite of assurances given to minorities, and Muslims in particular through several successive resolutions of the congress, the fact remains that we have not succeeded in rallying them to a common platform. The announcement of the formation of the Forward Bloc' has evoked such favourable reactions from minority communties that we are led to hope that through the instrumentality of the Forward Bloc' and its radical programme, we may be able to establish real unity.

Mr. Bose added, " I think even if we do not succeed in one stroke, we have no doubt the left wing of the congress, and the other non-congress movements will draw nearer one another in the immediate future thereby pave the way for the ultimate establishment of national unity."

Revolutionary Mentality

There were other things in the programme, said Mr. Bose, which would be known later. Asked what he meant by revolutionary mentality, Mr. Bose said, there were two aspects, destructive, and creative, He said, communalism in Russia after capture of power created a new order as also was the case in Ireland. In this country, there were signs of losing the revolutionary impulse. It was a wrong idea that revolution meant the shedding of the blood. England had achieved several bloodless revolutions.

As to whether congressmen should come out of office to prevent further weakening of revolutionary mentality, Mr. Bose said, the question could be answered by the ministers and legislators. If they feel that by their parliamentary activities they could no longer enhance the strength, and the prestige of the congress, by implementing the congress parliamentry programme then they should think of giving up office; but when that is done the issues must be clarified, and we must know exactly why the policy and programme cannot be furthered through legislation. If it is found that the inherent short comings of the Government of India Act are responsible either partly or wholly for our failure to implement the congress policy and programme, then the resignation will afford a powerful impetus for our attack on the present constitution. Mr. Bose did not find fault with the principle of office acceptance, but his opinion was that Ministers, and legislators had shown a slackening of speed on implementing the congress programme, and were losing the initiative and being absorbed with day to day administration. As far the question, whether the country was prepared for a fight at the moment, he said, that on the basis of his personal experience the country was prepared, but what was wanting was willingness on the part of the leaders to fight."

Forward Bloc

Speech at Baidyabate.

To those who opposed to the formation of the Forward Bloc" and who offered adverse criticism, we would say that this bloc will progress, gain strength, and gather added momentum. We have started this new after great deliberation, and mature thinking. In fact we have staked our political reputation in this movement."

Thus declared Sj. Subhas Chander Bose addressing a largely attended public meeting, wherein, an address welcome was presented to him on behalf of the citizens of Baidyabate. The birth of the Forward Bloc, proceeded, Sj. Bose, is not a matter of accident. It is not so much on historical necessity as a product of our national evolution. In the history of a nation's struggle there are different stages. The history of the past fifty years of the congress will show that there have been different phases in our national evolution. Such a phase has been the outcome of an idealogy that the congress adopted. The policy of non-violence propounded by Mahatma Gandhi in 1920 was a new chapter in the history of the congress. Today we are opening up another new chapter The Forward Bloc will live and grow, because it has come as a course of historical necessity. We hope that in no distant future it will be able to demonstrate that it has served a great object, and has proved of immense good to the country, and the nation.

Two Fold Programme

Reputing the criticism levelled against the Forward Bloc', that it has no other programme, than that of the congress, namely, non-violence, Sj. Bose asserted 'the goal of Forwad Bloc' is complete independence while its method is non-violent, non-co-operation, its object is different, its programme is different. The Forward Bloc' does not believe in Independence, through compromises, and pacts. We will have a two fold programme. We will stand by the existing programme of the congress, which is beneficial to the country, and will instil a revolutionary urge to give effect to it. The election manifesto, and many resolutions of the congress have not yet been implemented, because congress ministers after acceptance of office have lost their revolutionary mentality. Why is that in Soviet after the capture of power, they were able to revolutionise the whole country. Why is it that Mr. De-Valera in Ireland has during the last six years, been able to shake off the shackles of bondage one after another? Why is it that Mr. Cosgrave fail in leading the country forward? Our ministers can implement the election manifesto and the Faizpore resolution if they have that revolutionary urge, and not settle down to reformism.

Advanced Programme of Bloc

"Besides giving effect to the existing programme of the congress with a new fervour, and revolutionary zeal, it will be the aim of the Forward Bloc to pursue side by side a more advanced programme for preparing the country for the coming struggle. The advanced programme of the Forward Bloc will be inter-alia to conduct fight for freedom simaltaneously in British India, and Indian states ; to harness all anti-Imperialist forces in the country to bring in the fold of the congress those graps, and communities, who have not joined the congress, to organise a volunteer corps on an All India basis and to raise the slogan, " Prepare for the coming struggle."

Continuing Shriyut Subhas Bose made an impassioned appeal for giving a fair, and earnest trial to the programme of the Forward Bloc and expressed the hope, that through it the congress would gain strength, and attain complete independence. He appealed to the poor unemployed, labouring and agricultural classes to join the congress for carrying the struggle for freedom forward.

Referring to the response, and support that the Forward Bloc' would create a split in the congress, and weaken the great national organisation the speaker said, that sometimes split became necessary and it was not every split that was undesirable. There was split in the congress, when Ghandiji enunciated his policy of non-violent, non-co-operation. But those splits have not weakened the congress. Rather it has strengtnened the national movement. We wanted unity and we tried our level best to avoid split. But the split has become inevitable, and we hope it will strengthen congress, and eventually bring unity in our ranks.

'We have Right to form this Bloc'

We want unity of action. and not unity of inaction. We have a right to form this bloc. There are parties within the congress, such as the congress Socialist party the communist party etc. If there is no objection to these parties' why there should be any objection to the formation of Forward Bloc, the main object of which is consolidation of all Leftist forces in the country.

Concluding Sj. Bose analysed the cause of the reverses of the Leftists at Tripuri, and at the A. I. C. C. & stated that while the official bloc of the present day congress was a highly organised body, the Leftist elements lacked orgarisation and unity. There was supreme need for organising the Leftist forces into a well-knit unit. The Forward Bloc was brought into being to serve this purpose.

'More about Forward Bloc.'

The Forward Bloc is not the creation of the person. Its formation is based on the desire of the people. It pains me to find eminent intellectuals in our country repeating (repeatedly) that a split must be avoided under all circumstances—that unity must be preserved at any cost. But it is time for us to distinguish between a split that paves the way for synthesis and unity. It is also necessary for us to distinguish between the unity of action, and the unity of inaction.

I am afriad that—if we succumb to the slogan of unity at any cost and fall victims to the idea of avoiding a split under all circumstances—we shall stultify ourselves and paralyse our activity. What is worse, we shall unconsciously play the role of a Rightest inspite of all our Leftism. That is actually happening with so many of us today.

For From Truth.

During the last few days, various criticisms have been hurled against us from different points of view, and different angles of vision. We are told in the first place, that we have started the Forward Bloc' because we have been driven by a sense of resentment. Nothing is farther from the truth. As a matter of fact, in my first public utterence on the subject in Calcutta, I made it abundently clear that there was no personal factor behind the birth of the Bloc. I also said that inspite of all that may happen. I would continue to cherish the highest respect for Mahatma Gandhi's personality.

For those who cannot surrender to the uncompromising attitude of the Rightest leaders and who cannot accept blindly all that they think or do—there are but two courses open, namely to resort to inaction or to organise the entire Left on the platform of the Forward Bloc, and then stand up to the challenge of the Right. When we shall do that, we shall demand unity on honourable terms, and we shall get it. That will be the real unity—the unity of action which will strengthen and not weaken us and will enhance our fighting capacity."

June-17-1939

Objective of the Forward Bloc

Answering questions Mr. Bose explained his attitude towards federation, which the princes had recently adopted. Mr. Bose said, " I have not studied it properly Moreover I am not interested in what the princes talk about Federation. For me Federation is dead, and there is no hope of reviving it, unless and until the congress goes back on its declared policy.

Question :—Do you think there is any possibility of the congress going back on its policy. What I mean is that the congress attitude towards Federation will ultimately determine the decision of the British Government. Even if the Princes accept it, the British Government will not commit the folly of attempting to impose it on India, unless the congress alters its present policy.'

Forward Bloc

Regarding the object of the formation of the Forward Bloc, Mr. Subhas Chander Bose said :—" The immediate objective of the Forward Bloc is to rally all the Leftist elements in the congress, on a common platform on the basis of a minimum programme that will be acceptable to all of them. When we succeed in bringing about what I may call Left consolidation, we shall pave the way for real unity within the congress. Today the congress is dominated exclusively by one section, though that section may command majority. Those who do not belong to this section or wing are completely ignored. Consequently, unity today is possible only through the surrender of the Left Wing. Unity is not an end in itself, but a means. Unity is desirable, only if it increases our strength, but when unity demands the surrender of the progressive or radical section in the movement it no longer conduces to our strength and cannot therefore be desirable. During the last three decades the congress has passed through several crisis. In 1918 Moderates broke away. In 1920 Nationalist leaders like Mr. Jinnah, Mr. Bepin Chander Pal, and Mr. B. Chakarvarty severed their connection with the congress because they could not subscribe to the new method of non-violent non-co-operation. If the cry of the unity had been raised on such occasions, and attempt had been made to keep the world-beseceders, the congress would have stultified itself, and political advancement would not have taken place.

Splits

In the history of every political movement, we find instances, when political progress is achieved through the so-called splits. This historically fact can be justified philosphically too. According to the Hegelian Dielecties progress is made through a conflict between thesis, and synthesis, out of this conflict between thesis and antithesis is evolved synthesis. The formation of the Forward Bloc naturally involves a conflict within the congress. Out of this conflict, we shall evolve real unity for I have no doubt in my mind that once the Left elements in the congress are consolidated, the Right wing will change its attiude, and agree to an honourable compromise. This unity will be quite different in character from the unity that can be achieved today through complete surrender of the Left. When we bring about real unity with in the congress, we shall be able to stand upto the British Government and resume our struggle for complete Independence."

Left.

Question : How do you explain the term Left ?

Mr. Bose :—I am using the word Left in a broad sense to include all those, who consider the policy and programme of the present official block to be not sufficiently progressive or radical.

Question : What do you mean by an honourable compromise ?"

Mr. Bose :—The attitude of the Right Wing today is one of indifferent towards and perhaps contempt for the views of those who do not belong to their section. Consequently they do not feel like accommodating the views of the Left wingers on more important questions. Further they are opposed to a cabinet in which representatives of other shades of opinion would be represented. Their insistance on a homogeneous cabinet appeal to my mind as a desire to completely dominate the congress and its machinery. Once they are in a compromising mood, they will naturally take cognizance of and try to accommodate the views of the Left Wingers. This will bring about an honourable compromise between the two wings.

I must add in this connection that the Left Wing does not desire to dominate the congress, through the exclusion of the Right. On the contrary it desires that both wings should join hands and fight British Imperialism inspite of any difference that may exist today between one wing and another. Their desire is manifest in the theorey of a composite cabinet for which the Left wing stands.

Question :—If the Rightists had agreed to the inclusion of your two or four nominees on the working committee, do n't you think that the split could have been averted ?"

Mr. Bose :—Without going into the details of our negotiations, I may say that if we had found a spirit of accommodation on the other side, we would have done our best to avoid a split. When I communicated to Mahatma Gandhi my design to resign from the Presidentship, I said that since the other section was not prepared to accommodate us on a single detail, it was clear that there was no room for co-operation between the two sections. Consequently, the only course left for me was to submit my resignation, and thereby enable the majority party to run the congress according to their ideas and desires.

Question :—Should we understand that you have come to the parting of ways. If so, is there any chance, still of Mahatma Gandhi comenting the split, while acting as a peace-maker between the two wings ?

Mr. Bose:—Yes, we have of course come to parting of ways, but people often part to meet again. It may be so in the present case as well. As to whether Mahatma Gandhi can function as a mediator between the Right and the Left Wing is a question, which he alone can answer. During my Presidentship Gandhiji had on more than one occasion acted as a mediator. Personally I did expect that after the Tripuri Congress, he would intervene as a peace-maker, and bring about an honourable compromise. That is why in our Post-Tripuri correspondence, I remarked again and again that people were expecting Gandhiji to rise above parties, and work for the maintenance of unity within the congress. I must add to my regret that my expectation has not been fulfilled, and he has appeared during the last few months as a spokesman—and an ardent spokeman of the Rightest section of the congress.

As to what role Mahatma Gandhi will play in future, I do not know. The country naturally expects him even at this late hour to rise above parties and work for national unity.

Programme of the Forward Bloc.

Discussing the programme of the Forward Bloc in reply to a question Mr. Subhas Chander Bose said:— "At the outset, I should say that the programme is to be shaped in the light of our primary aim, and object namely the resumption of the national struggle for complete independence. There are certain items in the present Parlimentary and extra-Parlimentary programme of the congress, which are of a beneficial character, and which are conducive to our national strength. These items include for instance the Karachi resolution on Fundemental Rights the Faizpur resolution on agrarian questions, the congress Election Manifesto etc. These items should be retained, but should be implemented with great energy and vigour. This will require a more dynamic, and revolutionary spirit, and a more dynamic outlook. We shall be able to implement the above congress programme more successfully than in the past.

Not Enough.

But the present programme in not enough. We shall require a supplementary programme, if we are to prepare the country for an early resumption of the national struggle. This supplementary programme will have to be propagated and popularised by the Forward Bloc, so that ultimately the congress may adopt it.

It would be a mistake to condemn the present congress programme out right or on the other hand to regard it as entirely adequate for our present and future purposes. The supplementary programme should consist naturally of such items as will foster national unity, and increase our national strength. For instance, we must organise a volunteer corps on an All-India basis. We must mobilise the entire revolutionary energy of the nation by establishing a closer relation between the congress and the other anti-Imperialist organisations, like the Kisan Sabha, Trade Union congress, youth league, students' Federation etc. Thirdly we must extend our fighting front beyond the frontiers of British India. The alliance between the British government, and the Indian Princes must be met by an alliance between the Indian National Congress, and the States People's movement. The Haripura congress resolution on this question no longer satisfies the need of the times. On the contrary we have now to put before us the object of ultimately incorporating the States' Peoples movement within the Indian national Congress, and we shall have to work from now on in order to bring about consummation. The other details of the programme will be settled within a week from the date when we meet in Bombay. I have no doubt that if we work energetically from now onwards, we shall soon be able to bring about real unity within the congress. The problem before India is no longer how to resist, federation. The problem really is as to what we shall do if federation is quietly shelved, on this point my mind is perfectly clear. The times are so opportune that we shall be committing political suicide, if we do not avail ourselves of the opportunity by taking the initiative,and facing the issue of Purana Swaraja. In the present international situation, with the congress in power in eight Provinces, and with a nation wide awakening among the masses of both the British India, and the Indian states, if the congress speaks with one voice, and puts forward the National demand the British Government will have no option, but to concede it in its entirety. It is for our countrymen to answer if they will rise to the occasion."

April 25, 1940.

Forward Bloc.

"We do not believe that by hunger-strikes resorted to by certain individuals or groups of individuals the country could march towards its goal of freedom. What is needed is mass struggle whereby through the sufferings, and sacrifices of the people, the real swaraj will be odtained.

"Swami Sahajananda was a well-wisher of the Forward Bloc, although he was not a member of the Forward Bloc. The success of anti-compromise conference at Ramgarh was due to Swamiji. 'The Forward Bloc, observed Mr. Bose, was daily gaining strength, and the Government both Central and Provincial had come to realise it.

"At first the Government had ignored the organisation but now, from the many arrests made all over the country, the government was beginning to feel that it was no mere safe to ignore such a body.

Impending Struggle.

Speaking about the impending struggle, Mr. Bose warned the audience against the manner in which Mr. Gandhi or the Congress High command would launch a struggle, nothing would be achieved. By an individual's realisation, a nation cannot achieve Sawaraj.

"On their part, proceeded Mr. Bose, the struggle had begun. What was at present needed was the awakening of the masses, and good leadership. As for the awakening of the masses, the speaker maintained that they were fully conscious of the struggle ahead, or else they would not respond so well to the call of the leaders of the Forward Bloc'. He said that they would readily join the congress when it started a fight. But he was astonished to find that the congress Satyagarha pledge was meant to hoodwink the masses and to curb those organisations who did not see eye to eye with the congress High Command; and had already started a struggle. He was bewildered how some of the Leftists could accept a pledge of this nature".

National Week Speech At Calcutta.

Mr. Bose in the course of his speech first explained the significance of the observance of the national week; and remarked that its object was to awaken Indian from their age long political slumber. He remarked that they had observed this week, year, after year for the last 19 years not in memory of anything to be proud of but in memory of something of which they to a man were really ashamed? He hoped that the observance of the National week would bring them a massage of hope, and courage, which they would carry to the remotest part of the country. Mr. Bose said, that Indians had revived the memory of their glorious past of which they had for so long been forgetful. This was a really hearting sign. When they felt in their heart of hearts, the pangs of slavery, their present state would come to an end, and they would step into a new era.

Criticising the present attitude of the High command of the congress, Mr. Bose remarked, that the congress, when it came into existence in the year 1885, did not aim at full independence. Forty four years later, at its Lahore Session, it adopted complete independence as its goal. It might be asked why so much time had been taken to attain that new outlook. It was because the nation had lost almost all its self respect, and dignity as a result of the influence of British Imperialism. Indians, however, had gradually gained their political consciousness and begun to think that they must achieve their full stature. There were still many people in this country, who would be satisfied with 'Dominion Status', but 'We would not accept less than full independence'.

cease to exist. Mr. Bose said that their struggle had commenced with the National week, and they would continue to fight till their object is achieved.

Forward Bloc Slogans.

"Forward Bloc" Zindabad is no longer the slogan of the intellecual few. It has already become a slogan of the masses—otherwise thousands would not have greeted me, wherever I went.

"I gratefully acknowledge at the outset that Punjab has always had a soft corner for me, and this attitude towards my humble-self has often cut across local party divisions. The way, the Punjab delegates voted solidly for me at the last presidential election, and for which I shall always remain thankful to them, came as a surprise to many. But it did not cause any surprise to me, though the extent of the support I recieved surpassed my expectations. Having toured a large portion of the Punjab last year, I was well aware of the mind of the average Punjabi. The time, when I left Calcutta for Lahore, I was eager to know how I would be received in the Punjab after my resignation of the congress Presidentship. What I actually saw the moment, I reached the Lahore Station was a pleasant surprise to me, and exceeded all my expectations. It would be no exaggeration to say that the reception that was accorded to me, was even grander and more enthusiastic than the one I received last year. No doubt, many must have taken part in it, who do not see eye to eye with me on account of political problems.

Nevertheless, the mass enthusiasm that I witnessed would never have been possible but for a feeling of sympathy, which the general public entertained for my political views and programme. I can easily account for this. The temperament of the average Punjabi is such, and the political history of the Punjab is of such a nature that the punjab public cannot but sympathise with a Forward policy and programme, and with all those who stand for it. I have, therefore, no doubt in my mind that the Punjab as a whole will enthusiastically support the Forward Bloc. The crowds that came to cheer me at the intermediate Stations on my way to Lahore, and during my journey to Peshawar and back were a true index of the mass mind. "Forward Bloc Zindabad" is no longer the slogan of the intellectual few. It has already become a slogan of the masses —otherwise thousands would not have greeted me wherever I went.

Fire In Dormant Souls:

It has given me the greatest pleasure to see the enthusiasm in the faces of the crowds, I have met everywhere during the last few days. All of them do not certainly understand the principle, policy, and programme of the Forward Bloc. To expect this of women and children and of illiterate peasants and workers would be expecting too much indeed. What then has lit a fire in their dormant souls. What has roused their drooping, spirits, and their waving enthusiasm? What made their eyes with hope and joy, when they came forward to meet me? Surely they must have been feeling instrinctively that the policy, I was advocating, was a forward policy—that the stand, I had taken was a right one and it would bring us nearer to our cherished goal of Swaraj. That is why I told a Press representative the other day at Lahore that I was acting in consonance with the popular will. In all humility, I want to say once again that the Bloc has come to stay, because it is born out of historical necessity, and is inevitable phenomena in the history of our political advancement. One should easily understand that what is born out of historical causes and is the product of national needs, cannot die. It is bound to line and to thrive. That is why the 'Forward-Bloc' will grow from strength to strength, inspite of all internal and external obstacles that may appear before us today, and tomorrow. I am grateful to the Punjab public for giving me a new inspiration on the eve of my departure for Bombay to attend the All-India conference of the Forward Bloc. I appeal them, to organise the 'Forward Bloc' in such manner that the best elements available may find their place in it. "If this is done, it is quite possible that the organisation of the 'Forward Bloc' may open up a new chapter in the political history of the Punjab.

To visit the Frontier Province at long last was the fulfilment of a long cherished dream of mine. How happy I was when the train crossed the Attock and steamed into the Frontier Province—I could only feel but can hardly describe now.

"I was no longer the Congress President. Many regarded me as a rebel. I wondered therefore, how the brave Pathans would receive me. Reports had reached me earlier that some influential congress leaders as well as congress committees were going to non-co-operate with me. That only served to what my curiosity. But I was not disappointed. At every way side station, the people came to meet me in large crowds. It was a new experience for me and thrilled me. The Khudai Khidmatgars were officially non-co-operating with me, but I was agreeably surprised to find that the Red Shirts of Nowshera Tehsil were taking a prominent part in the reception and demonstrations. There was not the slightest indication that some influential congress leaders were non-co-operating with me, and if I were to judge from the enthusiastic receptions, I would never have guessed it. It was apparent that public enthusiasm had been roused to such a pitch that it had swept aside the dictates of some leaders.

The scene at Peshawar station and the subsequent procession through the town beggard all description. On every side I was told that whatever the Leaders might say the masses would warmly respond to the appeal of

"Forward Bloc". In fact I was told that if there was any province, where the Forward Bloc would prove to be an unparalleled success, it was the land of the brave and freedom loving Pathans. Their policy was always a forward policy—the policy of all lovers of freedom and democracy. Continuing Mr. Bose said that he could not form an opinion for himself until he met the workers and representatives from all over the Province, and saw the enthusiasm at the public meeting inspite of the 'silent ban' imposed by leaders. Seeing all that he became sure that the 'Forward Bloc' would be strongly entrenched in the Frontier Province. Pir Akbar Ali Shah. Pleader, Nowshera, had been appointed Provincial Secretary of the committee of the Forward Bloc'. Sikhs, and Hindus though in minority had assured him of their support. Mr. Bose said, "I have therefore left the Frontier Province full of hope and confidence regard- the future of 'Forward Bloc.'

Wail of Thatta.

Discussing the situation at Thatta in Campbellpore Distt. Mr. Subhas Bose made an appeal to the people of the province to help the workers in distress in that District, which was a citadel of reactionary forces. The awakening in such a district and particularly in the Rawalpindi District was a necessity for the province to make a headway. People there required not only sympathy, but funds to defend the workers. Help from the whole province was necessary. Mr. Bose added, "I would like to draw the attention of the Punjab

Provincial Congress Committee in particular to the wail of Thatta ".

Programme Of The All-India Forward Bloc

" The Forward Bloc will endeavour to implement the following programme to the best of its ability, and will at the same time carry on propaganda in its favour with a view to having it adopted by the Indian National Congress.

1. While every Indian should have full freedom of religious worship, religion and mysticism should not dominate politics, or political affairs Political affairs should be guided by political, economic, and scientific considerations alone.

2. Strenuous efforts should be made to fight Provincialism and communalism. which have been accentuated since the inaugeration of Provincial autonomy.

3. Any corruption that may exist today among congressmen—whether it be the result of an attempt to capture the congress ministry or whether it has appeared in the wake of office acceptance should be rooted out.

4. The congress should be freed from the influence of the vested interests, and from the domination of the congress Ministries. Democracy should be restored within the congress, and should replace the present authoritorian tendency. Simultaneously the congress organisations throughout the country should be redicalised and activised.

5. The Parliamentary programme of the congress should be implemented more vigorously and with a radical revolutionary mentality. Congress ministries should function not under the aegis of the British Government, but of the congress. Congress Ministries as well as the congress organisations in the country should keep before themselves the objective of developing a parallel government in the country.

6. The struggle of the Peasants and the workers for their economic emanicipation should be actively supported.

7. There should be close co-ordination between the congress on the one side and anti-Imperialist organisations like the Kisan Sabhas, Trade Unions, Youth leagues, Students Federations etc. on the other side.

8. A volunteer corps should be organised on an ll-India basis.

9. The congress should actively help the States' le in their struggle for responsible government d civil liberty. Close co-ordination should be developed between the congress and the States' People organisations with a view to making the states peoples organisation's an integral part of the Indian National congress. There should be a comprehensive plan for helping and guiding the states' peoples' movement throughout the country.

10. Uncompromising hostility should be offered to the federal scheme, and it should be combated by all peaceful, and legitimate means; should the British

government endeavour to fois the federal scheme on the Indian people.

11. All attempts should be made to prevent India being dragged into an Imperialist war by Great Britian. and to prevent Indian resources in men and money from being utilised, and exploited in the interests of British Imperialism.

12. The boycott of British goods, and of foreign cloth should be intensified once again. This is necessary not only to help Swadeshi industries in India, and the workers engaged in those industries, but also to thwart the war preparations of British Imperialism.

13. Provisions should be made for the proper training of political workers.

14. Steps should be taken from now to prepare the country for an early resumption of the national struggle for complete Independence.

15. In the realism of national re-construction, the "Forward Bloc" will stand for the idea of planning for India, and in particular of industrial planning. When the time and opportunity arrive, the Bloc will stand for industrial development through the medium of the state. The Bloc will also advocate a progressive sound policy which will be determined after consultation with other anti-Imperialist.

(2)

Dispute Forward Bloc—Gandhi

"Why I Resigned"

Bose May 7. "The voting at the last presidential election was unexpected in many quarters. It indicated how the mind of the general public and of congressmen in particular was working at the time. In my election appeal, I had stressed two principles to uphold which I would strive my utmost democracy within the congress and fight against the Federal Scheme. There was no reflection on either Mahatma Gandhi or his principles, or policy in any of my statements.

Nevertheless, after the result was declared Mahatma Gandhi issued a statement declaring that the defeat of Dr. Patabhai was his own defeat. This came as an utter surprise to everybody. Those congressmen, who had faith in Mahatmaji personally, but not in the high command were effected by this statement and withdrew their support from me. There is no doubt that a large majority of congressmen, who disliked the high command, were effected by this statement and withdrew their support from me. ..re is no doubt that a large majority of congressmen who disliked the high command, did not want to give up Mahatma Gandhi.

(3)

Gandhi Bose Correspondence etc.

"When I met Mahatma Gandhi at Wardha on the 15th February, he suggested that I should form a new working committee, leaving out the old members. We had a long discussion on the question

Missing Page

when I was somewhat better, and I found that our correspondence was not leading to a settlement, I became eager for a personal discussion with him. I was then so frantic in my desire to meet him that I was prepared to defy the Doctors, and go to Delhi for a couple of days. Unfortunately Mahatmaji had to leave for Rajkot suddenly, and we could not meet.

Could not accept his Advice.

Then came our meeting in Calcutta on the 27th April. Mahatmaji's position was virtually the same as at Wardha on the 15th February, and as he had consistently adopted in his letter to me in March and April. He wanted me to appoint a new working committee, leaving out the members, who had resigned. For reasons, which I detailed in my letters to him and in my statements before the All-India Congress Committee on the 29th April, I could not accept his advice. Such a committee would not have commanded Mahatmaji's confidence and would have therefore, militated against the requirements of Pandit Pant's resolution. Moreover, it would have been contrary to my own views, because I believed in the principle of a composite cabinet as being in the best interests of the country. Consequently, I repeatedly requested Mahatmaji in my letters, and in my talks in Calcutta to undertake the responsibility vested in him, by the Tripuri congress, and announced the personel of the working committee. Any decision of his would have been binding on me. Wherein Calcutta he finally declined to undertake this task, we arrived at a dead-lock. There appeared no alternative, but to place the matter before the All-India Congress Committee. In this juncture, it was suggested that I should discuss the matter with Dr. Rajendera Parshed, and other members of the old working committee and endeavour to arrive at an agreement as to the personnel of the new committee. I told Gandhiji that I would gladly do so. If this attempt had succeeded, I would have placed our informal agreement before the A. I. C. C. for formal ratification. But unfortunately we could not arrive at settlement. The question now is—why did we fall and who is responsible for the failure ?

Staggered

The negotiations commenced first with Dr. Rajendera Parshed. He suggested that four new members should be taken on the new working committee and I suggested four names. My proposal assured a majority in the working committee to the members, who had resigned but provided at the same time for fresh blood. After some discussions at Sodepur, we moved to Maulana Azad's residence for further talk. There I was told that the name, I had suggested were not acceptable. Some other names were proposed instead and Pandit Jawarlal's name was suggested for the office of General Secretary. I warmly welcomed the idea and pressed Mahatmaji to accept it. Before we could arrive at an agreement, we were faced with an entirely new proposal viz., that the

I had gathered from earlier talks, that there was no serious objection to the principle of having four new members and that the disagreement was about the names only. I was naturally staggered, when this new suggestion was moved and was supported by Gandhiji. I was told that sometime later two vacancies would occur, and two new members could be taken in their places.

On further enquiry, I was told that that was the maximum number of new members that I could have. I wanted to know, if the reply was in the negative. Apparently, the prestige of the old members demanded that the old committee should be appointed *ad-hoc*.

No Desire to Remain Dummy.

"To clarify the position further, I enquired, if in the two vaccancies, which would occur later on, my nominees would be acceptable to them, and I suggested names in this connection. Both these names were turned down. Then I enquired, if I could have a second secretary of my choice, who would be stationed in Calcutta. I told them that formerly there used to be three secretaries and I proposed to have two this year, one to be stationed at Allahabad and the other in Calcutta. This was absolutely necessary in order to help me in my work. Once again my proposal was turned down. The position therefore was that if I desired to retain the presidentship of the congress, I would have to re-appoint the old working committee *en hoc*. Further I would be offered only two vacancies at a future date, but in filling them up I, would have no choice in the matter of selecting the personnel. All these restrictions were to be imposed on, inspite of the fact that under the constitution of the congress, the president was to appoint his cabinet or working committee. When we reached this stage in our negotiations, I told Mahatma Gandhi that it was quite clear that in no single detail was my proposal acceptable to the others.

In the total absence of the spirit of accommodation on the other side, I did not see, how we could work together in future. I had no desire to remain a dummy President, or to hold on to the office at any cost. I would therefore place my resignation in the hand of the All-India Congress Committee, and thereby enable them to take steps to elect a new President, and a new working committee. I have no doubt in my mind that in submitting my resignation, I adopted the right course.

Against my Conviction.

Mr. Satish Chandera Dass Gupta, Editor of "Tashtriya Bani" has recently stated in an article that if I had appointed a new working committee leaving out the old members they (the old members) would not have opposed or obstructed me. The same statement was made by some of the old members of the committee before the Tripuri Congress. But we all know, what transpired at Tripuri, inspite of such assurances. It was not possible for me to appoint a purely Leftist cabinet not only because that was against my conviction, but also because it would have been in contravention of the Pant resolution which I had previously declared that I would implement.

" I should add in this connection that I had explicitly asked Mahatmaji, if he would empower me to announce before the A. I. C. C. that a Left Cabinet of my choice, commanded his implicit confidence in case I accepted his advice regarding a homogenous Leftist cabinet, and gave effect to that advice. Mahatmaji could not empower me to do so. Consequently, the appointment of homogenous Leftist cabinet would have amounted to an open defiance of the Tripuri Congress resolution.

As I have already repeatedly declared my resignation was decided upon in an entirely helpful spirit, and in my view, will prove to be in the best interests of the country. Self-respect honour, and duty towards my country demanded that I should resign, after having made all possible attempt to reach an honourable compromise and to avert a crisis within the congress.

(4)

Political and Economic Emancipation.

Address at All-India Students' Conference.

" Standing today in the midst of a complex situation it is just possible that you may feel perplexed for a while. The vacillating zig-zag policy of the Congress High Command increases one's bewilderment. The menacing attitude of some communal organisations adds to one's difficulties. The want of unity among the Leftists themselves will-nigh unnerves an ordinary mortal. But though you stand, with your backs to the wall, do not for one moment lose courage or self-confidence. Remember, comrades, that the Left movement today is on its trial. Its future will depend on how you and I come out of this ordeal.

Constituent Assembly.

" On the subject of constituent Assembly, Mr. Bose said, that a real constituent Assembly was one which was convened by a national government after the transference of power had taken place. An Assembly convened by and meeting under the aegis of an Imperialist government and elected on the basis of separate electorates would surely end in disaster to the congress, and to the Indian people. He, therefore, asked the people to raise their voice in protest against it. The problem before them, Mr. Bose added, " was the launching of the national struggle, and in case the congress working committee held back, each and everyone of the Leftists should march ahead with such strength and resources as they happened to possess. The struggle would be a national struggle, no matter who gave the call. It would be a fatal mistake to confuse the nature of the call with the nature of the struggle.

"The congress was much stronger today than it was in 1921, or 1930, or 1932 and if they had fought thrice with less strenght and resources, they should not quail before the present crisis.'

" It might be argued, continued Mr. Bose, " that the Congress Working Committee had not been sitting idle. A long winded resolution had been passed, and the congress ministries in eight Provinces had been withdrawn. War councils had been set up in several provinces, and there was talk of a volunteer camp, and volunteer organisation. " But what is all this talk of a three-month holiday indulged in by an ex-Premier? Why whispers on all sides that the congress ministries will soon return to office? The man in the street is naturally confused, and does not know what to do. To make confusion, worse confounded war councils have ordered to spin. We are now expected to spin our way to Swaraj. But how can we be convinced of the efficacy of this magre mautra of Mahatma Gandhi, when we knew that a century ago, when the Indian people, knew nothing, but khadi and handspinning, they fell a victim to foreign domination. It is time to call a spade, and to tell our people clearly that the idea of winning Swaraj through spinning is moonshine ".

Congress And Rightists.

"The members and sympathisers of the Forward Bloc in different parts of the country are now engaged in taking stock of the present situation in the country and in the congress, and are also doing a bit of heart—searching. Reports have been reaching us from several provinces that our members are not getting a square deal at the hands of the Rightists. My own belief, that by honest, and hard work, we shall be able to convert the majority in the congress to our point of view, has been considerably shaken of late. We now find that the Rightists are determined to maintain their present ascendancy in the congress by hook or by crook; and they will not scruple to go to any length in order to suppress or persecute us. The congress is therefore, becoming the close preserve of the Rightists, even as the Indian Association of Calcutta has been the close preserve of the liberals for a long time. We could have voluntarily submitted to the domination of the congress by the Rightists if they had pursued the correct line, and had taken the country forward along the path of struggle. But not only are they doing so, they are in addition adopting wrong measures, and wrong tactics, which are confounding the public mind, and which will ultimately lead the country into disaster. I am referring among other things to the demand for a fake constituent Assembly, and to the introduction of the spinning clause in the Independence Pledge. The position inside the congress is accordingly as follows:— Unfair and unscrupulous tactics are being used against us, and we have very little hope of securing a majority in the congress, if the Rightists continue in this way. The Rightist leaders are adopting wrong and harmful measures and tactics and we are unable to influence them in the least. Under such circumstances, shall we serve the interest of the nation if we continue to allow the Rightists to exploit us by our presence inside the congress. This question has assumed added importance because today we have a much larger mass appeal than they have. I am now simply putting this question but the Leftists and the 'Forward Bloc' will soon have to furnish the answer".

All India Students' Federation Conference.

"I have noticed in the press, several reports, about the recent Delhi Session of the All India Students Federation Conference, which are not wholly correct. The comments on such reports are even more misleading. Since I presided over that conference, it would be well to say a few words about the deliberations and the resolutions of that conference.

"In the first place, what struck me at the outset was that the vast majority of the students were Leftists in their political persuasions. The followers of the Rightist Leaders were comparatively few in number.

"Apart from the resolutions on non-controversial students' problems there were a few resolutions on what one may call political topics. These related to war, constituent Assembly, Independence Day, and Revolutionary Leadership. I participated only in the debate on the war resolution, on no other resolution did I speak.

War Resolution.

"The original war Resolution contained a paragraph demanding the speedy termination of the present war. Though a large number of Leftist students pressed for this paragraph in accordance with their conception of Peace, I considered it to be based on a wrong notion of Peace, and I therefore advised its deletion. My point of view was ultimately adopted by the conference.

Constituent Assembly.

The resolution on the constituent Assembly, which was ultimately adopted was a condemnation of the recent resolution of the Congress Committee, and of the new and strange interpretation of the Constituent Assembly now being put forwarded by the Congress Working Committee. The preamble to the original resolution contained a clause to the effect that confusion prevailed in the mind of the public regarding the meaning of a constituent Assembly. The amendment to the preamble which was carried was supported by some Leftists of communist, and socialist persuasion as well as by the Rightists. The intention of the amendment was to avoid costing any reflection on the present Congress Working Committee and naturally took many people by surprise.

Independence Day.

The same desire to avoid criticising the congress working committee revealed itself, when the resolution on Independence Day was moved and discussed. There was a clause in the resolution to the effect that the conference deplored the stress laid on spinning in the Independence Pledge.

"This clause was deleted by the joint votes of members of communist, socialist, and Rightist persuasion. This sort of voting on the part of the members of Communist, and Socialist persuasion naturally gave rise to both surprise and adverse criticism. One could understand the Rightists, who openly stood for the spinning clause in the Independence pledge, but one could not understand the communists, and socialists, who did not believe in it.

The resolution on Revolutionary leadership contained a paragraph which criticised the present leadership of the congress, and its weak and vacillating policy. This paragraph was ommitted by the joint votes of communists, socialists and Rightists. The voting on the political resolutions did not indicate by any mean the strength of the Rightists among the students. They were comparatively few in number and would not consequently have been able to carry any resolution or amendment with their own votes. That is why they invariably joined hands with communists and socialists over the above amendment.

What gave me the most unpleasant surprise was the argument put forward by some students of Leftist persuasion to the effect that the platform of the students' Federation should be a non-party, and non-political one. As long as political resolution sponsored by them were carried by the house, no such argument was thought of but the argument was preferred when a political resolution was moved, which they did not approve of. Personally, I hold the view that students are not only entitled to participate in politics; but to discuss political resolutions at their conference, if they so desire

Leftists Elements Should Unite

We want country to be free immediately.

Mr. Subhas Bose's address at Radical Youth conference.

Lahore:— The exposition of the circumstances which actuated the formation of the Forward Bloc in the congress and its objective and programme was given by Mr. Subhas Chander Bose while speaking at the Radical Youth conference in the Town Hall Gardens last night.

Mr. Bose rose to speak amidst prolonged cheers and loud and continuous slogans of Subhas Chander Zindabad.

The audience numbering over thousands which had been waiting to hear Mr. Bose grew restive afterlong patience and refused to hear other speakers and made a persistent demand that Mr. Bose be requested to speak to them.

"*Loving Reception*".

After thanking the people for the great and loving

reception of the honour they had done him since his arrival at Lahore, Mr. Bose said that he had not expected he would be honoured thus even after having resigned the presidentship of the congress. But after what he had seen at Lahore, he had convinced that the Punjab was in agreement with his policy and programme and that he was acting in consonance with the popular will.

Mr. Bose added that it was no matter of surprise that the punjab which had been in the vanguard of all struggles and which had made unique and innumerable sacrifices in the cause of the country's freedom in the past, should now be supporting those who want to march forward.

"Drift Towards Constitutionalism".

Answering his own question whether India was :epared to achieve her immediate goal of independ- ıce, Mr. Bose admitted that under Gandhiji's adership, the country had made great progress wards its cherished goal. But they were still under reign yoke. He regretted that they were drifting ·wards constitutionalism after the acceptance of inistries in the Congress Majority provinces.

Many congress workers, he pointed out, have :gun to think that freedom would now be won by nstitutional means and there would be no necessity launch a struggle for achieving independence. ıat was the greatest harm done by the acceptance the offices.

"Need of Revolutionary Mentality".

The Leftists believe that it would be impossible to achieve independence without struggle and a struggle was impossible without the revolutionary mentality and an urge to be free. They wanted to revive that mentality.

Continuing Mr. Bose made it plain that their quarrel with the Rightists today was not with regard to the creed but over the method. "We want the country to be free immediately", said Mr. Bose and added, "The Rightists want to wait". They think the country is not at present prepared for the fight. But we hold that the country is prepared for it.

It is a matter of regret that while Gandhiji is clear in his view that the country is not prepared for the struggle today, there are lacks of people both in the congress and outside it who believe that the country has a power even today to face the British Government. If we accept Gandhiji view and advice, we shall have to wait for Swaraj. Gandhiji is now waiting for light' before he can lead the country of another struggle for which he definitely and clearly says the country is not prepared. But we, of the Left are not prepared to wait till Gandhiji gets the light. We believe the country is prepared to launch another struggle for the achievement of our goal of independence and so we are not prepared to wait.

"Formation of Forward Bloc".

Such being the circumstances, the formation of the Forward Bloc was necessary for rallying all the Left Elements which believe in the creation of revolutionary mentality and preparing the country for an immediate struggle for the achievement of our goal.

Unity at present would have meant nothing but submission of the views of the Left in its entirety to Gandhiji. That unity would have been of no use as it would not have given us any strength but on the other hand weakened us. We of the Left Wing are not prepared to surrender our views to Gandhiji because we know and we do not want the opportunity to passby.

"Would Bring About Real Unity".

Out of the present split would be born real unity that would prove beneficial to the congress and the country. That unity would arise from the consolidation of all the Left element.. Today the Rightists were united and would have their real strength, they acted together and had one leader to guide them in whom they had faith. They wielded a power and so they did not care for the views of those in the Left Wing. When all the element in the Left Wing are united, a revolution will be created in the congress when that comes to happen the Rightist will be forced to have an honourable compromise with the Left.

Mr. Bose referring to the question of a homogenous or a composite congress Cabinet attacked the present working committee saying that it did not enjoy confidence of all sections of the Congress because those sections were not represented on it. If all sections were represented on the Congress Cabinet, it would command greater confidence and have more power at its back than it had today.

"Leftists should unite".

Making an appeal to the Left elements to unite Mr. Bose said that if once they were organised, they would be able to bring about real unity and not false unity in action.

Citing the instance of the Swarajaya Party and the conflict which arose at Gaya, Mr. Bose said a real unity would be achieved out of present conflict as it happened there when the Congress adopted the programme of the Swaraj Party ultimately.

Concluding Mr. Bose dwelt upon the programme of the Forward Bloc and said that they wanted a new slogan to be raised in the country. That slogan was "Be prepared for the coming struggle".

" BE PREPARED FOR THE STRUGGLE ".

'Slogan of Forward Bloc'

Mr. Bose's presidential address.

Congress Ministries criticized.

Bombay 22: The aims and objects of the Forward Bloc and the necessity for its creation were explained in detail by Mr. Subhas Bose, Presiding over the First All-India Forward Bloc Radical Conference this evening.

Mr. Bose explained that a Left wing was necessary in any organisation to prevent stagnation and to hasten progress. Further it had a philosphical justification. The law of human progress had ordained that it was only through conflicts that there would be emerge progress. Such splits of a temporary nature that might arise as a result of the formation of Left wings were in fact land-marks in our History.

'Uncompromising'

After referring to the rise of the Left wing since 1922 Mr. Bose said that the attitude of the majority party in the congress at present had become uncompromising and there was complete absence of efforts on their part to accommodate the other side. He referred to the composition of the working committee and said that the Committee should be a homogenous one even as various groups with different ideoligies were permitted to be in the congress.

The Forward Bloc, Mr. Bose maintained, was for real unity within the congress, " Unity that leads to action and strength and not unity at any cost, which leads to inaction and stagnation. The present majority party did not want a fighting programme.

Proceeding Mr. Bose referred to Mahatma Gandhi's 'new technique " and remarked, " According to the new technique we should consider all our activities and sacrifices since 1920 as waste. Why did the congress launch civil disobedience again and again? I see no difference between this new technique and the policy of our moderators" (Cheers).

No money from Rome, or Berlin

Reverting to the formation of the Forward Bloc, Mr. Bose said that its opponents were spreading all sorts of malicious remours and false stories about the Bloc. It was even suggested that the Forward Bloc was based on voilence and that it was financed from abroad. Mr. Bose emphatically denied the rumours and said "There is no money coming from Rome, Berlin, Tokyo, or Moscow. This is but mischievious propaganda by our opponents to belittle our movement to ridicule us and to condemn us by any means fair or foul (Cries of shame).

"Congress Ministries".

Referring to the present policy of the Congress, Mr. Bose observed that the congress should make more serious efforts to implement this programme. In the Parliamentary sphere he suggested there should be a more vigorous check and expressed the opinion that with real revolutionary mentality more good could be done to the masses. It appeared to him that the ministries were not doing all they could, simply because they had not the "revolutionary urge" in them. Apart from the present programme he stressed the need "for a supplementary programme which would hasten our march to swaraj".

"Religion & Politics".

Mr. Bose also wanted that religion should be completely eschewed from politics. "Religion" he said, "should be the concern of individuals who should be given complete freedom to practice what ever religion they liked but politics should not be guided by RELIGOUS or mystical considerations. It should guided only by economic, political and scientific considerations.

Speaking on the subject of Indian States, *vis-a-vis* the congress, Mr. Bose said, that in practice there had been some welcome departure from the principle laid down in the Haripura resolution. The policy of non-intervention should now be given a deliberate go-by and it was high time that a new decision was taken: The policy of the British Government was one of "United front" to save the princes, and even so the policy of the congress should be one of the United front to stand by the states subjects.

Enlarging on the question of the congress Ministries. Mr. Bose desired that an enquiry committee should conduct investigation in camera on the present state of affairs, what the Ministers had done so far and what they could do. For his part he was of the opinion that much more good than had at present generally achieved, could have been done if only the Ministries had the revolutionary mentality. He cited as example the case of Ireland whether the Cosgrave Government which was in power for the last 10 years failed to rise to the occasion whereas De. Valera Government with the same constitution was able to achieve more. If the congress machinery in office was properly utilised, he had no doubt greater good could be done to the masses.

The pace at which the congress ministries functioned really disheartened him. He critisized the congress ministries participation in the "Home Ministers Conference" where decisions not conducive to the freedom movement, were taken.

A Great Role.

Regarding the future of the Forward Bloc, Mr. Bose had no doubts. It was destined to play a great role. The Forward Bloc, he asserted had come to stay. "Its slogans will be "Be prepared for the struggle". We shall contest all elections to the different cogress Committees. There are various important questions that remain to be settled. Our fundamental aim is that all Left Unite. We should take course of each other.

Sir Cowasij Jehangir Hall, where the conference was held, was packed to over-flowing. A large number of delegates were present.

Mr. Bose's Letter to Government.

Bombay, March 10 (by mail):— Mr. Subhas Chánder Bose has released the following letter which he wrote to the Home Secretary, Government of India for publication:—

"Whenever my sister-in-law Mrs. Biwahati Bose, interviewed you at Delhi on or about the 18th February 1937, you practically assured her that even if I was not released on my arrival at Bombay, I would be allowed to stay where I chose and that interviews with relatives at least would be permitted without police interference. When sometime during my stay in Jubbulpore Jail, Mrs. Bose wired to you from Jubbulpore enquiring about the conditions of my stay in Bombay prior to embarkation, you replied telegraphically to the effect that instructions had been issued to the Bombay Government in the same sense as to the Central Provinces Government.

Since I had been permitted interviews with my people in Jubbulpore Jail without any police restrictions, whatsoever your message was naturally construed to mean that at least, five interviews with relatives would be allowed in Bombay. Thereupon some of my relatives [illegible]e up to Bombay to see me off in addition to several friends from different parts of the country. These friends including gentlemen like Dr. Deshmukh, Ex-mayor of Bombay were not even allowed to approach me or see me. My relatives were not allowed to approach me till noon though I had reached the boat at 9-45 A. M. and they were allowed only after I had shouted at the policemen more than once for their unwarranted harrasment. And when at last my relatives were permitted to come they were surrounded by the Police.

There is one other matter to which I shall refer before I close. The original order of the Government of

India embodying the government offer which you sent to my brother Mr. Satish Chander Bose desires to go to Europe and the necessary arrangements are made by his relatives for the passage from Bombay, he will be allowed to embark and will be granted a passport for France and Switzerland. The order under regulation III will then be withdrawn. This could only mean that at the time of embarkation or sailing an order would be served on my withdrawing the previous order of detention under Regulation III of 1818. This procedure was followed in 1927 when I was brought back from Burma as a state prisoner and subsequently released in Calcutta. I have however received no release order this time though I repeatedly asked the Bombay Police for it. Does this mean that the order of detention still holds in respect of and in opposition to the original order of the Government of India on the basis of which arrangements were made for my voyage to and treatment in Europe.

If the failure to serve the release order on me at Bombay be deliberate as I trust it is not then the conduct of the Government deserves to be condemned.

However I am writing this to request you to send a copy of the release order to my relatives in Calcutta or Patna and to me through the British Council at Vienna.

Mr. Subhas Bose Accuses Police of Harrassment.

"The 'Reconciliation' a monthly organ of the Christian Pacifist congregational crusade at London, publishes the following article from Mr. Subhas Chander Bose. On the Bengal situation with an editorial note saying that it is of the highest importance that those who desire peace in India, shall hear what such a representative of Bengal as Mr. Subhas Bose has to say about the Government of India's policy in relation to atrrorism :—

"In their evidence before the joint committee on Indian constitutional Reforms in November last, Mr. J. C. French late of the Indian civil service, and Mr. S. H. Mills late of the Indian Police Service,. endeavoured to prove that the only way to tackle the situation in Bengal was to continue the present official policy in that province, and to deny a decent measure of self-government to her in future. To support this contention, it was asserted among other things that after the great war, and again in 1927-28 when amensty was granted to political prisoners, in Bengal, it was followed by a further recrudescence of revolutionary activity.

Challenge to Government.

As against this assertion, I desire to state, with a sense of responsibility:—

(a) that a generous measure of amensty was never granted.

(b) that no attempt has ever been made to explore the fundemental causes of the revolutionary movements.

(c) that no serious attempts have ever been made to come to an understanding with the Leaders or the members of the Revolutionary Party.

Regarding (a) I can state from personal knowledge that whenever the Government proposed an amensty; the political branch of the Police always opposed it. This happened also in my own case 1927, when the political Branch of Bengal Police opposed the proposal of my release till the very last day and but for the intervention of the Bengal Governor (Sir Stanley Jackson) I would never have got out of the clutches of the Bengal ordinance.

Police Harrassment.

It is a matter of common knowledge among political prisoners in Bengal that even when they are relesed, both before and after their release they have to undergo a great deal of harrassment. Before their release they are periodically interviewed by the Police officers who try to find out if the mentality of the political prisoners has undergone such change as to warrant their release from detention. And after their release they are so closely followed by the watch-dogs of the Intelligence Department as to make their life of comparative freedom almost as torture. The net result of all this experience is that the soothing effect of an amnesty is not felt by any political prisoner.

Regarding (b) It would interest people to know that a proposal was made by responsible medical men for a scientific enquiry into the causes of revolutionary movement. And the author of the proposal was no less a man than Lt. Col. Barkley Hill, a distinguished member of the Indian Medical Service, and a specialist in mental disease. The rejection of the proposal of Lt. Col. Barkley Hill would not have mattered, if the government had conducted a systematic and scientific enquiry into the problem, instead of being content with diagnosis and remedy suggested by the police.

No Attempt to Understand.

Regarding (c) it is a fact that though attempts have been made from time to time to an understanding with the leaders of the political movement in India. no such attempt has ever been made to come to an understanding with the Revolutionary Party. This would not have been necessary if the leaders of the political movement had taken it upon themselves to speak on behalf of the Revolutionary Party as well. But since they have not done that the Government should have realized the necessity of coming to an understanding with the revolutionary party separately. But I must admit in this connection that Sir Stanley Jackson when he was Governor of Bengal, did attempt an understanding through the mediation of the late Mr. J. M. Sen Gupta. But these negotiations should be carried on directly between the government and themselves and not through police officers; but to this the government would not agree and so the negotiations came to a premature end.

How Negotiations Suffer.

The initiative in the matter of an understanding with the Revolutionary party has to be taken by the government for the simple reason that it is extremely risky for a public man in India to do so. I know of at least two cases in which public men who went out of their way to attempt the task themselves came under the suspicion of the police, and were subsequently clapped into prison.

There are many people in Bengal who sincerely feel that the chief stumbling block in the way of an understanding is the Political Branch of the police. They desire to carry on in their own way and they are therefore never tired of saying that the revolutionaries are "*irreconcilable*". But is not the Indian National Congress which stands for 'Complete Independence' equally irreconcilable? If, nevertheless, understanding with the political leaders could be attempted, I see no reason why it could not be attempted in the case of the revolutionary party as well.

XXV

INDO-BRITISH TRADE RELATIONS

One of the most remarkable facts in connection with the growth of the foreign trade of India is that the percentage share of the United Kingdom has almost continuously been on the decline for the last fifty years or more, though the actual amount of Indo-British trade has shown very great development. This means that the progress of Indo-British trade has not kept pace with that of our total trade; in other words, trade with non-British countries has grown at a faster rate than that with Great Britian. Till the middle of the 19th century, the growth of our foreign commerce was practically synonymous with the development of our trade with the united Kingdom.

It lies beyond the scope of the present article to trace the beginnings of our commerce with Great Britain which led to her occupying the almost monopolistic position in India's foreign trade. The subsequent developments have been in the direction of a gradual divergence of both our imports and exports from the United Kingdom to other countries, especially the Continental countries of Europe, and to U. S. A. and Japan with the result as noted above. The following figures are illustrative of the fact :—

Percentage share of U. K. in the Total Trade of India.

1875-76	...	...	62·2
1880-81	...	...	58·7
1890-91	...	...	50·9
1900-01	...	...	45·1
1905-06	...	...	42·9
1910-12	...	...	39·1
1915-16	...	...	47·4
1920-21	...	...	41·8
1925-26	...	...	32·1

This decline in the percentage share of the United Kingdom has been more marked in our export trade. It is true that the share of Great Britain has always been larger in our imports than in our exports; but smaller as the volume of exports has been, its decline has still been relatively more marked than that of imports, as the following figures will reveal :—

Percentage share of U. K. in India's Import and Export Trade.

		Import	Export
1875-76	...	83·0	48·3
1880-81	...	82·8	41·6
1890-91	...	76·4	32·7
1900-01	...	65·6	30·7
1905-06	...	68·5	25·1
1910-11	...	62·1	24·8
1915-16	...	60·4	38·1
1920-21	...	58·8	19·4
1925-26	...	50·9	21·0

In our imports, Great Britian continued to retain more than half the total trade and occupied by far the most important position, the share of the country coming next namely, Japan, being only 8 percent in 1925-26. But as a consumer of Indian goods, she had long ceased to hold a similar position. Japan and the U. S. A. followed her at close quarters, the percentage shares of U. K., Japan and the U. S. A. in India's export trade being respectively 21·0, 15·0 and 10·4 in the year 1925-26.

II

The causes of this decline in the percentage share of the United Kingdom in India's foreign trade are not far to seek. The pre-eminence of that country in the earlier days was due to a number of peculiar facilities which she enjoyed in her relations with India. She was politically supreme in this country. Our trade had to depend almost entirely on British shipping; most of the exporting and importing firms were British concerns; so were the exchange banks and insurance companies. The railways of India were mostly built up with British capital and conducted by British companies which furthered the interests of British commerce.

Many of the agricultural industries (some of them with British capital) were initiated and developed with a view to supplying the British market.

The agricultural policy of the Government was also directed to the encouragement of the cultivation of such raw materials and foodgrains as jute, cotton, wheat, and oilseeds, with the object of stimulating their export to Britian. On the other hand, the United Kingdom was the foremost industrial country of the world, supplying most of the demands of India for manufactured goods, in some of which (cotton manufactures) the imports were directly encouraged by the tariff legislation of the Government of India, indirectly restricting the growth of those manufacturing industries in India that were likely to hinder the progress of our import trade with that country.

The preponderance of the United Kingdom in our foreign trade was, therefore the outcome of a combination of two causes ; the political and economic subordination of India to that country and the industrial supremacy of Great Britian among the countries of the world.

Subsequently, direct trade connections came to be established with almost all the important countries of the world ; and with the gradual progress of trade with them, Britian's share has steadily declined. This growth of Indian trade with non-British countries was no doubt made possible by the free trade policy pursued by the British Government in relation to the Indian market. The specific reasons will be found in the fact that while in the first half of the 19th century, the United Kingdom was the only great industrial country, subsequent industrial developments in countries like Germany, U.S.A., and Japan have resulted in large quantities of manufactured goods being imported from them, mostly at the expense of Great Britian.

On the other hand, these industrially developed countries have found in India a veritable store-house of raw materials with which to foster their manufacturing industries. But the keen competition which they had to meet in capturing the Indian market from British hands for their own commodities was absent in the case of the purchase of raw materials from India. For, while the progress in our imports from other countries was being fought against and restricted at every step by Britian, India could sell her raw produce to any country which offered her the best price. It was, therefore, comparatively easier for the non-British countries to show greater developments in consuming Indian goods than in replacing British imports by their own manufactures.

Hence, with the economic advancement of non-British countries and the establishment of commercial relations with them, our trade was diverted more and more towards these countries.

III

From the above, it should not be supposed that there was an actual decline in the amount of Indo-British trade. On the other hand, the United Kingdom showed the greatest progress in the net addition to the amount of trade transacted between India and any other country as the following figures will indicate:—

	Value in Lakhs of Rupees. Exports to the U. K.	Imports from the U. K.	Total amount of the Indo-British trade.
1875-76	2809	3228	6087
1880-81	3105	4403	7508
1890-91	3227	5502	8779
1900-01	3205	5310	8516
1905-06	4070	7685	11755
1910-11	5224	8311	13533
1915-16	7600	8352	15952
1920-21	5297	20460	25757
1925-26	8097	1532	19629

Thus, during the period 1875-76, to 1925-26, the amount of our trade with Britian increased by about 136 crores of rupees. an amount, which was in itself greater than that transacted with any other country. The gradual decline in the percentage share of the United Kingdom was, therefore, due to her inability to keep pace with the general growth of India's total trade, the extent of which can further be gauged from the following index numbers :—

	Total Indian Trade	Indo-British Trade
1875-76	100	100
1880-81	131	124
1890-91	177	145
1900-01	194	141
1905-06	282	194
1910-11	354	224
1915-16	348	264
1920-21	634	426
1925-26	630	325

As has already been observed, the preponderance of Great Britian has been more complete in India's import trade. This has been reflected in the fact that our total imports have shown identical movements with those from the United Kingdom. Fluctuations in the imports from that country in either direction have invariably been followed by similar fluctuations in our total imports. This has, however, not been the case with the exports which have shown contrary movements in some particular years to those from the United Kingdom. This is, of course, due to the exports to Britian being only a fraction of our total exports. But the supremacy of that country has been so complete in India's import trade that irrespective of the developments with other countries, our total imports have in every year moved along with those from Britian.

The outstanding article of importance that has contributed to the bulk of our import trade with Great Britian is cotton manufactures. England is the greatest cotton manufacturing country in the world, and India has been her best customer. Indeed, India occupies the foremost place among the countries importing cotton piece-goods. This single article has represented more than 50 percent of India's total imports from the United Kingdom.

The other articles of importance are metals, machinery and mill-work, and railway plant and rolling stock. Each of these amounted to more than ten crores of rupees in the latest years of the period under study. Besides these, there is a host of other minor articles. The bulk is, however, made up of cotton goods, metals and manufactures thereof, and the progress of Indo-British trade has been mainly limited to these commodities.

Besides the facts that the exports to Britian have represented a smaller value than the imports therefrom and that the progress in them has been slower than in the latter, there is another point of contrast to be noted. On the import side, cotton goods have represented the bulk of the trade whereas, on the export side, there has been no such predominent article. On the contrary, while the important articles of import kept up their relative positions all through, those of export underwent the greatest changes in their growth and relative importance.

In the earlier days, raw cotton occupied the first place among the objects of exports. Right down to 1884-85 the output and export of jute which were being highly encouraged by the establishment and progress of the jute manufacturing industry in Dundee, held the first place. Then, the export of tea which was fast driving away the Chinese stuff from the British market along with the rapid growth of the newly-established Indian industry, took the place of honour for the first time in 1890-91. Thus in 1890-91 tea, foodgrains, raw jute and cotton respectively occupied the first four places, the value of the exports of each of these being between 4 and 5 crores of rupees.

Since then, while the exports of raw cotton fell heavily amounting only 21 lakhs of rupees in 1899-1900, those of the other three commodities continued to grow in volume; and for the next few years, these interchanging the first three places amongst themselves. By the end of the century, tea, however, came definitely to hold the formost place; and though in certain abnormal years, the exports of food-grains exceeded those of tea, the latter have since then continued to hold the premier position. This rising preponderance of tea in relation to food-grains and jute was due to the following causes.

India herself being a densely-populated country, subject to shortage of crops and famines, the exports of grains could show expansion only within certain limits and were liable to grear fluctuations. In the case of jute, growth of the manufacturing industry in India and here restricted the exports to the United Kingdom. But tea was not subject to any of these influences. The home consumption was negligible and there was no great demand from other countries.

The industry was started and fostered with a view to supply the demands of Britian which has continued to be almost the single market for Indian tea, the exports to other countries being quite small. Had it not been for tea, the exports to the United Kingdom would have shown still greater percentage decline.

The other articles of importance in our export trade with that country are hides and skins, jute manufactures, oil-seeds, raw wool. lac. coffee and teak wood.

IV

It will be noted from the above study of the growth of Indo-British trade that most of the articles of import and export suffer from double-sided competition.

The chief commodities of import, as already observed, are cotton goods and metal manufactures, both of which were liable to competition from home and abroad. In the case of the former, the increasing home-production and the keen competition from Japan came greatly in the way of the United Kingdom. Indeed, in recent years, the import of cotton goods from England have shown considerable decline in volume. As regards metal and manufactures, while in the earlier days England had no competitor on the field, towards the close of the last century, Belgium and Germeny came to be keen rivals of Great Britian. Indeed, by the beginning of this century, in certain kinds of metal manufactures, especially in iron and steel, the imports from Belgium and Germany to a great extent replaced those from the former. Lately the U. S. A. also joined them. Then there was the growth of Indian iron and steel industry, which was raising its head under a system of protection.

In the case of exports, the trade in raw materials like jute, hides and skins, and seeds was restricted by a keener demand from Continental countries, and was thus being diverted from the United Kingdom to non-British countries ; on the other hand, the trade in articles like coffee, cotton, and tea had to meet the competition of foreign countries in supplying the British market and was thus being replaced by exports from the latter. There is a third class of commodities like foodgrains and wool, the exports of which were restricted both by the available home supply and foreign competition. It will be seen that except tea (the exports of which are also to some extent liable to foreign competition), the exports of all other articles had gradually been diverted from the United Kingdom to other countries. Great Britian would not import Indian raw cotton or jute manufactures, while India found other markets, not only for these commodities but also for her raw jute, oilseeds, hides and skins and other raw materials.

V

Another very important point to be noted in connection with the growth of Indo-British trade is that it has more or less kept pace with the progress of the foreign trade of Great Britian. This means that while the United Kingdom declinad in her relative importance in India's foreign trade, India fully retained hers in Great Britian. Indeed till the outbreak of the last war, India was actually gaining in her relative importance, the growth of Indo-British trade being ahead of that of Britian's total trade. Since then, India slightly declined in her position, the subsequent development in the United Kingdom's foreign trade being a little quicker than those with India. On the whole, the percentage share of India in Britian's trade remained more or less the same, while her percentage share in India's trade was continuously on the decline. It is, therefore, important to note in connection with the prospects of British trade in India that the United Kingdom showed as much progress in her trade with India as with other countries. The contrast is indeed striking. The following are the corroborative index numbers:—

		Total trade of U. K.	Indo-British trade.
Average	1875-79	100	100
,,	1885-89	104	144
,,	1895-99	121	141
,,	1905-09	178	210
,,	1910-13	208	265
,,	1914-18	301	270
Year	1920	585	428
,,	1921	822	327
,,	1925	388	326

Regarding the percentage share of India in Britian's total trade it should be observed that India occupies no such eminent position as the United Kingdom does in India. Indo-British trade represents only a fraction of Britian's total trade. It is true that as a consumer of British goods, India occupies the foremost place; but while these represent about 50 percent of our total imports, they scarcely amount to 12 percent of Britian as a consumer of Indian goods. Thus while the share of the United Kingdom in our export trade amounted to 25 : 5 per cent. in 1924-25, India's share in Britian's import trade amounted to only 5. 7 per cent in 1924.

The following figures bring out more clearly the position India occupies in the foreign trade of Great Britian :—

Year 1924 Exports from U. K. To		Value in Millions of £ Imports into U. K. From	
India	90.6	U. S. A.	222.6
Australia	60.7	Argentina	75.2
U. S. A.	53.8	India	65.1
Germany	42.6	Canada	62.7

Considered as a whole, during the year 1924, India's share in the total trade of the United Kingdom was only 8 per cent while Britian's share in that of India was as much as 86 per cent.

VI

It has been observed that the decline in the percentage share of the United Kingdom in our foreign trade was more in the exports sent thereto than in the imports received thereform.

An important change, however, took place since the close of the war. While the exports from India retained the pre-war level, the imports from the United Kingdom fell far short of it. During the period 1920-21 to 1925-26, the share of Britian in our import trade declined from 58.8 per cent to 50.9 per cent, whereas the same in our import trade rose from 19.4 per cent to 21.0 per cent.

This is also observable in the trade of the United Kingdom.

Percentage share of India in U. K's Export and Import Trade.

		Export	Import
1910	...	10.69	5.53
1913	...	13.38	5.48
1922	...	12.80	4.25
1923	...	11.21	5.76
1925	...	11.12	...

Previous to 1922, India was gaining in relative importance in Britian's export trade and losing in her import trade. The subsequent developments were in the opposite direction. The causes of this change in the trend of Indo-British trade will reveal a few important truths regarding the strength of Britian's hold on the Indian market.

During the war period, the import of British goods into India was naturally restricted, and countries like Japan and U. S. A. took full advantage of the situation in pushing the sale of their goods. The result was that when the United Kingdom regained her normal conditions, she found that the market had to a great extent been captured by those countries whom it was now very difficult to drive away. Japan had come to be a formidable competitor not only in Indian market but elsewhere, as well in the supply of cotton goods which are by far the most important article of our import trade with Britian. Moreover, the raising of the import duty and the abolition of the excise gave an advantage to Indian manufactures which they had never enjoyed before. Thus in the post-war period, the imports of British cotton goods came to be seriously affected by competition from within the country as well as from Japan. On the other hand, the fact that Germany and Belgium could very soon recover the Indian market in spite of the complete collapse of their trade with India during the war period while the United Kingdom was unable to do so, points to the inability of Britian to compete with those countries in certain classes of commodities. The development of new industries in India also came in the way of the growth of British imports, *e.g.*, the iron and steel industry. It will thus be seen that British imports in the post-war period became subjected to very keen competition from home and abroad.

With exports from India, such was not the case. The stimulus that they had received during the war led to their subsequent growth. Moreover, the policy of Imperial Preference and the preferential duties levied on certain Indian goods in the United Kingdom caused some slight developments in our exports to that country.

Hence it was that in the postwar period, the exports sent from India to the United Kingdom showed greater developments than the imports received therefrom, while the reverse had been the case so long.

VII

From the above study, important conclusions may be drawn regarding the future prospects of Indo-British trade. True, we have not taken into account the latest developments in as much as we have left the last four years out of our study; nor have we considered the possible reactions of the recent Swadeshi movement on our trade, especially with Britian. Nevertheless, the historical perspective of half a century will, in our opinion, be a surer guide in the matter than the passing events of a few abnormal years.

In view of the fact that the United Kingdom has now come under the sway of far greater competition in the import trade of India both from home as well as from foreign countries, some of which are decidedly better situated in supplying many of the manufactured goods required in India, we can expect very little progress, if not a positive decline in our import trade with Britian.

In the case of exports sent from India, we may expect some slight developments in future, especially in view of the fact that the import of Empire products is being encouraged in the United Kingdom and that systematic efforts are being made to consume a greater amount of colonial goods. But here, also, the prospects are not very bright. Canada and Australia, with their vast agricultural resources, are showing great progress in their exports to Britian. It i future some of the articles from India will be replaced by those from these colonies. In the case of wheat, they have already almost completely ousted India from the British market.

Moreover, it should not be lost sight of that the total amount of Indo-British trade has reached such huge dimensions for a poor country like India that the possibilities of further expansion are limited. While the import of British goods is restricted by competition from India and foreign countries, the exports from India are likely to be restricted by the competition from the colonies in supplying the British market and by the greater demand for Indian goods from non-British countries.